THE ARCHITECTURE
OF CONCURRENT
PROGRAMS

Prentice-Hall
Series in Automatic Computation

MARTIN, *Design of Real-Time Computer Systems*
MARTIN, *Future Developments in Telecommunications*, 2nd ed.
MARTIN, *Principles of Data-Base Management*
MARTIN, *Programming Real-Time Computing Systems*
MARTIN, *Security, Accuracy, and Privacy in Computer Systems*
MARTIN, *Systems Analysis for Data Transmission*
MARTIN, *Telecommunications and the Computer*, 2nd ed.
MARTIN, *Teleprocessing Network Organization*
MARTIN and NORMAN, *The Computerized Society*
MCKEEMAN, et al., *A Compiler Generator*
MEYERS, *Time-Sharing Computation in the Social Sciences*
MINSKY, *Computation: Finite and Infinite Machines*
NIEVERGELT, et al., *Computer Approaches to Mathematical Problems*
PLANE and MCMILLAN, *Discrete Optimization*
POLIVKA and PAKIN, *APL: The Language and Its Usage*
PRITSKER and KIVIAT, *Simulation with GASP II: A FORTRAN-based Simulation Language*
PYLYSHYN, ed., *Perspectives on the Computer Revolution*
RICH, *Internal Sorting Methods Illustrated with PL/1 Programs*
RUDD, *Assembly Language Programming and the IBM 360 and 370 Computers*
SACKMANN and CITRENBAUM, eds., *On-Line Planning: Towards Creative Problem-Solving*
SALTON, ed., *The SMART Retrieval System: Experiments in Automatic Document Processing*
SAMMET, *Programming Languages: History and Fundamentals*
SCHAEFER, *A Mathematical Theory of Global Program Optimization*
SCHULTZ, *Spline Analysis*
SCHWARTZ, et al., *Numerical Analysis of Symmetric Matrices*
SHAH, *Engineering Simulation Using Small Scientific Computers*
SHAW, *The Logical Design of Operating Systems*
SHERMAN, *Techniques in Computer Programming*
SIMON and SIKLOSSY, eds., *Representation and Meaning:
    Experiments with Information Processing Systems*
STERBENZ, *Floating-Point Computation*
STOUTEMYER, *PL/1 Programming for Engineering and Science*
STRANG and FIX, *An Analysis of the Finite Element Method*
STROUD, *Approximate Calculation of Multiple Integrals*
TANENBAUM, *Structured Computer Organization*
TAVISS, ed., *The Computer Impact*
UHR, *Pattern Recognition, Learning, and Thought:
    Computer-Programmed Models of Higher Mental Processes*
VAN TASSEL, *Computer Security Management*
VARGA, *Matrix Iterative Analysis*
WAITE, *Implementing Software for Non-Numeric Application*
WILKINSON, *Rounding Errors in Algebraic Processes*
WIRTH, *Algorithms + Data Structures = Programs*
WIRTH, *Systematic Programming: An Introduction*
YEH, ed., *Applied Computation Theory: Analysis, Design, Modeling*

To my father

THE ARCHITECTURE OF CONCURRENT PROGRAMS

PER BRINCH HANSEN

University of Southern California

PRENTICE-HALL, INC. Englewood Cliffs, New Jersey 07632

Library of Congress Cataloging in Publication Data

Brinch Hansen, Per,
    The architecture of concurrent programs.

    (Prentice-Hall series in automatic computation)
    Summary in Danish.
    Bibliography: p.
    Includes index.
    1. Concurrent Pascal (Computer programming language)
2. Operating systems (Computers)   I. Title.
QA76.73.C65B73 1977   001.6'424   77-4901
ISBN 0-13-044628-9

© 1977 by Prentice-Hall, Inc., Englewood Cliffs, New Jersey 07632

All rights reserved. No part of this book may be
reproduced in any form, by mimeography or by any
means, without permission in writing from the publisher.

10 9 8 7 6 5 4 3 2 1

Printed in the United States of America

PRENTICE-HALL INTERNATIONAL, INC., *London*
PRENTICE-HALL OF AUSTRALIA PTY. LTD., *Sydney*
PRENTICE-HALL OF CANADA, LTD., *Toronto*
PRENTICE-HALL OF INDIA PRIVATE LIMITED, *New Delhi*
PRENTICE-HALL OF JAPAN, INC., *Tokyo*
PRENTICE-HALL OF SOUTH EAST ASIA PTE. LTD., *Singapore*
WHITEHALL BOOKS LIMITED, Wellington, *New Zealand*

CONTENTS

PREFACE

CONCURRENT PROGRAMMING

This book describes a method for writing concurrent computer programs of high quality. It is written for professional programmers and students who are faced with the complicated task of building reliable computer operating systems or real-time control programs.

The motivations for mastering concurrent programming are both economic and intellectual. Concurrent programming makes it possible to use a computer where many things need attention at the same time — be they people at terminals or temperatures in an industrial plant. It is without doubt the most difficult form of programming.

This book presents a systematic way of developing concurrent programs in a structured language called *Concurrent Pascal* — the first of its kind. The use of this language is illustrated by three non-trivial concurrent programs: a single-user operating system, a job-stream system, and a real-time scheduler. All of these have been used successfully on a PDP 11/45 computer. The book includes the complete text of these three programs and explains how they are structured, programmed, tested, and described.

In an earlier book, *Operating System Principles* [Prentice-Hall, 1973],

I tried to establish a background for studying existing operating systems in terms of basic concepts. This new text tells the other side of the story: how concurrent programs can be constructed systematically from scratch. It also illustrates details of important design problems — the management of input/output, data files, and programs — which were deliberately omitted from the first book. So it is useful both as a practical supplement to operating system courses and also as a handbook on structured concurrent programming for engineers.

COMPILATION AND TESTING

A concurrent program consists of sequential processes that are carried out simultaneously. The processes cooperate on common tasks by exchanging data through shared variables. The problem is that unrestricted access to the shared variables can make the result of a concurrent program dependant on the relative speeds of its processes. This is obvious if you think of a car and a train passing through the same railroad crossing: it is the relative timing of these "processes" that determines whether they will collide.

Unfortunately, the execution speed of a program will vary somewhat from one run to the next. It will be influenced by other (unrelated) programs running simultaneously and by operators responding to requests. So you can never be quite sure what an incorrect, concurrent program is going to do. If you execute it many times with the same data you will get a different result each time. This makes it hopeless to judge what went wrong. Program testing is simply useless as a means of locating time-dependent errors.

Some of these errors can no doubt be located by proofreading. I have seen a programmer do this by looking at an assembly language program for a week. But, to proofread a large program, you must understand it in complete detail. So the search for an error may involve all of the people who wrote the program, and even then you cannot be sure it will be found.

Well, *if we cannot make concurrent programs work by proofreading or testing, then I can see only one other effective method at the moment: to write all concurrent programs in a programming language that is so structured that you can specify exactly what processes can do to shared variables and depend on a compiler to check that the programs satisfy these assumptions.* Concurrent Pascal is the first language that makes this possible.

In the long run it is not advisable to write large concurrent programs in machine-oriented languages that permit unrestricted use of store locations and their addresses. There is just no way we will be able to make such programs reliable (even with the help of complicated hardware mechanisms).

CONCURRENT PASCAL

From 1963–65 I was one of ten programmers who wrote a Cobol compiler in assembly language. This program of 40,000 instructions took 15 man-years to build. Although it worked well, the compiler was very difficult to maintain since none of us understood it completely.

Five years later, compiler writing was completely changed by the sequential programming language *Pascal*, invented by Niklaus Wirth. Pascal is an abstract language that hides irrelevant machine detail from the programmer. At the same time it is efficient enough for system programming. It is easily understood by programmers familiar with Fortran, Algol 60, Cobol, or PL/I.

In 1974 Al Hartmann used Sequential Pascal to write a compiler for my new programming language, called *Concurrent Pascal*. This compiler is comparable to a machine program of 35,000 instructions. But, written in Pascal, the program text is only 8,300 lines long and can be completely understood by a single person. The programming and testing of this compiler took only 7 months.

The aim of Concurrent Pascal is to do for operating systems what Sequential Pascal has done for compilers: to reduce the programming effort by an order of magnitude.

Concurrent Pascal extends Sequential Pascal with *concurrent processes* and *monitors*. The compiler prevents some time-dependent programming errors by checking that the private variables of one process are inaccessible to another. Processes can only communicate by means of monitors.

A monitor defines all the possible operations on a shared data structure. It can, for example, define the send and receive operations on a message buffer. The compiler will check that processes only perform these two operations on a buffer.

A monitor can delay processes to make their interactions independent of their speeds. A process that tries to receive a message from an empty buffer will, for example, be delayed until another process sends a message to it.

If a programmer can design a process or monitor correctly, the rest of a program will not be able to make that component behave erratically (since no other part of the program has direct access to the variables used by a component). *The controlled access to private and shared variables greatly reduces the risk of time-dependent program behavior caused by erroneous processes.*

MODEL OPERATING SYSTEMS

This book stresses the *practice* of concurrent programming. It contains a complete description of three model operating systems written in Concurrent Pascal.

Chapter 5 describes a single-user operating system, called *Solo*. It supports the development of Sequential and Concurrent Pascal programs on the PDP 11/45 computer. Input/output are handled by concurrent processes. Pascal programs can call one another recursively and pass arbitrary parameters among themselves. This makes it possible to use Pascal as a job control language. Solo is the first major example of a hierarchical concurrent program made of processes and monitors.

Chapter 6 presents a *job-stream system* that compiles and executes short Pascal programs which are input from a card reader and are output on a line printer. Input, execution, and output take place simultaneously, using buffers stored on disk.

Chapter 7 discusses a *real-time scheduler* for process control applications in which a fixed number of concurrent tasks are carried out periodically with frequencies chosen by an operator.

These chapters not only describe how to build different kinds of operating systems but also illustrate the main steps of the program development process.

The Solo system shows how a concurrent program of more than a thousand lines can be *structured* and *programmed* as a sequence of components of less than one page each. The real-time scheduler is used to demonstrate how a hierarchical, concurrent program can be *tested* systematically. The job-stream system illustrates how a program structure can be derived from *performance* considerations.

LANGUAGE DEFINITION AND IMPLEMENTATION

I have tried to make this book as readable as possible to share an architectonic view of concurrent programming effectively. Formalism is often a stumbling block in the first encounter with a new field, and the practice of structured concurrent programming is not commonplace yet. So I have assumed in chapters 3 and 4 that you are so familiar with one or more programming languages that it is sufficient to show the flavor of Sequential and Concurrent Pascal by examples before describing the model operating systems.

But when you wish to use a new programming language in your own work, a precise definition of it becomes essential. So the *Concurrent Pascal report* is included in chapter 8.

The whole purpose of this work is to show how much a concurrent programming effort can be reduced by using an abstract language that suppresses as much machine detail as one can afford to without losing control of program efficiency. For this reason the introduction to Concurrent Pascal ignores the question of how the language is implemented.

Chapter 9 is an overview of the *language implementation* for those who feel uncomfortable unless they have a dynamic feeling for what their programs make the machine do. I suspect that most of us belong to that group. Once you understand what a machine does, however, it is easier to forget the details again and start relying completely on the abstract concepts that are built into the language.

TEACHING AND ENGINEERING

Very few operating systems are so well-structured and well-documented that they are worth studying in detail. And few (if any) computing centers make it possible for students to write their own concurrent programs in an abstract language. Since students can neither study nor build realistic operating systems it is almost impossible to make them feel comfortable about the subject.

This book tries to remedy that situation. It defines an abstract language for concurrent programming that has been implemented on the PDP 11/45 computer. The compiler can be moved to other computers since it is written in Sequential Pascal and generates code for a simple machine that can be simulated efficiently by microprogram or machine language.

The book also offers complete examples of model operating systems that can be studied by students.

If you are a professional programmer you can seldom choose your own programming language for large projects. But you can benefit from new language constructs — such as processes and monitors — by taking them as models of a systematic programming style that can be imitated as closely as possible in other languages (including assembly languages).

The system kernel that is described in chapter 9 illustrates this. It is an assembly language program written entirely by means of *classes* (a concept similar to monitors). Since this concept is not in the assembly language it is described by comments only.

The book can also be used as a handbook on the design of small operating systems and significant portions of larger ones.

If you are a software engineer you may feel that the operating systems described here are much smaller than those you are asked to build. This raises the question of whether the concepts used here can help you build huge systems. My recommendation is to use abstract programming concepts (such as processes and monitors) wherever you can. This will probably solve most programming problems in a simple manner and leave you with only a few really machine-dependent components (such as a processor scheduler and a storage allocator). As a means of organizing your thoughts, Concurrent Pascal can only be helpful.

But I should also admit that I do not see a future for large operating systems. They never worked well and they probably never will. They are just too complicated for the human mind. They were the product of an early stage in which none of us had a good feeling for what software quality means. The new technology that supports wide-spread use of cheap, personal computers will soon make them obsolete.

Although operating systems have provided the most spectacular examples of the difficulty of making concurrent programs reliable, there are other applications that present problems of their own. As an industrial programmer I was involved in the design of *process control programs* for a chemical plant, a power plant, and a meteorological institute. These real-time applications had one thing in common: they were all unique in their software requirements.

When the cost of developing a large program cannot be shared by many users the pressure to reduce the cost is much greater than it is for general-purpose software, such as compilers and operating systems. The only practical way of reducing cost then is to give the process control engineers an abstract language for concurrent programming. To illustrate this I rewrote an existing real-time scheduler from machine language into Concurrent Pascal (chapter 7).

The recent reduction of hardware costs for microprocessors will soon put even greater pressure on software designers to reduce their costs as well. So there is every reason for a realistic programmer to keep an eye on recent developments in programming methodology.

PROJECT BACKGROUND

In 1971, Edsger Dijkstra suggested that concurrent programs might be easier to understand if all synchronizing operations on a shared data structure were collected into a single program unit (which we now call a *monitor*).

In May 1972 I wrote a chapter on *Resource Protection* for *Operating System Principles*. I introduced a language notation for monitors and pointed out that resource protection in operating systems and type checking in compilers are solutions to the same problem: to verify automatically that programs only perform meaningful operations on data structures. My conclusion was that *"I expect to see many protection rules in future operat-*

ing systems being enforced in the cheapest possible manner by type checking at compile time. However, this will require exclusive use of efficient, well-structured languages for programming." This is still the idea behind Concurrent Pascal.

I developed Concurrent Pascal at the California Institute of Technology from 1972-75. The compiler was written by Al Hartmann. Robert Deverill and Tom Zepko wrote the interpreter for the PDP 11/45. I built the model operating systems, and Wolfgang Franzen made improvements to one of them (Solo).

ACKNOWLEDGEMENT

The Institute of Electrical and Electronics Engineers, North-Holland Publishing Company, and John Wiley and Sons kindly granted permission to reprint parts of the papers:

> "The programming language Concurrent Pascal."
> *IEEE Transactions on Software Engineering 1*,
> 2, June 1975.

> "Universal types in Concurrent Pascal."
> *Information Processing Letters 3*,
> 6, July 1975.

> "The Solo operating system."
> *Software — Practice & Experience 6*,
> 2, April–June 1976.

The development of Concurrent Pascal was partly supported by the National Science Foundation under grant number DCR74-17331.

Giorgio Ingargiola, Luis Medina, and Ramon Varela all gave helpful comments on the text. I also wish to thank Christian Gram, Ole-Johan Dahl, and Peter Naur for a constructive, detailed evaluation of this work.

PER BRINCH HANSEN
University of Southern California

PROGRAMMING TOOLS

1

DESIGN PRINCIPLES

This book describes a method for writing concurrent programs of high quality. Since there is no common agreement among programmers about the qualities a good program should have, I will begin by describing my own requirements.

1.1 PROGRAM QUALITY

A good program must be *simple*, *reliable*, and *adaptable*. Without simplicity one cannot expect to understand the purpose and details of a large program. Without reliability one cannot seriously depend on it. And without adaptability to changing requirements a program eventually becomes a fossil.

Fortunately, these essential requirements go hand in hand. Simplicity gives one the confidence to believe that a program works and makes it clear how it can be changed. Simplicity, reliability, and adaptability make programs *manageable*.

In addition, it is desirable to make programs that can work efficiently on several different computers for a variety of similar applications. But *efficiency*, *portability*, and *generality* should never be sought at the expense of simplicity, reliability, and adaptability, for only the latter qualities make it possible to understand what programs do, depend on them, and extend their capabilities.

The poor quality of much existing software is, to a large extent, the result of turning these priorities upside down. Some programmers justify extremely complex and incomprehensible programs by their high efficiency. Others claim that the poor reliability and efficiency of their huge programs are outweighed by their broad scope of application.

Personally I find the efficiency of a tool that nobody fully understands irrelevant. And I find it difficult to appreciate a general-purpose tool which is so slow that it cannot do anything well. But these are matters of taste and style and are likely to remain so.

Whenever program qualities appear to be in conflict with one another I shall consistently settle the issue by giving first priority to manageability, second priority to efficiency, and third priority to generality. This boils down to the simple rule of limiting our computer applications to those which programmers fully understand and which machines can handle well. Although this is too narrow a view for experimental computer usage it is sound advice for professional programming.

Let us now look more closely at these program qualities to see how they can be achieved.

1.2 SIMPLICITY

We will be writing concurrent programs which are so large that one cannot understand them all at once. So we must reason about them in smaller *pieces*. What properties should these pieces have? Well, they should be so small that any one of them is trivial to understand in itself. It would be ideal if they were no more than *one page* of text each so that they can be comprehended at a glance.

Such a program could be studied page by page as one reads a book. But in the end, when we have understood what all the pieces do, we must still be able to see what their combined effect *as a whole* is. If it is a program of many pages we can only do this by ignoring most of our detailed knowledge about the pieces and relying on a much simpler description of what they do and how they work together.

So our program pieces must allow us to make a clear separation of their detailed behavior and that small part of it which is of interest when we consider combinations of such pieces. In other words, we must distinguish between the *inner and outer behavior* of a program piece.

Program pieces will be built to perform well-defined, simple functions. We will then combine program pieces into larger *configurations* to carry out more complicated functions. This design method is effective because it splits a complicated task into simpler ones: First you convince yourself that the pieces work individually, and then you think about how they work together. During the second part of the argument it is essential to be able to forget how a piece works in detail — otherwise, the problem becomes too complicated. But in doing so one makes the fundamental assumption that the piece always will do the same when it carries out its function. Otherwise, you could not afford to ignore the detailed behavior of that piece in your reasoning about the whole system.

So *reproducible behavior* is a vital property of program pieces that we wish to build and study in small steps. We must clearly keep this in mind when we select the kind of program pieces that large concurrent programs will be made of. The ability to repeat program behavior is taken for granted when we write sequential programs. Here the sequence of events is completely defined by the program and its input data. But in a concurrent program simultaneous events take place at rates not fully controlled by the programmer. They depend on the presence of other jobs in the machine and the scheduling policy used to execute them. This means that a conscious effort must be made to design concurrent programs with reproducible behavior.

The idea of reasoning first about *what* a pieces does and then studying *how* it does it in detail is most effective if we can repeat this process by explaining each piece in terms of simpler pieces which themselves are built from still simpler pieces. So we shall confine ourselves to *hierarchical structures* composed of *layers* of program pieces.

It will certainly simplify our understanding of hierarchical structures if each part only depends on a small number of other parts. We will therefore try to build structures that have *minimal interfaces* between their parts.

This is extremely difficult to do in *machine language* since the slightest programming mistake can make an instruction destroy any instruction or variable. Here the *whole store* can be the interface between any two instructions. This was made only too clear in the past by the practice of printing the contents of the entire store just to locate a single programming error.

Programs written in *abstract languages* (such as Fortran, Algol, and Pascal) are unable to modify themselves. But they still have broad interfaces in the form of *global variables* that can be changed by every statement (by intention or mistake).

We will use a programming language called *Concurrent Pascal*, which makes it possible to divide the global variables into smaller parts. Each of these is accessible to a small number of statements only.

The main contribution of a good programming language to simplicity is to provide an abstract *readable notation* that makes the parts and structure of programs obvious to a reader. An abstract programming language *suppresses machine detail* (such as addresses, registers, bit patterns, interrupts, and sometimes even the number of processors available). Instead the language relies on *abstract concepts* (such as variables, data types, synchronizing operations, and concurrent processes). As a result, program texts written in abstract languages are often an order of magnitude shorter than those written in machine language. This *textual reduction* simplifies program engineering considerably.

The fastest way to discover whether or not you have invented a simple program structure is to try to *describe* it in completely readable terms — adopting the same standards of clarity that are required of a survey paper published by a journal. If you take pride in your own description you have probably invented a good program structure. But if you discover that there is no simple way of describing what you intend to do, then you should probably look for some other way of doing it.

Once you appreciate the value of description as an early warning signal of unnecessary complexity it becomes self-evident that program structures should be described (without detail) *before* they are built and should be described by the *designer* (and not by anybody else). *Programming is the art of writing essays in crystal clear prose and making them executable.*

1.3 RELIABILITY

Even the most readable language notation cannot prevent programmers from making mistakes. In looking for these in large programs we need all the help we can get. A whole range of techniques is available

> correctness proofs
> proofreading
> compilation checks
> execution checks
> systematic testing

With the exception of correctness proofs, all these techniques played a vital role in making the concurrent programs described in this book work.

Formal proofs are still at an experimental stage, particularly for concurrent programs. Since my aim is to describe techniques that are immediately useful for professional software development, I have omitted proofs here.

Among the useful verification techniques, I feel those that reveal errors at the earliest possible time during the program development should be emphasized to achieve reliability as soon as possible.

One of the primary goals of Concurrent Pascal is to push the role of *compilation checks* to the limit and reduce the use of *execution checks* as much as possible. This is not done just to make compiled programs more efficient by reducing the overhead of execution checks. In program engineering, compilation and execution checks play the same roles as preventive maintenance and flight recorders do in aviation. The latter only tell you why a system crashed; the former prevents it. This distinction seems essential to me in the design of real-time systems that will control vital functions in society. Such systems must be highly reliable *before* they are put into operation.

Extensive compilation checks are possible only if the language notation is *redundant*. The programmer must be able to specify important properties in at least two different ways so that a compiler can look for possible inconsistencies. An example is the use of declarations to introduce variables and their types before they are used in statements. The compiler could easily derive this information from the statements — provided these statements were always correct.

We shall also follow the crucial principle of language design suggested by Hoare: *The behavior of a program written in an abstract language should always be explainable in terms of the concepts of that language and should never require insight into the details of compilers and computers.* Otherwise, an abstract notation has no significant value in reducing complexity.

This principle immediately rules out the use of machine-oriented features in programming languages. So I shall assume that *all programming will take place in abstract programming languages.*

Dijkstra has remarked that *testing* can be used only to show the presence of errors but never their absence. However true that may be, it seems very worthwhile to me to show the presence of errors and remove them one at a time. In my experience, the combination of careful proofreading, extensive compilation checks, and systematic testing is a very effective way to make a program so dependable that it can work for months without problems. And that is about as reliable as most other technology we depend on. I do not know of better methods for verifying large programs at the moment.

I view programming as the art of building *program pyramids* by adding one brick at a time to the structure and making sure that it does not collapse in the process. The pyramid must remain *stable* while it is being built. I will regard a (possibly incomplete) program as being stable as long as it behaves in a predictable manner.

Why is program testing so often difficult? Mainly, I think, because the addition of a new program piece can spread a burst of errors throughout the rest of a program and make previously tested pieces behave differently. This clearly violates the sound principle of being able to assume that when you have built and tested a part of a large program it will continue to behave correctly *under all circumstances.*

So we will make the strong requirement that *new program pieces added on top of old ones must not be able to make the latter fail.* Since this property must be verified before program testing takes place, it must be done by a compiler. We must therefore use a language notation that makes it clear what program pieces can do to one another. This strong *confinement of program errors* to the part in which they occur will make it much easier to determine from the behavior of a large program where its errors are.

1.4 ADAPTABILITY

A large program is so expensive to develop that it must be used for several years to make the effort worthwhile. As time passes the users' needs change, and it becomes necessary to modify the program somewhat to satisfy them. Quite often these modifications are done by people who did not develop the program in the first place. Their main difficulty is to find out how the program works and whether it will still work after being changed.

A small group of people can often succeed in developing the first version of a program in a low-level language with little or no documentation to support them. They do it by talking to one another daily and by sharing a mental picture of a simple structure.

But later, when the same program must be extended by other programmers who are not in frequent contact with the original designers, it becomes painfully clear that the "simple" structure is not described anywhere and certainly is not revealed by the primitive language notation used. It is important to realize that *for program maintenance a simple and well-documented structure is even more important than it is during program development.* I will not talk about the situation in which a program that is neither simple nor well documented must be changed.

There is an interesting relationship between programming errors and changing user requirements. Both of them are sources of *instability* in the program construction process that make it difficult to reach a state in which you have complete confidence in what a program does. They are caused by our inability to fully comprehend at once what a large program is supposed to do in detail.

The relative frequencies of program errors and changing requirements are of crucial importance. If programming introduces numerous errors that are difficult to locate, many of them may still be in the program when the user requests changes of its function. And when an engineer constantly finds himself changing a system that he never succeeded in making work correctly in the first place, he will eventually end up with a very unstable product.

On the other hand, if program errors can be located and corrected at a much faster rate than the system develops, then the addition of a new piece (or a change) to the program will soon lead to a stable situation in which the current version of the program works reliably and predictably. The engineer can then, with much greater confidence, adapt his product to slowly changing needs. This is a strong incentive to make program verification and testing fast.

A hierarchical structure consists of program pieces that can be studied one at a time. This makes it easier to read the program and get an initial understanding of what it does and how it does it. Once you have that insight, the consequences of changing a hierarchical program become clear. When you change a part of a program pyramid you must be prepared to inspect and perhaps change the program parts that are on top of it (for they are the only ones that can possibly depend on the one you changed).

1.5 PORTABILITY

The ability to use the same program on a variety of computers is desirable for economic reasons: Many users have different computers; sometimes they replace them with new ones; and quite often they have a common interest in sharing programs developed on different machines.

Portability is only practical if programs are written in abstract languages that hide the differences between computers as much as possible. Otherwise, it will require extensive rewriting and testing to move programs from one machine to another. Programs written in the same language can be made portable in several ways:

(1) by having *different compilers* for different machines. This is only practical for the most widespread languages.

(2) by having a *single compiler* that can be modified to generate code for different machines. This requires a clear separation within the compiler of those parts that check programs and those that generate code.

(3) by having a *single computer* that can be simulated efficiently on different machines.

The Concurrent Pascal compiler generates code for a simple machine tailored to the language. This machine is simulated by an assembly language program of 4 K words on the PDP 11/45 computer. To move the language to another computer one rewrites this interpreter. This approach sacrifices some efficiency to make portability possible. The loss of efficiency can be eliminated on a microprogrammable machine.

1.6 EFFICIENCY

Efficient programs save time for people waiting for results and reduce the cost of computation. The programs described here owe their efficiency to

> special-purpose algorithms
> static store allocation
> minimal run-time checking

Initially the loading of a large program (such as a compiler) from disk took about 16 sec on the PDP 11/45 computer. This was later reduced to 5 sec by a disk allocation algorithm that depends on the special characteristics of program files (as opposed to data files). A scheduling algorithm that tries to reduce disk head movement in general would have been useless here. The reasons for this will be made clear later.

Dynamic store algorithms that move programs and data segments around during execution can be a serious source of inefficiency that is not under the programmer's control. The implementation of Concurrent Pascal does not require garbage collection or demand paging of storage. It uses static allocation of store among a fixed number of processes. The store requirements are determined by the compiler.

When programs are written in assembly language it is impossible to predict what they will do. Most computers depend on hardware mechanisms to prevent such programs from destroying one another or the operating system. In Concurrent Pascal most of this protection is guaranteed by the compiler and is not supported by hardware mechanisms during execution. This drastic reduction of run-time checking is only possible because all programs are written in an abstract language.

1.7 GENERALITY

To achieve simplicity and reliability we will depend exclusively on a machine-independent language that makes programs readable and extensive compilation checks possible. To achieve efficiency we will use the simplest possible store allocation.

These decisions will no doubt reduce the usefulness of Concurrent Pascal for some applications. But I see no way of avoiding that. To impose *structure* upon yourself is to impose *restrictions* on your freedom of programming. You can no longer use the machine in any way you want (because the language makes it impossible to talk directly about some machine features). You can no longer delay certain program decisions until execution time (because the compiler checks and freezes things much earlier). But the freedom you lose is often illusory anyhow, since it can complicate programming to the point where you are unable to cope with it.

This book describes a range of small operating systems. Each of them provides a special service in the most efficient and simple manner. They show that Concurrent Pascal is a useful programming language for minicomputer operating systems and dedicated real-time applications. I expect that the language will be useful (but not sufficient) for writing large, general-purpose operating systems. But that still remains to be seen. I have tried to make a programming tool that is very convenient for many applications rather than one which is tolerable for all purposes.

1.8 CONCLUSION

I have discussed the programming goals of

> simplicity
> reliability
> adaptability
> efficiency
> portability

and have suggested that they can be achieved by careful design of program structure, language notation, compiler, and code interpreter. The properties that we must look for are the following:

> structure: hierarchical structure
> small parts
> minimal interfaces
> reproducible behavior
> readable documentation
>
> notation: abstract and readable
> structured and redundant
>
> compiler: reliable and fast
> extensive checking
> portable code
>
> interpreter: reliable and fast
> minimal checking
> static store allocation

This is the philosophy we will follow in the design of concurrent programs.

1.9 LITERATURE

For me the most enjoyable thing about computer programming is the insight it gives into problem solving and design. The search for simplicity and structure is common to all intellectual disciplines.

Here are a historian and a biologist talking about the importance of recognizing structure:

"It is a matter of some importance to link teaching and research, even very detailed research, to an acceptable architectonic vision of the whole. Without such connections, detail becomes mere antiquarianism. Yet while history without detail is inconceivable, without an organizing vision it quickly becomes incomprehensible . . . What cannot be understood becomes meaningless, and reasonable men quite properly refuse to pay attention to meaningless matters."

William H. McNeill [1974]

"There have been a number of physicists who suggested that biological phenomena are related to the finest aspects of the constitution of matter, in a manner of speaking below the chemical level. But the evidence, which is almost too abundant, indicates that biological phenomena operate on the 'systems' level, that is, above chemistry."

Walter M. Elsasser [1975]

A linguist, a psychologist, and a logician have this to say about writing and notation:

"Omit needless words. Vigorous writing is concise. A sentence should contain no unnecessary words, a paragraph no unnecessary sentences, for the same reason that a drawing should have no unnecessary lines and a machine no unnecessary parts. This requires not that the writer make all his sentences short, or that he avoid all detail and treat his subject only in outline, but that every word tell."

William Strunk, Jr. [1959]

"How complex or simple a structure is depends critically upon the way in which we describe it. Most of the complex structures found in the world are enormously redundant, and we can use this redundancy to simplify their description. But to use it, to achieve the simplification, we must find the right representation."

Herbert A. Simon [1969]

"There is something uncanny about the power of a happily chosen ideographic language; for it often allows one to express relations which have no names in natural language and therefore have never been noticed by anyone.

Symbolism, then, becomes an organ of discovery rather than mere nota-tion."

Susanne K. Langer [1967]

An engineer and an architect discuss the influence of human errors and cultural changes on the design process:

"First, one must perform perfectly. The computer resembles the magic of legend in this respect, too. If one character, one pause, of the incantation is not strictly in proper form, the magic doesn't work. Human beings are not accustomed to being perfect, and few areas of human activity demand it. Adjusting to the requirement for perfection is, I think, the most difficult part of learning to program."

Frederick P. Brooks, Jr. [1975]

"Misfit provides an incentive to change . . . However, for the fit to occur in practice, one vital condition must be satisfied. It must have time to hap-pen. The process must be able to achieve its equilibrium before the next cul-ture change upsets it again. It must actually have time to reach its equilibrium every time it is disturbed — or, if we see the process as continu-ous rather than intermittent, the adjustment of forms must proceed more quickly than the drift of the culture context."

Christopher Alexander [1964]

Finally, here are a mathematician and a physicist writing about the beauty and joy of creative work:

"The mathematician's patterns, like the painter's or the poet's, must be beautiful; the ideas, like the colours or the words, must fit together in a harmonious way. Beauty is the first test: there is no permanent place in the world for ugly mathematics."

G. H. Hardy [1967]

"The most powerful drive in the ascent of man is his pleasure in his own skill. He loves to do what he does well and, having done it well, he loves to do it better. You see it in his science. You see it in the magnificence with which he carves and builds, the loving care, the gaiety, the effrontery. The monuments are supposed to commemorate kings and religions, heroes, dogmas, but in the end the man they commemorate is the builder."

Jacob Bronowski [1973]

REFERENCES

ALEXANDER, C., *Notes on the synthesis of form*. Harvard University Press, Cambridge, MA, 1964.

BRONOWSKI, J., *The ascent of man*. Little, Brown and Company, Boston, MA, 1973.

BROOKS, F. P., *The mythical man-month. Essays on software engineering*. Addison-Wesley, Reading, MA, 1975.

ELSASSER, W. M., *The chief abstractions of biology*. American Elsevier, New York, NY, 1975.

HARDY, G. H., *A mathematician's apology*. Cambridge University Press, New York, NY, 1967.

LANGER, S. K., *An introduction to symbolic logic*. Dover Publications, New York, NY, 1967.

MCNEILL, W. H., *The shape of European history*. Oxford University Press, New York, NY, 1974.

SIMON, H. A., *The sciences of the artificial*. M.I.T. Press, Cambridge, MA, 1969.

STRUNK, W., and WHITE, E. B., *The elements of style*. Macmillan, New York, NY, 1959.

2

PROGRAMMING CONCEPTS

We will construct large concurrent programs as hierarchies of smaller components. Each component should have a well-defined function that can be implemented and tested as an almost independent program. The components and their combinations should have reproducible behavior. And the verification and testing of such programs must take place much faster than they will change due to new requirements.

This chapter introduces the kind of components we will use and describes how to connect them. Our programming tool is a language called *Concurrent Pascal.* It extends the sequential programming language Pascal with new concepts called *processes, monitors,* and *classes.*

This is an informal description of Concurrent Pascal. It uses examples, pictures, and words to bring out the creative aspects of new programming concepts without getting into their finer details. Other chapters will introduce a language notation for these concepts and define them concisely. This form of presentation is perhaps not precise from a formal point of view. But it is, I hope, more effective from a human point of view.

2.1 CONCURRENT PROCESSES

I will introduce the language by solving a simple and useful problem: How can text be copied as fast as possible from a card reader to a line printer?

Figure 2.1 shows a card reader, a line printer, and a program that copies data from one to the other. The card reader and line printer can transfer 1000 and 600 lines/min (corresponding to 60 and 100 msec/line).

The simplest solution to the problem is a cyclical, sequential program

cycle input; output **end**

that inputs one line at a time from the card reader and outputs it to the line printer.

Unfortunately, this is very inefficient since it forces the card reader and line printer to alternate

input, output, input, output, . . .

so that one of them always waits while the other operates. As a result the copying speed is only 375 lines/min (or 160 msec/line).

We can only increase the speed by letting the card reader and the line printer operate *simultaneously* (Fig. 2.2). The copy program now consists of two sequential processes that are executed simultaneously

card process: cycle input; send **end**
printer process: cycle receive; output **end**

A card process inputs one line at a time from the card reader and sends it through a buffer to a printer process that receives and outputs it to the line printer. This program copies text at the speed of the slowest device (600 lines/min).

Since we are interested in abstract programming it is not important

CARD READER   LINE PRINTER

PROGRAM

Fig. 2.1 Data copying

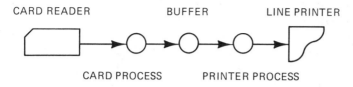

CARD READER   BUFFER   LINE PRINTER

CARD PROCESS   PRINTER PROCESS

Fig. 2.2   Data flow among concurrent processes

how *concurrent processes* are implemented on a computer. All we need to know is that they are executed simultaneously so that they can make peripherals run at the same time.

On some computers, a single processor will be multiplexed among concurrent processes by means of clock interrupts. On other computers, each process will be executed by its own processor. We will deliberately ignore these details and assume that they are taken care of by the machine which executes the compiled code of our abstract concurrent programs. (Chapter 9 describes the implementation of Concurrent Pascal on the PDP 11/45 computer.)

Our refusal to be concerned with machine detail makes it impossible to predict the absolute and relative speeds of concurrent processes. We will, however, assume that all processes have positive speeds. (After all, why write a piece of program unless we know that the machine will execute it?) The machine will often be much faster than its peripherals so that we can expect processes to run roughly at the speed of the devices they control.

2.2   PRIVATE DATA

We will build concurrent programs out of sequential processes that are executed simultaneously. This is quite attractive since most programmers already have a deep intuitive understanding of sequential programming.

A *sequential process* consists of a data structure and a sequential program that operates on it (Fig. 2.3). The program statements are executed strictly one at a time.

The important thing about a sequential program is that it always gives

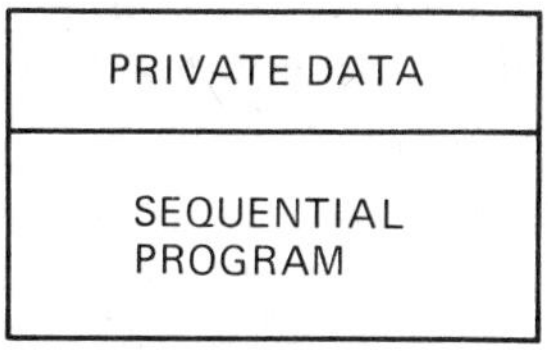

```
┌─────────────────────────┐
│  PRIVATE DATA           │
├─────────────────────────┤
│  SEQUENTIAL             │
│  PROGRAM                │
│                         │
└─────────────────────────┘
```

Fig. 2.3   A process

the same results when it operates on the same data *independently of how fast it is executed.* All that matters is the *sequence* in which operations are carried out.

A *programming error* in a sequential program can always be located by repeating the execution of the program several times with the data that revealed the error. In each of these *experiments*, the values of selected variables are recorded to determine whether or not a certain program part works. This process of elimination continues until the error has been located.

When a program part has been found to behave correctly in one test we can ignore that part (and its variables) in subsequent tests because it will continue to behave in exactly the same manner each time the program is executed with the same data. So *our ability to test a large, sequential program in small steps depends fundamentally on the reproducible behavior of the program.*

The time-independent behavior of a sequential process is guaranteed, however, only if its variables are inaccessible to other processes. But if a process uses the values of a variable which another process changes, then the result depends on the relative speeds of the processes.

When a concurrent program is executed several times with the same data, the relative speed of the processes will always vary somewhat. In a multiplexed computer the execution of a process will be influenced by the presence of other (perhaps unrelated) processes. And in a multiprocessor system, execution speeds will depend on how fast operators react to program requests.

If a concurrent program contains an error that makes one process change the variables of another process at unpredictable times, then that program will give different results each time it is executed with the same data.

Such unpredictable program behavior makes it impossible to locate an error by systematic testing. It can perhaps be found by studying the program text in detail for days. But this can be very frustrating (if not impossible) when it consists of thousands of lines and one has no clues about where to look.

If we wish to succeed in building large, concurrent programs which are reliable, we must use programming languages that are so well structured that a compiler can catch most time-dependent errors (because nobody else can). So we will choose a language notation that clearly shows which variables a process owns. The compiler will then make sure that these *private variables* are inaccessible to other processes.

2.3 PERIPHERALS

Peripheral devices are a potential source of erratic program behavior that deserves careful attention. The classical programming technique for simultaneous input and processing of data is to use a *double buffer* that is accessible both to a sequential program and its input device.

The program inputs the first data item in a buffer variable x. While the program operates on x, the device inputs the second data item in another buffer variable y. The program then processes y while the third data item is being input to x, and so on.

More than one programmer has made the mistake of referring to a data item before it has been input completely. This makes the program result depend on the relative speed of program execution and input transfers.

The problem is that this programming technique turns a program and its peripherals into concurrent processes that can refer to each other's "private" variables by mistake.

In Concurrent Pascal a peripheral device can only be accessed by an operation *io* that delays the calling process until the input/output has been completed. So a variable is at any time accessible either to a single process or to a single device (but not to both of them). A data transfer is just another sequential operation with a completely reproducible result.

While a process is waiting for the completion of a data transfer, the computer can execute other processes. So this approach does not necessarily make the machine idle. Simultaneous input and processing of data items can be done by two processes connected by a buffer (Fig. 2.2).

Another benefit of making input/output an *indivisible* operation is that *peripheral interrupts become irrelevant to the programmer*. They are handled completely at the machine level.

When computer problems first arise they are often solved in very complicated ways. It takes a long time to discover the obvious solutions. And then it takes a while longer to get used to them. The programming of input/output illustrates this well.

2.4 SHARED DATA

Although it is vital to make sure that some variables are private to processes, they must also be able to share data structures (such as a buffer). Otherwise, concurrent processes cannot exchange data and cooperate on common tasks. But since shared data are the major pitfall of concurrent programming we must proceed with extreme care and define exactly what processes can do with such data structures.

The *buffer* in the copying program is a data structure shared by two concurrent processes (Fig. 2.2). The details of how such a buffer is constructed are irrelevant to its users. All the processes need to know is that they can *send* and *receive* data through it. If they try to operate on the buffer in any other way it is probably either a programming mistake or an example of tricky programming. In both cases, one would like a compiler to detect such misuse of a shared data structure.

To make this possible, we must introduce a language construct that will enable a programmer to tell a compiler how a shared data structure can be used by processes. This kind of system component is called a *monitor*. A monitor can synchronize concurrent processes and transmit data among them. It can also control the order in which competing processes use shared, physical resources.

A monitor defines a *shared data* structure and all the operations processes can perform on it (Fig. 2.4). These synchronizing operations are called *monitor procedures*. A monitor also defines an *initial operation* that is executed when its data structure is created.

We can define a *buffer* as a monitor. It will consist of shared variables defining the *contents* of the buffer. It will also include two monitor procedures, *send* and *receive*. The initial operation will make the buffer *empty* to begin with.

Processes cannot operate directly on shared data. They can only call monitor procedures (such as send and receive) that have access to the data. A monitor procedure is executed as part of the calling process (just like any other procedure).

If concurrent processes simultaneously call monitor procedures which operate on the same shared data, these procedures must be executed strictly one at a time. Otherwise, processes might find the data structure in some (unknown) intermediate state, which would make the results of monitor calls unpredictable.

This means that the machine must be able to delay processes for short periods of time until it is their turn to execute monitor procedures. We will not be concerned about how this is done, but will just notice that a process

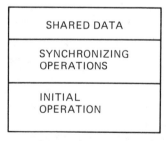

Fig. 2.4   A monitor

has *exclusive access* to shared data while it executes a monitor procedure. (Chapter 9 explains the implementation details of this.)

So the machine on which concurrent processes run will handle *short-term scheduling* of simultaneous monitor calls. But the programmer must also be able to delay processes for longer periods of time until their requests for data and other resources can be satisfied. For example, if a process tries to receive data from an empty buffer it must be delayed until another process sends more data.

Concurrent Pascal includes a simple data type, called a *queue*, that can be used by monitor procedures to control *medium-term scheduling* of processes. A monitor can either *delay* a calling process in a queue or *continue* a process waiting in a queue.

It is not important yet to understand how these queues work except for the following rule: *A process has exclusive access to shared data only as long as it continues to execute statements within a monitor procedure. As soon as a process is delayed in a queue it loses its exclusive access until another process calls the same monitor and continues its execution.*

A compiler will check that processes only access a monitor through its procedures. This has dramatic consequences for program *reliability*. It means that once a monitor has been implemented correctly other parts of a program cannot make it fail. It remains a *stable, correct component* no matter what the rest of the program does. Compile-time protection of private variables has the same effect on processes.

Programming languages, such as Fortran, Cobol, PL/1, and Pascal use common data structures ("global variables") as interfaces between separate program parts. This makes it easy for one part of a program to crash another by changing its data structure in unexpected ways.

Concurrent Pascal is based on the assumption that *procedures are a much safer interface mechanism than common data structures*. Procedures associated with a data structure make it possible for a programmer to define all the possible operations on the data and depend on a compiler to prevent the rest of a program from using the data in any other way.

2.5 ACCESS RIGHTS

So far I have only introduced the *components* from which concurrent programs can be constructed, namely processes and monitors. But we still need a precise way of describing how these components can be *connected* to form *hierarchical structures*.

Figure 2.2 makes it obvious that data flow from a card process through a buffer to a printer process. We will call this a *data flow graph*.

Figure 2.5 shows the same system from a different viewpoint. The circles are *system components*, and the arrows are the *access rights* of these

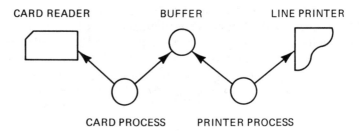

CARD READER   BUFFER   LINE PRINTER

CARD PROCESS   PRINTER PROCESS

Fig. 2.5   System components and their access rights

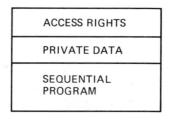

Fig. 2.6   A process with access rights

components. They show that both processes can *use* the buffer, but that only the card process can use the card reader, and only the printer process can use the line printer. This kind of picture is an *access graph*.

The access rights of the processes only enable them to call the *send* and *receive* procedures defined by the *buffer* monitor. They do not give them the right to operate directly on the data structure that represents the buffer. (I remark in passing that *peripheral devices* can be looked upon as monitors implemented in hardware which can only be accessed by a single procedure *io.*)

This will be our structuring mechanism: to connect program components by access rights into hierarchical systems in which concurrent processes communicate by calling monitors.

In a large concurrent program these access rights should be written down to make the program structure obvious to a reader and verifiable to a compiler. So we will extend a *process* with *access rights* (Fig. 2.6). The access rights mention the monitors the process can call.

Although the copying example does not show this, monitor procedures should also be able to call procedures defined within other monitors. Otherwise, the language will not be very useful for hierarchical design. So a *monitor* can also have *access rights* to other monitors (Fig. 2.7).

Processes can only communicate by means of monitors. A compiler will check that a process only uses the monitors it has access to.

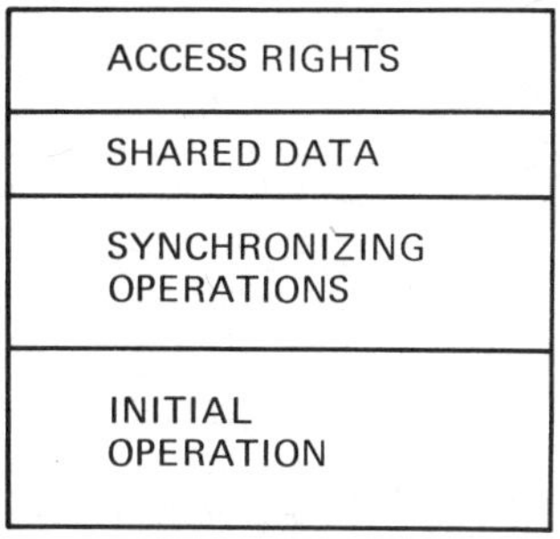

```
┌─────────────────────────┐
│                         │
│      ACCESS RIGHTS      │
│                         │
├─────────────────────────┤
│                         │
│      SHARED DATA        │
│                         │
├─────────────────────────┤
│      SYNCHRONIZING      │
│      OPERATIONS         │
│                         │
├─────────────────────────┤
│                         │
│      INITIAL            │
│      OPERATION          │
│                         │
└─────────────────────────┘
```

Fig. 2.7   A monitor with access rights

2.6 ABSTRACT DATA TYPES

A process executes a sequential program — it is an active component. A monitor is just a collection of procedures which do nothing until they are called by processes — it is a passive component. But there are strong similarities between a process and a monitor: both define a data structure (private or shared) and the meaningful operations on it. The main difference between processes and monitors is the way they are scheduled for execution.

It seems natural, therefore, to regard processes and monitors as *abstract data types* defined in terms of the operations one can perform on them. They are abstract because the rest of a program only knows *what* one can do with them without depending on *how* the data are structured and manipulated. It is even possible to change the *data representation* without influencing the rest of a program as long as the operations remain the same.

In the copying system the buffer can be represented either by a single line slot, an array of lines, a linked list, or a tree structure. And it can be stored either in core or on disk. The processes do not care as long as they can send and receive lines through it. This gives the programmer the freedom to experiment with different data representations to improve performance.

The hiding of implementation details within an abstract data type makes it easier to tune a program locally. It also makes it easier to understand what the program does as a whole, since all these different data representations implement the same abstract idea of sending and receiving.

Since a compiler can check that these operations are the only ones carried out on the abstract data structure we can hope to be able to build very reliable, concurrent programs in which *controlled access* to data and physical resources is guaranteed before these programs are put into operation (or even tested). This will solve to a large extent the *resource protection* problems in the cheapest possible manner (without hardware mechanisms and run-time overhead).

CARD READER   BUFFERS   LINE PRINTER

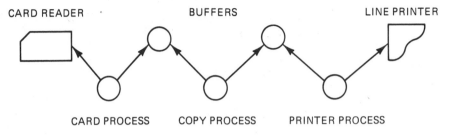

CARD PROCESS   COPY PROCESS   PRINTER PROCESS

Fig. 2.8   A pipeline system

A useful concept can be used over and over again (and not just once). So we will define processes and monitors as data types and make it possible to use several instances of each of them in a system. We can, for example, use *two buffers* to build a *pipeline system* in which data pass through a card process, a copy process, and a printer process (Fig. 2.8).

The *copy process* will format the text so that each file begins and ends with a blank page, each page begins and ends with a blank line, and each line is surrounded by blank margins.

Since input/output and execution alternate strictly within peripheral processes it is desirable to keep their data processing minimal to make the devices run as fast as possible. This is achieved by formatting the text in a separate process that can run while the other processes are waiting for input/output. This extension of the copying system also has the advantage of leaving all the previous components unchanged (Fig. 2.5). So here we have an example of how one can adapt a program to new requirements without changing it completely.

In a concurrent program the programmer only *defines* the buffer *type* once but *declares* two *instances* of it. I will distinguish between definitions and instances of components by calling them *system types* and *system components*. Access graphs (such as Fig. 2.8) will always show system components (not system types).

During program execution the machine creates a separate data structure for each system component. But components of the same type share a single copy of the procedures associated with the data. So the pipeline system uses two copies of the buffer variables but only one copy of the send and receive procedures.

To make the programming language useful for hierarchical system design it should permit the division of a system type, such as the copy process, into smaller system types. Let us assume that the buffers in Fig. 2.8 transmit whole lines of text between the processes. The text formatting can then be done one step at a time by means of three abstract data types inserted between the copy process and its output buffer (Fig. 2.9).

The copy process calls a *file maker* which adds blank pages to each text

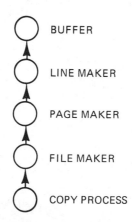

Fig. 2.9   Decomposition of the copy process

file. The file maker in turn calls a *page maker* which adds blank lines to each text page. The page maker then calls a *line maker* which adds a margin to each text line before sending it through the buffer.

The file, page, and line makers are only used by the copy process. Such components which can only be called by a single other component will be called *classes*.

A class defines a data structure and the possible operations on it (just like a monitor). The exclusive access of a process to class variables can be guaranteed completely at compile time. The machine does not have to schedule simultaneous calls of class procedures at run time, because such calls cannot occur. This makes class calls considerably faster than monitor calls.

2.7 HIERARCHICAL STRUCTURE

If we put all the components of the pipeline system together we get a complete picture of its structure. In Fig. 2.10, classes, monitors, and processes are marked, *C*, *M*, and *P*.

In an access graph a process is a node that no other node has access to. A class is one that a single other node has access to. And a monitor is one that two or more other nodes have access to. (The phrase "has access to" also means "points to.")

Some years ago I was part of a team that built a multiprogramming system in which processes can appear and disappear dynamically [Brinch Hansen, 1970]. In practice, this system was used mostly to set up a fixed configuration of processes. This is to be expected, since most concurrent programs control computers with a fixed configuration of peripherals and perform a fixed number of control tasks in some environment.

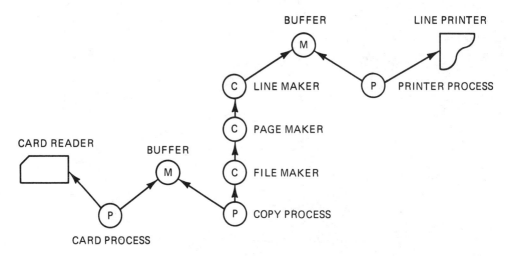

Fig. 2.10   Hierarchical system structure

Dynamic process deletion certainly complicates the meaning and implementation of a programming language considerably. And since it seems to be unnecessary in many real-time applications, it is probably wise to exclude it altogether. So *a concurrent program will consist of a fixed number of processes, monitors, and classes.* These components and their data structures will exist forever after system initialization. A concurrent program can, however, be extended by recompilation.

It remains to be seen whether this restriction will simplify or complicate operating system design. But the poor quality of most existing operating systems clearly demonstrates an urgent need for simpler approaches.

In other programming languages the data structures of processes, monitors, and classes would be called *global data.* This term would be misleading in Concurrent Pascal, where each data structure can be accessed by a single component only. It seems more appropriate to call them *permanent data structures.*

A Concurrent Pascal compiler will check that the private data of a process are accessed only by that process. It will also check that the data structure of a class or monitor is accessed only by its procedures.

Figure 2.10 shows that the *access rights* within a concurrent program normally are not tree structured. Instead they form a directed graph. This partly explains why the traditional *scope rules* of block structured languages are inconvenient for concurrent programming (and, I believe, for sequential programming as well). In addition, the access rights to variables in these languages are not very selective (a block can use not only its own variables but also those defined in all blocks surrounding it). In Concurrent Pascal, a program component has access to only a small number of other components. And these components are accessible only through well-defined procedures.

Since the execution of a monitor procedure will delay the execution of further calls of the same monitor, we must prevent a monitor from calling itself recursively. Otherwise, processes can become *deadlocked* waiting (in vain) for themselves to leave monitors before they reenter them. So the compiler will check that the access rights of system components are hierarchically ordered (or, if you like, that there are no cycles in the access graph).

The *hierarchical ordering* of system components has vital consequences for system design and testing:

A hierarchical, concurrent program can be *tested* component by component, *bottom up* (but could, of course, be conceived *top down* or by *iteration*). Here the "bottom" of a program is all the components which do not use any other components, while the "top" is those components which no other components use.

When an incomplete program has been shown to work correctly (by proof or testing), a compiler can guarantee that this part of the system will continue to work correctly when new untested components are added on top of it. Programming errors within new components cannot make old components fail because old components do not call new components, and new components only call old components through well-defined procedures that have already been tested.

Several other reasons besides program correctness make a hierarchical structure attractive:

(1) A hierarchical system can be studied in a stepwise manner as a sequence of *abstract machines* simulated by programs [Dijkstra, 1971].

(2) A partial ordering of process interactions permits one to use *mathematical induction* to prove certain overall properties of the system (such as the absence of deadlocks) [Brinch Hansen, 1973b].

(3) *Efficient resource utilization* can be achieved by ordering the program components according to the speed of the physical resources they control (with the fastest resources being controlled at the bottom of the system) [Dijkstra, 1971].

(4) A hierarchical system designed according to the previous criteria is often *nearly decomposable* from an analytical point of view. This means that one can develop stochastic models of its dynamic behavior in a stepwise manner [Simon, 1969].

It seems most natural to represent a hierarchical system, such as Fig. 2.10, by a two-dimensional *picture*. But in order to *write* a concurrent program, we must somehow represent these access rules by linear text. This limitation of written language tends to obscure the simplicity of the original structure. That is why I have tried to explain the purpose of Concurrent Pascal by means of pictures instead of language notation.

The next two chapters introduce the language notation of Sequential and Concurrent Pascal and present a complete, executable program for the pipeline system.

3

SEQUENTIAL PASCAL

The purpose of this work is to experiment with a small number of concepts for concurrent programming. Instead of inventing a new programming language from scratch I have used an existing sequential language *Pascal* as a host for these ideas. The resulting language is *Concurrent Pascal*.

The model operating systems described here are written in Concurrent Pascal. All other programs are written in Sequential Pascal: compilers, editors, input/output drivers, job control interpreters, disk allocators, and user programs.

This is a short, informal overview of Sequential Pascal. It is neither complete nor concise. But it should be sufficient to understand the programs described later. For historic reasons there are minor differences between the most recent version of Pascal [Jensen and Wirth, 1974] and the one used here. Since these differences do not change the direction of this work they will be ignored.

The representation of basic symbols is somewhat restricted by the character set used (ASCII). I have improved this slightly by using bold face types for word symbols in this book. Apart from this, the programs are presented in their original executable form. I have become used to this program representation and find it as readable as any other.

3.1 PROGRAM STRUCTURE

A Sequential Pascal program consists of declarations of

> constants
> data types
> variables
> routines

and a sequence of *statements* that operate on these objects. The statements will be executed one at a time.

An outline of a program is shown below.

```
const linelength = 132;

type line = array (.1..linelength.) of char;

var pageno, maxno: integer; ok: boolean;

procedure writetext(text: line);
var i: integer; c: char;
begin
   i:= 0;
   repeat
     i:= i + 1;
     c := text(.i.);
     display(c);
   until c = ' ';
end;
.....
begin
   .....
   if pageno = maxno then
   begin
     writetext('filelimit ');
     ok:= false;
   end;
   .....
end.
```

The program defines a constant *linelength* with the value 132 and a data type *line* which is an array of characters numbered 1, 2, 3, . . . , linelength.

It uses three variables: two integers, called *pageno* and *maxno*, and a boolean *ok*.

The program also defines a procedure *writetext* which uses a line para-meter named *text*. The procedure has two local variables: an integer *i* and a character *c*. One of the program statements calls this procedure to write the text string 'filelimit'.

The objects used by the programs have *unique identifiers*

> linelength
> line
> pageno
> maxno
> ok
> writetext
> . . . . .

These identifiers are *introduced* by declarations before they are *used* in state-ments. This redundancy enables a compiler to detect misspelled or ambigu-ous identifiers. (Strictly speaking, the same identifier can be used for differ-ent objects within different routines and data structures, but this is not important here.)

3.2 CONSTANTS AND VARIABLES

If a *constant* is used several times in a program it is useful to define its value once and refer to it elsewhere by an identifier

> **const** pagelength = 512; firstline = 2;

This makes it easy to change the value later if necessary.

ASCII characters are numbered 0 to 127. These *ordinal values* can be used to define unprintable characters such as NL (new line) and EM (end medium)

> **const** nl = '(:10:)'; em = '(:25:)';

One can also name string constants and real constants

> **const** pass5 = 'spass5';
> oneday = 86400.0 "seconds";

A *comment*, such as "seconds", has no effect on the program. In Pascal a *variable v* must always be of some fixed *type* T

$$var \ v: T$$

The type defines all the possible values of the variable. The declarations

$$var \ pageno, \ maxno: integer;$$
$$ok: boolean;$$

restrict the variables *pageno* and *maxno* to *integer* values

$$\ldots -2, -1, 0, 1, 2, \ldots$$

and limit the variable *ok* to *boolean* values

$$false, \ true$$

The basic operations on variables are *assignment* of values

$$maxno := 255$$
$$pageno := pageno + 1$$
$$ok := false$$

and *comparisons* for equality

$$if \ pageno = maxno \ then \ldots$$

or inequality

$$while \ status <> complete \ do \ldots$$

The fixed types of variables enhance the readability of programs by making some of their assumptions explicit. The declaration

$$var \ pageno: integer$$

reveals that the programmer only intends to assign integer values to the variable *pageno*, perform arithmetic operations on it, and compare it to other integers. Anything else is a mistake on his part.

This explicit assumption enables a compiler to detect meaningless statements, such as an assignment of a boolean value to an integer variable

$$pageno := false$$

or a comparison of integer and boolean variables

$$if\ pageno = ok\ then\ ...$$

Although a computer may represent the boolean values *false* and *true* by 0 and 1, it is essential to consider booleans and integers as different concepts in a programming language. Otherwise, a compiler cannot perform this kind of *type checking*.

3.3 SIMPLE DATA TYPES

The data type concept plays a central role in abstract programming because it clarifies the assumptions of programs and makes them partly verifiable during compilation.

The *simple data types* consist of values that can only be operated upon as a whole. They are either *enumerations* or *reals*. The types

        type integer = (–32768, –32767, ... 0, 1, ... 32767)

        type boolean = (false, true)

        type char   = (nul, soh, ... '#', '$', ... '0', '1', ... 'a', 'b', ... del)

are enumerations. Each of them defines a finite, ordered set of values. These standard types need not be defined by the programmer. This is only done here to show their values.

The language notation does not reveal how these values are represented in a computer. The integer values might be stored as two's complement bit patterns, the boolean values as 0 and 1, and the character values as 0 to 127. *Pascal enables the programmer to ignore details of machine representation and consider integers, booleans, and characters as distinct, abstract concepts.*

The programmer can also define his own enumeration types. For example, the definition

> **type** iooperation = (input, output, move, control)

introduces a new data type called *iooperation*. Its values are called *input*, *output, move,* and *control.* A computer might represent these values by 0, 1, 2, and 3, but this is irrelevant to the programmer.

Other examples of new enumeration types are

> **type** iodevice = (typedevice, diskdevice, tapedevice,
>   printdevice, carddevice)
>
> **type** ioresult = (complete, intervention, transmission,
>   failure, endfile, endmedium, startmedium)

Enumeration variables are declared as follows

> **var** count, lineno, charno: integer;
>
> ok: boolean;
>
> c: char;
>
> status: ioresult;

An enumeration value can be used to *select* a statement to be executed

> **if** count < 0 **then** write('–') **else** write(' ')
>
> **if** (count = pagelength) **or** (c = em) **then**
> **begin** write(text); count:= 0 **end**
>
> **case** status **of**
>   complete:
>   ok:= true;
>   intervention:
>   **begin** wait; ok:= false **end**;
>   transmission, failure:
>   **begin** write('errors'); ok:= false **end**
> **end**

or to *repeat* the execution of a statement

> **for** lineno:= 1 **to** firstline – 1 **do** write(nl)

> **while** (c $<>$ '#') & (charno $<$ linelength) **do**
> **begin** write(c); charno:= charno + 1; read(c) **end**

> **repeat** read(c) **until** c = em

An enumeration type can also be a *subrange* of another one

> **type** fileno = 1..2;
>
> > digit = '0'..'9';
> >
> > iomark = endfile..startmedium;
>
> **var** f: fileno; d: digit; m: iomark;

These declarations restrict the variable *f* to the values 1 and 2, the variable *d* to the values '0', '1', . . . '9', and the variable *m* to the values *endfile, endmedium,* and *startmedium.* For example

> f:= 2; d:= '3'; m:= endmedium;

The standard type *real* consists of a finite set of the real numbers

> **var** seconds: real;
>
> seconds:= seconds + 1.0;
>
> **if** seconds $>=$ oneday **then** seconds:= seconds – oneday;

The following standard functions *convert* values of one simple type to another

ord(x)	The ordinal value of the character x.
chr(x)	The character with the ordinal value x.
conv(x)	The real corresponding to the integer x.
trunc(x)	The integer corresponding to the real x.

Example:

```
const onemin = 60.0 "seconds";
var min, sec: integer; rem: real;
sec:=trunc(rem - conv(min) * onemin)
```

Example:

```
var digit: char; rem: integer;
digit:= chr(abs(rem mod 10) + ord('0'))
```

3.4 STRUCTURED DATA TYPES

Arrays, records, and sets are data structures composed of simpler types. They can be operated upon either as a whole or component by component.

An *array* is a data structure with a fixed number of components of the same type. A text line, for example, can be defined as an array of characters

```
type line = array (.1..132.) of char
```

The individual characters have *indices* from 1 to 132.

The declarations

```
var text, error: line; charno: integer;
```

introduce two line variables, *text* and *error*, and an integer variable, *charno*.

Lines can be operated upon as a whole

```
if status <> complete then text:= error
```

or character by character

```
for charno:= 1 to 132 do error(.charno.):= '?'
```

An array element is *selected* by means of its index

```
error(.charno.)
```

During program execution the machine checks that indices are within the range of the arrays (here 1 to 132).

A *record* is a data structure with a fixed number of components that may be of different types. For example, to output a line on a printer one uses a record that defines the input/output operation and its result

```
type ioparam = record
            operation: iooperation;
            status: ioresult;
            arg: integer
        end
```

This data type is called an *ioparam*. It contains three *fields* named *operation*, *status*, and *arg*. These fields are of types *iooperation*, *ioresult*, and *integer* defined earlier.

A line is printed as follows

```
var param: ioparam; text: line;

param.operation:= output;
repeat io(text, param, printdevice)
until param.status = complete;
```

(The extra argument in the record is only used for disks and magnetic tapes.)
A record field is *selected* by means of its identifier

```
param.operation
param.status
```

Instead of repeatedly qualifying record fields with the same record identifier one can do it once by means of a *with* statement

```
with param do
begin
    operation:= output;
    repeat io(text, param, printdevice)
    until status = complete;
end
```

The data type

$$\text{type characters} = \textbf{set of } \text{char}$$

defines all the possible *subsets* of characters, among others

```
var empty, signs, digits: characters;
empty:= (..)
signs:= (.'+', '-'.)
digits:= (.'0', '1', '2', '3', '4', '5', '6', '7', '8', '9'.)
```

Another example of a set type is

$$\text{type cylinder} = \textbf{set of } \text{sector}$$

where

$$\text{type sector} = 0..23$$

which defines a disk cylinder as a set of sectors numbered 0 to 23.
     In general, a *set* type

$$\textbf{set of } \text{T}$$

defines all the possible subsets of the values of an enumeration type T.
     The basic set operations are

or	union
&	intersection
−	difference
in	membership

Example:

```
var numeric: characters;
```

```
numeric:= signs or digits
```

Example:

> **var** pool: cylinder; next: sector;
>
> **while not** (next **in** pool) **do**
> next:= (next+1) **mod** 24;
> pool:= pool – (.next.)

We will occasionally use a variable that can have values of different types, such as boolean, integer, or identifier. A possible notation for this might be

> var param: **either** boolean, integer, **or** identifier;
>
> param:= boolean(false)
> param:= integer(15)
> if param = identifier('backup') **then** ...

This idea is a bit more cumbersome to express in Pascal. The variable must be defined as a record that contains either a boolean field, an integer field, or an identifier field. This record must include a *tag field* that defines which of the three *variants* is being represented by the other record field

> **type** argtag = (booltype, inttype, idtype);
> **type** argtype = **record**
>   **case** tag: argtag **of**
>   booltype: (bool: boolean);
>   inttype: (int: integer);
>   idtype: (id: identifier)
>   **end**;
> var param: argtype;

The type *argtag* defines the possible values of the tag field. The type *argtype* defines a record with three variants. If the tag field has the value *booltype* then the rest of the record is a boolean field named *bool*. On the other hand, if the tag value is *inttype* the record contains an integer field called *int*, and so on.

This variant record can be used as follows

> **with** param **do**
> **begin** tag:= booltype; bool:= false **end**

> **if** param.tag = idtype **then** ...

The programmer pays a price for the flexibility of variant types. Every time a program refers to a variant field the machine will check whether the tag value is consistent with the variant assumed.

3.5 ROUTINES

A routine is a sequence of statements with parameters that have been combined into a single action. Data types and routines are the main components of Sequential Pascal programs. There are two kinds of routines: *procedures* and *functions*.

Example:

```
procedure readpage(addr: integer; var block: page);
var param: ioparam;
begin
  with param do
  begin
    operation:= input;
    arg:= addr;
    repeat io(block, param, diskdevice)
    until status = complete;
  end;
end
```

where

> **type** page = **array** (.1..512.) **of** char

This procedure is called *readpage*. Its parameters are an integer and a disk page, called *addr* and *block*. The procedure can use the values of both parameters but can only change the second one. The distinction between *constant* and *variable parameters* is made by omitting or writing the symbol *var* before the parameters

> addr: integer   **var** block: page

The procedure also uses a local variable *param* to perform disk input.

The procedure can be executed by being *called* with *arguments* corresponding to those specified in its definition

> var pageno: integer; slot: page;
>
> readpage(pageno, slot)

A function is a routine that computes a single value

```
function hash(id: identifier): integer;
var key, i: integer; c: char;
begin
  key:= 1; i:= 0;
  repeat
    i:= i + 1; c:= id(.i.);
    if c <> ' ' then
      key:= key * ord(c) mod tablelength + 1;
  until (c = ' ') or (i = idlength);
  hash:= key;
end
```

This function converts an identifier

```
const idlength = 12
type identifier = array (.1..idlength.) of char
```

into an integer value called its hash key

```
var name: identifier; key: integer;
key:= hash(name)
```

3.6 SCOPE RULES

A program is much easier to understand if each of its statements operate only on a small number of variables and if each variable is accessible only to a small part of the program. This part of the program is called the *scope* of the variable.

The variables declared at the beginning of a Sequential Pascal program are accessible throughout the program. These *global variables* exist as long as the program is being executed.

The variables declared within a routine are only accessible to that routine. These *local variables* exist only while the routine is being executed.

The compiler checks these *scope rules*.

Since the local variables disappear after the execution of a routine they can only be used to hold *temporary results*. More *permanent results* must be stored in global variables. This tends to make the global data structures large and complicated for nontrivial programs. It also makes programs hard to understand since every statement can potentially change the global data.

Programs can become somewhat obscure when routines change global variables that are not passed to them as parameters. The following is an example of these *side effects*

```
var header: line; endinput: boolean;
    out: record count: integer; text: line end;

.....

procedure initialize(text: line);
begin
  header:= text;
  endinput:= true;
  out.count:= 0;
end
```

Instead of letting this procedure change the global variables *header, endinput,* and *out* without prior warning, one could ask the programmer to pass them as explicit arguments to the routine. However, the intention of this programming style is to show that these three arguments are *always* the same. This assumption would be hidden throughout the program (and might be violated by mistake) if all arguments had to be explicit.

The problem is simply that this routine needs local variables that are permanent rather than temporary. But Sequential Pascal does not make it possible for the programmer to restrict the access to a permanent variable to one (or just a few routines). It is accessible either to all routines or to none. This problem with global variables is solved in Concurrent Pascal.

3.7 TYPE CHECKING

In Pascal every constant, variable, and expression has a type that is known during compilation. This enables a compiler to check that operands are *compatible* with the operations performed on them. The compiler does this by simulating the execution of statements using the types of the operands instead of their values.

An example will show how this works

> var ok: boolean; codelength: integer;
>
> if ok & (codelength > 0) then savefile

By replacing the operands with their types we get the abstract statement

> if boolean & (integer > integer) then statement

The comparison of two integers is a legal subexpression that produces a boolean result (since it is either true or false). This reduces the expression to

> if boolean & boolean then statement

The *and* operation on two booleans produces a boolean result

> if boolean then statement

So the whole expression has a boolean value which is exactly what is required by a conditional statement.

On the other hand, the statement

> if ok & codelength then savefile

will be found incorrect since an *and* operation cannot be performed on a boolean and an integer

> if boolean & integer then statement

Type checking depends on a comparison of declarations and statements written in different parts of a program text. This textual separation makes it difficult to find type errors by proofreading the text. It is therefore vital to design a programming language such that these obscure errors can be discovered during compilation.

Automatic type checking assumes that *the types of all operands and the possible operations on them are known during compilation.* In Sequential Pascal all operands have fixed types, and the elementary operations on the standard types (boolean, char, integer, and real) are known as well (&, or, not, +, -, *, /, <, =, >, and so on).

But when the programmer introduces a structured data type, such as

> **type** diskfile = **record**
>   unit: disk;
>   map: filemap;
>   opened: boolean
>   **end**

and defines four operations on it

> **procedure** open(file: diskfile; mapaddr: integer)
> **procedure** close(file: diskfile)
> **procedure** read(file: diskfile; pageno: integer; **var** block: page)
> **procedure** write(file: diskfile; pageno: integer; block: page)

the language does not make it possible to tell the compiler that these are supposed to be the *only* operations one can perform on disk files.

In Concurrent Pascal type checking is extended to data structures as well. The problem of doing this is closely related to the problem of limiting the scope of permanent variables to a small number of routines.

Occasionally, a system programmer must be able to relax the rules of type checking somewhat. This can be done without going to the other extreme of introducing variables that are treated as typeless bit patterns throughout the program (as assembly languages and some implementation languages do).

Consider again an operating system procedure that outputs a page of data to a disk file

> **procedure** write(file: diskfile; pageno: integer; block: page)
> **begin** ..... **end**

where a page is defined as a text string

> **type** page = **array** (.1..512.) **of** char

This procedure can be used to output a text string x as page number i on a disk file f

> var f: diskfile; i: integer; x: page;
> write(f, i, x)

But if we insist that the arguments of a procedure call must be of the same types as the parameters defined within the procedure, then we cannot use the same procedure to output a page of another type, say an array of integers

> type intpage = **array** (.1..256.) **of** integer
> var g: diskfile; j: integer; y: intpage;
> write(g, j, y)

We could, of course, suggest the use of a type definition that mentions all the possible variants of a disk page. But this is unrealistic. When a system programmer writes a disk file routine he cannot anticipate all the possible data types that users will assign to disk pages in the future. All the programmer knows and can depend on when he writes the disk file procedure is the *physical length* of a disk page. This is one of the few cases in which one cannot hope to hide machine detail.

To make the output procedure more general we will define the disk page as a *universal parameter*

> **procedure** write(file: diskfile; pageno: integer;
> block: **univ** page)

The symbol *univ* indicates that the procedure can be called with any argument that occupies the same number of store locations as a disk page. It can now be called with the integer page y as an argument. Before and after the call, the variable y is regarded strictly as an integer page. And within the procedure, the parameter is considered strictly as a disk page. Type checking is only relaxed at the point where the procedure is being called.

3.8 LITERATURE

Hoare [1973] and Wirth [1976b] discuss philosophies of language design and evaluation. In *Structured programming*, Hoare [1972] summarizes the fundamental concepts of data types and structures.

Wirth's books [1973 and 1976a] are very readable introductions to systematic programming in Sequential Pascal. The *User manual and report* by Jensen and Wirth [1974] is a short overview and concise definition of Pascal.

REFERENCES

DAHL, O. J., DIJKSTRA, E. W., and HOARE, C. A. R., *Structured programming.* Academic Press, New York, NY, 1972.

HOARE, C. A. R., *Hints on programming language design.* Computer Science Department, Stanford University, Stanford, CA, Dec. 1973.

JENSEN, K., and WIRTH, N., "Pascal — user manual and report," *Lecture notes in computer science 18*, Springer-Verlag, New York, NY, 1974.

WIRTH, N., *Systematic programming: an introduction.* Prentice-Hall Inc., Englewood Cliffs, NJ, 1973.

WIRTH, N., *Algorithms + data structures = programs.* Prentice-Hall Inc., Englewood Cliffs, NJ, 1976a.

WIRTH, N., *Programming languages: what to demand and how to assess them.* Institut für Informatik, Eidgenössische Technische Hochschule, Zurich, Switzerland, 1976b.

4

CONCURRENT PASCAL

Earlier I explained the concepts of Concurrent Pascal informally by means of pictures of a hierarchical pipeline that copies text from a card reader to a line printer and formats it. I will now use the same example to introduce a language notation. The presentation is still informal — it shows the concepts of the language rather than its details.

We will program the components of the pipeline program one at a time (Fig. 2.10).

4.1 INPUT/OUTPUT

The standard procedure

$$io(block, param, device)$$

makes a peripheral *device* input or output a data *block* as defined by an additional *parameter*. The calling process is delayed until the operation is completed.

We will write the pipeline program for a computer on which the device and its parameter must be of the following types

<pre>
        type iodevice = (typedevice, diskdevice, tapedevice,
                           printdevice, carddevice)

        type ioparam = record
                           operation: iooperation;
                           status: ioresult;
                           arg: integer
                       end
</pre>

where

<pre>
        type iooperation = (input, output, move, control)

        type ioresult = (complete, intervention, transmission,
                           failure, endfile, endmedium, startmedium)
</pre>

A process defines an input/output *operation* and its *argument* before starting a device. After the data transfer the device returns one of the following *results*

complete	The operation succeeded.
intervention	The operation failed, but can be repeated after manual intervention.
transmission	The operation failed due to a transmission error, but can be repeated immediately.
failure	The operation failed and cannot be repeated until the device has been repaired.
endfile	An end of file mark was reached.
endmedium	An end of medium mark was reached.
startmedium	A start of medium mark was reached.

The types of a *data block* and the *extra argument* within an io parameter vary from device to device but will be fairly self-evident in each case (see Chapter 8 for details).

The *card reader* and *line printer* can transfer one *line* at a time

> **const** linelength = 132
> **type** line = **array** (.1..linelength.) **of** char

The card reader inputs 80 characters per line (without a termination character). The line printer outputs a variable number of characters on each line terminated by a NL or FF character

$$\textbf{const } nl = '(:10:)'; \textit{ff} = '(:12:)';$$

A concurrent program must ensure that its devices are used by at most one process at a time (since the machine does not check this).

4.2 PROCESSES

Although we only need one *printer process*, we may as well define it as a general system type of which several copies may exist

> **type** printerprocess =
> **process**(buffer: linebuffer);
>
> **var** param: ioparam; text: line;
>
> **begin**
>   param.operation:= output;
>   **cycle**
>   buffer.receive(text);
>   **repeat** io(text, param, printdevice)
>   **until** param.status = complete;
>   **end;**
> **end;**

A printer process has access to a *buffer* of type *linebuffer* (to be defined later). The process has two variables, *param* and *text*, of *ioparam* and *line* types.

A process type defines a *sequential program:* in this case, an endless cycle that receives a line from the buffer and outputs it to the printer.

The *receive* operation on the buffer

$$\text{buffer.receive(text)}$$

returns a line of text.

The output of a line is repeated until it is successfully completed (that is, until the operator turns on the power of the line printer and puts it under computer control).

The next component type is a *card process*.

```
type cardprocess =
process(buffer: linebuffer);

var param: ioparam; text, error: line;
    charno: integer;

begin
   for charno:= 1 to 80 do error(.charno.):= '?';
   param.operation:= input;
   with param do
   cycle
      repeat io(text, param, carddevice)
      until status <> intervention;
      if status <> complete then text:= error;
      buffer.send(text);
   end;
end;
```

A card process has access to a line *buffer*. It uses four private variables: an io *parameter*, two lines called *text* and *error*, and an integer called *charno*.

The process inputs lines from the card reader and sends them through the buffer. If the power of the card reader is turned off, the input is repeated until the operator intervenes. A card input with transmission errors is replaced by question marks.

Finally, we need a *copy process* that can transmit data from one buffer to another.

```
type copyprocess =
process(inbuffer, outbuffer: linebuffer);

var consumer: filemaker; text: line;

begin
   init consumer(outbuffer);
   with inbuffer, consumer do
   cycle receive(text); write(text) end;
end;
```

A copy process has access to an *input* and an *output buffer*. It has two private variables: a *consumer* of type *filemaker* (defined later) and a *text* line.

The statement

> init consumer(outbuffer)

initializes the consumer and connects it to the output buffer. This is explained in more detail later.

To begin with, a concurrent program is executed as a single, sequential process called the *initial process*. It contains declarations of the other processes and monitors

> var inbuffer, outbuffer: linebuffer;
> reader: cardprocess;
> copier: copyprocess;
> printer: printerprocess;

The system components are a card process, a copy process, and a printer process called the *reader*, *copier*, and *printer*. They are connected by *input* and *output buffers*.

The initial process starts the reader process by an *init* statement

> init reader(inbuffer)

which allocates storage for the *private variables* of the process and starts its execution with access to the input buffer. The *access rights* of a process to other system components, such as the input buffer, are also called its *parameters*.

A process can only be initialized once. After initialization, the parameters and private variables of a process exist forever. They are called *permanent variables*.

The init statement can be used to start concurrent execution of several processes and define their access rights. The statement

> init reader(inbuffer),
> copier(inbuffer, outbuffer),
> printer(outbuffer)

starts concurrent execution of the reader process (with access to the input buffer), the copier process (with access to both buffers), and the printer process (with access to the output buffer).

A process can only access its own parameters and private variables. The latter are not accessible to other system components. Compare this with the more liberal *scope rules* of block-structured languages in which a routine can access not only its own parameters and local variables but also those declared globally.

In Concurrent Pascal all variables accessible to a system component are declared within its type definition. This access rule and the init statement make it possible for a programmer to state access rights explicitly and have them checked by a compiler. They also make it possible to study a system type as a self-contained program unit.

Although the examples do not show this, one can also define constants, data types, and procedures within a process. These objects can only be used within the process type.

4.3 MONITORS

A *line buffer* is a monitor type.

```
type linebuffer =
monitor

var contents: line; full: boolean;
    sender, receiver: queue;

procedure entry receive(var text: line);
begin
   if not full then delay(receiver);
   text:= contents; full:= false;
   continue(sender);
end;

procedure entry send(text: line);
begin
   if full then delay(sender);
   contents:= text; full:= true;
   continue(receiver);
end;

begin full:= false end;
```

The monitor defines a set of *shared variables:* The *contents* of the buffer is a single line. A boolean defines whether or not the buffer is *full.* Two variables of type *queue* are used to delay the *sender* and *receiver* processes until the buffer becomes empty and full, respectively.

The monitor defines two procedures, *send* and *receive.* These *monitor procedures* are marked with the word *entry* to distinguish them from local procedures used within the monitor only (there are none of these in this example).

Receive delays the calling process until the buffer is full. It then returns a text line to the process. Finally, the procedure continues the execution of a sending process (if it is waiting in the sender queue).

Send delays the calling process until the buffer is empty. It then puts a text line into the buffer and continues the process (if any) waiting in the receiver queue. (The queueing mechanism will be explained in detail shortly.)

The *initial statement* of a line buffer makes it empty to begin with.

A line buffer is declared and initialized as follows within the initial process

```
var inbuffer: linebuffer;
init inbuffer
```

The *init* statement allocates storage for the shared variables of the input buffer and executes its initial statement. A monitor can be initialized only once. After initialization, the shared variables of a monitor exist forever. They are called *permanent variables.*

The parameters and local variables of a monitor procedure exist only while it is being executed, however. They are called *temporary variables.*

A monitor procedure can only access its own temporary and permanent variables. These variables are not accessible to other system components. Other components can, however, call procedure entries within a monitor (provided they have access to it).

While a monitor procedure is being executed, it has *exclusive access* to the permanent variables of the monitor. If concurrent processes try to call procedures within the same monitor simultaneously, these procedures will be executed strictly one at a time.

Only monitors and constants can be permanent parameters of processes and monitors. This rule ensures that processes communicate only by means of monitors.

It is possible to define constants, data types, and local procedures within monitors (and processes). These local objects of a system type can only be used within that system type.

To prevent *deadlocks* of monitor calls and ensure that access rights are hierarchical the following rules are enforced: A routine must be declared before it can be called; routine definitions cannot be nested and cannot call themselves; and a system type cannot call its own routine entries.

The absence of recursion makes it possible for a compiler to determine the store requirements of all system components. This and the use of permanent components make it possible to use a *fixed store allocation* in a computer that does not support paging (see Chapter 9 for details).

Since system components are permanent they must be declared as permanent variables of other components.

4.4 QUEUES

A monitor procedure can delay a calling process for any length of time by executing a *delay* operation on a queue variable. Only one process at a time can wait in a queue. When a calling process is delayed by a monitor procedure it loses its exclusive access to the monitor variables until another process calls the same monitor and executes a *continue* operation on the queue in which the first process is waiting.

The continue operation makes the calling process return from its monitor procedure. If another process is waiting in the selected queue, that process will immediately resume its execution of the monitor procedure in which it was delayed. After being resumed, the process again has exclusive access to the permanent variables of the monitor.

A single-process queue is the simplest tool that gives the programmer complete control of the medium-term scheduling of individual processes. A queue is still a fairly abstract concept which allows one to ignore the identity of a process and think of it merely as "the calling process" or "the process waiting in this queue." It also hides the details of processor scheduling that take place during preemption and resumption of a process.

A queue must be declared as a permanent variable within a monitor type. The larger programs described later show how multiprocess queues can be built from single-process queues.

4.5 CLASSES

A *file maker* is defined as a class type. It has access to a line *buffer*. Its permanent variables define a *page maker*, called the *consumer*, and a boolean *eof* denoting the end of a text file.

The class defines a procedure entry *write* that skips a page at the beginning and the end of a file and transmits its text lines to the page maker.

It also includes a local function *more* that defines whether or not a line contains text or an end of file mark. (The latter is a card consisting of the character # followed by blanks.)

The *initial statement* of a file maker initializes its page maker and sets the boolean eof to true.

A class can only be initialized once. After initialization, its parameters and private variables exist forever. A class routine can only access its own temporary and permanent variables. These cannot be accessed by other components.

```
type filemaker =
class(buffer: linebuffer);

var consumer: pagemaker; eof: boolean;

function more(text: line): boolean;
var charno: integer;
begin
   if text(.1.) <> '#' then
      more:= true else
   begin
      charno:= 80;
      while text(.charno.) = ' ' do
         charno:= charno - 1;
      more:= (charno <> 1);
   end;
end;

procedure entry write(text: line);
begin
   if eof then
   begin consumer.skip; eof:= false end;
   if more(text) then
      consumer.write(text) else
   begin consumer.skip; eof:= true end;
end;

begin init consumer(buffer); eof:= true end;
```

A class is a system component that cannot be called simultaneously by several other components. This is guaranteed by the following rule: A class must be declared as a permanent variable within a system type; a class can be passed as a permanent parameter to another class (but not to a process or monitor). So a chain of nested class calls can only be started by a single process (possibly from within a monitor). Consequently, it is not necessary to schedule simultaneous class calls at run time — they simply cannot occur.

A *page maker* is also a class.

```
type pagemaker =
class(buffer: linebuffer);

var consumer: linemaker; lineno: integer;

procedure newpage;
var text: line;
begin
   text(.1.):= ff; consumer.write(text);
   text(.1.):= nl; consumer.write(text);
   lineno:= 1;
end;

procedure entry skip;
begin newpage end;

procedure entry write(text: line);
begin
   consumer.write(text);
   if lineno = 60 then newpage else
      lineno:= lineno + 1;
end;

begin init consumer(buffer); newpage end;
```

A page maker defines a procedure entry that *skips* the rest of a page and another one that *writes* 60 lines per page.

The page maker uses another class called a *line maker*.

```
type linemaker =
class(buffer: linebuffer);

var image: line; charno: integer;
```

```
      procedure entry write(text: line);
      begin
        for charno:= 27 to 106 do
          image(.charno.):= text(.charno - 26.);
        buffer.send(image);
      end;

      begin
        for charno:= 1 to 26 do
          image(.charno.):= ' ';
        image(.107.):= nl;
      end;
```

This class extends a text line with a left margin of 26 characters and terminates it with a NL character before sending it through the buffer.

4.6 A COMPLETE PROGRAM

We can now put all these components together into a complete, concurrent program. A Concurrent Pascal program consists of nested definitions
of system types (processes, monitors, and classes). The outermost of these
is the initial process which declares and initializes the other processes and
the monitors that connect them.

When the execution of a process (such as the initial process) terminates,
its permanent variables continue to exist. This is necessary because these
variables may be monitors that are used by other processes.

The following is a complete program for the *pipeline system*. It has been
running on a PDP 11/45 computer.

```
      "***********************
      *    input/output types    *
      ***********************"

      type iodevice = (typedevice, diskdevice, tapedevice,
                        printdevice, carddevice);

      type iooperation = (input, output, move, control);

      type ioresult = (complete, intervention, transmission,
                        failure, endfile, endmedium, startmedium);
```

```
type ioparam = record
                 operation: iooperation;
                 status: ioresult;
                 arg: integer
               end;

const linelength = 132;
type line = array (.1..linelength.) of char;

const nl = '(:10:)'; ff = '(:12:)';


"**************
*    linebuffer    *
**************"

type linebuffer =
monitor

var contents: line; full: boolean;
    sender, receiver: queue;

procedure entry receive(var text: line);
begin
   if not full then delay(receiver);
   text:= contents; full:= false;
   continue(sender);
end;

procedure entry send(text: line);
begin
   if full then delay(sender);
   contents:= text; full:= true;
   continue(receiver);
end;

begin full:= false end;


"*************
*    linemaker    *
*************"

type linemaker =
class(buffer: linebuffer);
```

```
var image: line; charno: integer;

procedure entry write(text: line);
begin
   for charno:= 27 to 106 do
      image(.charno.):= text(.charno - 26.);
   buffer.send(image);
end;

begin
   for charno:= 1 to 26 do
      image(.charno.):= ' ';
   image(.107.):= nl;
end;


"***************
*    pagemaker    *
***************"

type pagemaker =
class(buffer: linebuffer);

var consumer: linemaker; lineno: integer;

procedure newpage;
var text: line;
begin
   text(.1.):= ff; consumer.write(text);
   text(.1.):= nl; consumer.write(text);
   lineno:= 1;
end;

procedure entry skip;
begin newpage end;

procedure entry write(text: line);
begin
   consumer.write(text);
   if lineno = 60 then newpage else
      lineno:= lineno + 1;
end;

begin init consumer(buffer); newpage end;
```

```
"*************
*   filemaker   *
*************"

type filemaker =
class(buffer: linebuffer);

var consumer: pagemaker; eof: boolean;

function more(text: line): boolean;
var charno: integer;
begin
  if text(.1.) <> '#' then
    more:= true else
  begin
    charno:= 80;
    while text(.charno.) = ' ' do
      charno:= charno - 1;
    more:= (charno <> 1);
  end;
end;

procedure entry write(text: line);
begin
  if eof then
  begin consumer.skip; eof:= false end;
  if more(text) then
    consumer.write(text) else
  begin consumer.skip; eof:= true end;
end;

begin init consumer(buffer); eof:= true end;


"***************
*   cardprocess   *
***************"

type cardprocess =
process(buffer: linebuffer);

var param: ioparam; text, error: line;
    charno: integer;
```

```
begin
  for charno:= 1 to 80 do error(.charno.):= '?';
  param.operation:= input;
  with param do
  cycle
    repeat io(text, param, carddevice)
    until status <> intervention;
    if status <> complete then text:= error;
    buffer.send(text);
  end;
end;

"***************
*    copyprocess    *
***************"

type copyprocess =
process(inbuffer, outbuffer: linebuffer);

var consumer: filemaker; text: line;

begin
  init consumer(outbuffer);
  with inbuffer, consumer do
  cycle receive(text); write(text) end;
end;

"******************
*    printerprocess    *
******************"

type printerprocess =
process(buffer: linebuffer);

var param: ioparam; text: line;

begin
  param.operation:= output;
  cycle
    buffer.receive(text);
    repeat io(text, param, printdevice)
    until param.status = complete;
  end;
end;
```

```
"********************
*       initial process      *
********************"
```

var inbuffer, outbuffer: linebuffer;
    reader: cardprocess;
    copier: copyprocess;
    printer: printerprocess;

begin
    init inbuffer, outbuffer,
        reader(inbuffer),
        copier(inbuffer, outbuffer),
        printer(outbuffer);
end.

4.7 EXECUTION TIMES

Section 8.15.9 defines the execution times for Concurrent Pascal state-ments on a PDP 11/45 computer. We will use these figures to illustrate how one estimates the execution time of a statement, such as

for charno:= 27 to 106 do
    image(.charno.):= text(.charno – 26.)

which is the bottleneck of the copying process in the pipeline system. The *assignment* statement takes the following time (in μsec)

image	40	indexed enumeration
(.charno.)	10	enumeration variable
:=	8	enumeration assignment
text	40	indexed enumeration
(.charno	10	enumeration variable
–	9	enumeration subtraction
26.)	7	enumeration constant

124 μsec

So the whole *for* statement takes

$$82 + (69 + 124) * 80 = 15522 \ \mu sec$$

or about 16 msec. Since the printing of a line takes 100 msec, there is more than enough time to do the formatting simultaneously.

The following figures give a feeling for the cost of routine calls and processor multiplexing

simple routine call	58 μsec
class routine call	80 μsec
monitor routine call (no processor switching)	200 μsec
delay or continue (processor switching)	600 μsec
io	1500 μsec

To call a class routine is almost as fast as calling a simple routine. The short-term scheduling of simultaneous monitor calls make them almost three times slower than class calls. If a monitor call delays the calling process or continues another process waiting in a queue, the resulting processor switching takes another 0.6 msec. Input/output, which usually causes the processor to switch from one process to another twice (before and after the transfer), uses about 1.5 msec of processor time.

Although the exact timing of processor multiplexing is unknown to a Concurrent Pascal programmer, the execution figures make it possible to predict the total amount of processor time used by the pipeline program per line copied and estimate the cycle time of each process roughly.

4.8 CONCLUSION

We have constructed a nontrivial, concurrent program from small, trivial components that can be studied in almost any order you please. We will now pause and look at Concurrent Pascal in the light of the programming principles presented in Chapter 1.

Program structure

The pipeline program consists of 4 processes, 3 classes, and 1 monitor type which are connected hierarchically. Each component is small (10–20 lines) and uses a small number of other components (1–3). The program and its components have reproducible behavior and will print a text correctly each time it is input independently of its speed of execution.

Language notation

Concurrent Pascal is an abstract programming language that hides most of the machine details which make assembly language programming so troublesome

> registers and store locations
> data representation
> variable addresses
> machine instructions and jumps
> peripheral instructions and interrupts
> processor and store allocation

Compared to assembly language, Concurrent Pascal reduces the text of a program by an order of magnitude and makes it clear what the program components are and how they are connected.

The declaration of objects before they are used is a redundancy that makes it possible to check automatically whether a program satisfies some of the assumptions on which it was built.

Compiler

The Concurrent Pascal compiler for the PDP 11/45 computer performs extensive checks of

> program syntax
> declarations
> type compatibility
> access rights
> hierarchical structure

Almost none of these consistency checks are possible for a machine language program which is an unstructured sequence of instructions operating on typeless, global variables that do not have to be declared (but can be accessed by computing arbitrary addresses).

The Concurrent Pascal compiler generates code for an abstract computer simulated by a machine program. It can be moved to other computers by rewriting this interpreter of 4 K words.

The compiler has been running without errors since January 1975. It compiles about 10 lines/sec on a PDP 11/45 computer using a slow disk (50 msec/transfer) for intermediate storage of code.

Interpreter

The abstract code generated by the compiler is about 60 per cent slower than the corresponding machine code. In practice, however, concurrent programs are often limited by the speed of peripherals rather than by the interpreter (as shown in Section 4.7).

Operating systems which handle user programs written in machine language must necessarily take the pessimistic view that *all* programs could turn out to be random bit patterns. To prevent such programs from crashing a system, the designer must depend heavily on hardware protection mechanisms. The RC 4000 multiprogramming system is one of those heroic systems that try to make concurrent programs reliable at the machine level (Brinch Hansen, 1970).

The exclusive use of abstract programming languages changes the approach to reliability completely. When all programs are certified by a reliable compiler one can eliminate hardware protection mechanisms entirely as we have done on the PDP 11/45 computer. The Concurrent Pascal interpreter only checks that array indices are within range. This is one of the few cases in which abstract programming is even more efficient than machine programming.

The static store allocation among processes makes it possible for concurrent programs to execute efficiently at fairly predictable speeds.

We will now apply this programming technique to more complicated concurrent tasks.

4.9 LITERATURE

The classes in Concurrent Pascal are a restricted form of those invented by Dahl [1972] for the Simula 67 language. Simula 67 makes the variables of a class directly accessible both inside and outside that class. Concurrent Pascal classes can only be accessed by procedure calls.

Dijkstra suggested the idea of monitors in 1971. I proposed the first language notation for them [Brinch Hansen, 1973]. In 1972 I suggested the use of queue variables (called "events") for process scheduling. Hoare [1974] used a first-come, first-served variant of these queues (called "conditions"). In defining Concurrent Pascal, I finally decided to use the simplest possible form of queues (with a single process waiting in each) [Brinch Hansen, 1975].

REFERENCES

BRINCH HANSEN, P., "Structured multiprogramming," *Comm. ACM 15*, 7, pp. 574–78, July 1972.

BRINCH HANSEN, P., *Operating system principles*. Prentice-Hall Inc., Englewood Cliffs, NJ, July 1973b.

BRINCH HANSEN, P., "The programming language Concurrent Pascal," *IEEE Transactions on Software Engineering 1*, 2, pp. 199–207, June 1975.

DAHL, O. J., DIJKSTRA, E. W., and HOARE, C. A. R., *Structured programming*. Academic Press, New York, NY, 1972.

DIJKSTRA, E. W., "Hierarchical ordering of sequential processes," *Acta Informatica 1*, 2, pp. 115–38, 1971.

HOARE, C. A. R., "Monitors: an operating system structuring concept," *Comm. ACM 17*, 10, pp. 549–57, Oct. 1974.

CONCURRENT PROGRAMS

5

THE SOLO OPERATING SYSTEM

This is a description of the first operating system *Solo* written in the programming language *Concurrent Pascal*. It is a simple, but useful single-user operating system for the development and distribution of Pascal programs for the PDP 11/45 computer. It has been in use since May 1975.

5.1 OVERVIEW

From the user's point of view there is nothing unusual about the Solo system. It supports editing, compilation, and storage of Sequential and Concurrent Pascal programs. These programs can access either console, cards, printer, tape or disk at several levels (character by character, page by page, file by file, or by direct device access). Input, processing, and output of files are handled by concurrent processes. Pascal programs can call one another recursively and pass arbitrary parameters among themselves.

To the system programmer, however, Solo is quite different from many other operating systems

(1) Less than 4 per cent of it is written in machine language. The rest is written in Sequential and Concurrent Pascal.

(2)   In contrast to machine-oriented languages, Pascal does not contain low-level programming features, such as registers, addresses, and interrupts. These are all handled by the virtual machine which executes compiled programs.

(3)   System protection is achieved largely by means of compile-time checking of access rights. Run-time checking is minimal and is not supported by hardware mechanisms.

(4)   Solo is the first major example of a hierarchical concurrent program implemented by means of abstract data types (classes, monitors, and processes).

(5)   The complete system consisting of more than 100,000 machine words of code (including two compilers) was developed by a student and myself in less than a year.

To appreciate the usefulness of Concurrent Pascal one needs a good understanding of at least one operating system written in the language. The purpose of this section is to look at the Solo system from the user's point of view before studying its internal structure. It tells how the user operates the system, how data flow inside it, how programs call one another and communicate, how files are stored on disk, and how well the system performs in typical tasks.

Job Control

The user controls program execution from a display (or a teletype). He calls a program by writing its name and parameters, for example

>   move(5)
>   read(maketemp, seqcode, true)

The first command positions a magnetic tape at file number 5. The second one inputs the file to disk and stores it as *sequential code* named *maketemp*. The boolean *true* protects the file against accidental deletion in the future.

If the user forgets which programs are available, he may for example type

>   help

(or anything else). The system responds by writing

not executable, try
            list(catalog, seqcode, console)

The suggested command lists the names of all sequential programs on the console.

If the user knows that the disk contains a certain program, but is uncertain about its parameter conventions, he can simply call it as a program without parameters, for example

read

The program then gives the necessary information

try again
            read(file: identifier; kind: filekind; protect: boolean)
using
            filekind = (scratch, ascii, seqcode, concode)

Still more information about a program can be gained by reading its manual

copy(readman, console)

A user session may begin with the input of a new Pascal program from cards to disk

copy(cards, sorttext)

followed by a compilation

pascal(sorttext, printer, sort)

If the compiler reports errors on the program listing

pascal:
            compilation errors

the next step is usually to edit the program text

edit(sorttext)

...

and compile it again. After a successful compilation, the user program can now be called directly

sort(...)

The system can also read job control commands from other media, for example

do(tape)

A task is preempted by pushing the BEL key on the console. This causes the system to reload and initialize itself. The command *start* can be used to replace the Solo system with any other concurrent program stored on disk, for example

start(jobstream)

This starts the job stream system described in Chapter 6. The Solo system can be restarted by pushing the BEL key.

Data Flow

Figure 5.1 shows the data flow inside the system when the user is processing a single text file sequentially by copying, editing, or compiling it.

The input, processing, and output of text take place simultaneously. Processing is done by a *job process* that starts input by sending an argument through a buffer to an input process. The argument is the name of the input device or disk file.

The *input process* sends the data through another buffer to the job process. At the end of the file the input process sends an argument through yet another buffer to the job process indicating whether any transmission errors occurred during the input.

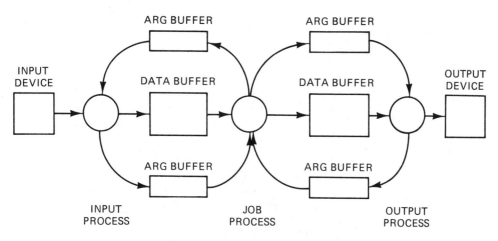

Fig. 5.1　Processes and buffers

Output is handled similarly by an *output process* and another set of buffers.

In a single-user operating system it is desirable to process a file continuously at the highest possible speed. So the data are buffered in core instead of on disk. The capacity of each buffer is 512 characters.

Control Flow

Figure 5.2 shows what happens when the user types a command such as

edit(cards, tape)

After system loading the machine executes a Concurrent Pascal program (Solo) consisting of three processes. Initially the input and output processes both load and call a sequential program *io* while the job process calls another sequential program *do*. The do program reads the user command from the console and calls the *edit* program with two parameters, *cards* and *tape*.

The editor starts its input by sending the first parameter to the io program executed by the input process. This causes the io program to call another program *cards* which then begins to read cards and send them to the job process.

The editor starts its output by sending the second parameter to the io

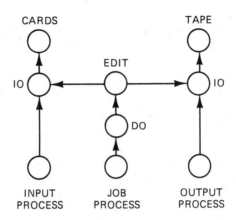

Fig. 5.2   Concurrent processes and sequential programs

program executed by the output process. The latter calls a program *tape* which receives data from the job process and puts them on tape.

At the end of the file the cards and tape programs return to the io programs which then await further instructions from the job process. The editor returns to the do program which continues to read and interpret the next command from the console.

It is worth observing that the operating system itself has no built-in drivers for input/output from various devices. Data are simply produced and consumed by Sequential Pascal programs stored on disk. The operating system contains only the mechanism to call these. This gives the user complete freedom to supplement the system with new devices and simulate complicated input/output such as the merging, splitting, and formatting of files without changing the job programs.

Most important is the ability of Sequential Pascal programs to call one another recursively with arbitrary parameters. In Fig. 5.2, for example, the do program calls the edit program with two identifiers as parameters. This removes the need for a separate (awkward) job control language. *The job control language is Pascal.*

This is illustrated more dramatically in Fig. 5.3, which shows how the command

pascal(sorttext, printer, sort)

causes the do program to call the program *Pascal*. The latter in turn calls seven compiler passes one at a time, and (if the compiled program is correct) Pascal finally calls the filing system to store the generated code on disk.

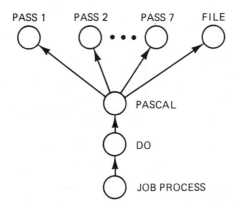

Fig. 5.3 Compilation

A program does not know whether it is being called by another program or directly from the console. In Fig. 5.3 the Pascal program calls the filing system. The user may, however, also call the file system directly

$$file(protect, sort, true)$$

to protect his program against accidental deletion.

The Pascal *pointer* and *heap* concepts give programs the ability to pass arbitrarily complicated data structures among each other, such as symbol tables during compilation [Jensen and Wirth, 1974]. In most cases, however, it suffices to use identifiers, integers, and booleans as program parameters.

Store Allocation

The run-time environment of Sequential and Concurrent Pascal is a kernel of 4 K words. This is the only program written in machine language. The user loads the kernel from disk into core by means of the operator's panel. The kernel then loads the Solo system and starts it. The Solo system consists of a fixed number of processes. They occupy fixed amounts of core store determined by the compiler.

All other programs are written in Sequential Pascal. Each process stores the code of the currently executed program in a fixed core segment. After termination of a program called by another, the process reloads the previous program from disk and returns to it. The data used by a process and the programs called by it are all stored in a core resident stack of fixed length.

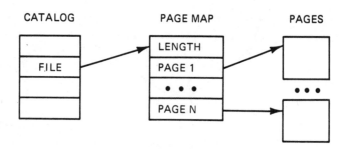

Fig. 5.4   File system

File System

The backing store is a slow *disk* with removable packs. Each user has his own disk pack containing the system and his private files. So there is no need for a hierarchical file system.

A disk pack contains a *catalog* of all files stored on it. The catalog describes itself as a file. A *file* is described by its name, type, protection, and disk address. Files are looked up by hashing.

All system programs check the *types* of their input files before operating on them and associate types with their output files. The Sequential Pascal compiler, for example, will take input from an ascii file (but not from a scratch file), and will make its output a sequential code file. The possible file types are *scratch, ascii, seqcode,* and *concode.*

Since each user has his own disk pack, files need only be *protected* against accidental overwriting and deletion. All files are initially unprotected. To protect one the user must call the file system from the console as described in the section on control flow.

To avoid compacting of files (lasting several minutes), file pages are scattered on disk and addressed indirectly through a *page map* (Fig. 5.4). A file is opened by looking it up in the catalog and bringing its page map into core.

The resident part of the Solo system implements only the most frequently used file operations: *lookup, open, close, get,* and *put.* A nonresident, sequential program, called *file,* handles the more complicated and less frequently used operations: *create, replace, rename, protect,* and *delete* file.

Disk Allocation

The disk always contains a scratch file of 255 pages called *next.* A program creates a new file by outputting data to this file. It then calls the file

system to associate the data with a new name, a type, and a length ($\leqslant 255$).
Having done this the file system creates a new instance of *next*.

This scheme has two advantages

(1) All files are initialized with typed data.

(2) A program creating a file need only call the nonresident file system
once (after producing the file). Without the file *next* the file system would
have to be called at least twice: before output to create the file, and after
output to define its final length.

The disadvantage of having a single file *next* is that a program can only
create one file at a time.

Unused disk pages are defined by a set of page indices stored on disk.

On a slow disk special care must be taken to make *program loading* fast.
If program pages were scattered randomly on the disk it would take 16
sec to load the compiler and its input/output drivers. An algorithm described later reduces this to 5 sec. When the system creates the file *next* it
tries to place it on consecutive pages within neighboring cylinders as far as
possible (but will scatter the pages somewhat if it has to). It then rearranges
the page indices within the page map to minimize the number of disk revolutions and cylinder movements needed to load the file. Since this is done
before a program is compiled and stored on disk it is called *disk scheduling
at compile time*.

The system uses a different allocation technique for the two temporary
files used during compilation. Each pass of the compiler takes input from a
file produced by its predecessor and delivers output to its successor on
another file. A program *maketemp* creates these files and interleaves their
page indices (making every second page belong to one file and every second
one to the other). This makes the disk head sweep slowly across both files
during a pass instead of moving wildly back and forth between them.

Operator Communication

The user communicates with the system through a console. Since a task
(such as editing) usually involves several programs executed by concurrent
processes these programs must identify themselves to the user before asking
for input or making output

```
do:
edit(cards, tape)
edit:
...
do:
...
```

Program identity is only displayed every time the user starts talking to a different program. A program that communicates several times with the user without interruption (such as the editor) only identifies itself once.

Normally only one program at a time tries to talk to the user (the current program executed by the job process). But an input/output error may cause a message from another process

tape:
inspect

Since processes rarely compete for the console, it is sufficient to give a process *exclusive access* to the user for input or output of a single line. A conversation of several lines will seldom be interrupted.

A Pascal program only calls the operating system once with its identification. The system will then automatically display it when necessary.

Size and Performance

The Solo system consists of an operating system written in Concurrent Pascal and a set of system programs written in Sequential Pascal.

Program	Pascal lines	Machine words
operating system	1300	4 K
do, io	700	4 K
file system	900	5 K
concurrent compiler	8300	42 K
sequential compiler	8300	42 K
editor	400	2 K
input/output programs	600	3 K
others	1300	8 K
	21800	110 K

(The two Pascal compilers can be used under different operating systems written in Concurrent Pascal — not just Solo.)

The amounts of code written in different programming languages are

	Per cent
machine language	4
Concurrent Pascal	4
Sequential Pascal	92

This clearly shows that a good sequential programming language is more important for operating system design than a concurrent language. But although a concurrent program may be small it still seems worthwhile to write it in a high-level language that enables a compiler to do thorough checking of data types and access rights. Otherwise, it is far too easy to make time-dependent programming errors, which are extremely difficult to locate.

The kernel written in machine language implements the process and monitor concepts of Concurrent Pascal and responds to interrupts. It is independent of the particular operating system running on top of it.

The Solo system requires a core store of 39 K words for programs and data.

kernel	4 K words
operating system	11 K words
input/output programs	6 K words
job programs	18 K words
core store	39 K words

This amount of space allows the Pascal compiler to compile itself.

The speed of text processing using disk input and tape output is

copy	11600 char/sec
edit	3300–6200 char/sec
compile	240 char/sec

All these tasks are 60–100 per cent disk limited. These figures do not distinguish between time spent waiting for peripherals and time spent executing operating system or user code since this distinction is irrelevant to the user. They illustrate an overall performance of a system written in a high-level language using straightforward code generation without any optimization.

Final Remarks

The compilers for Sequential and Concurrent Pascal were designed and implemented by Al Hartmann and myself in half a year. I wrote the operating system and its utility programs in 3 months. In machine language this would have required 20–30 man-years and nobody would have been able to understand the system fully. The use of an efficient, abstract programming language reduced the development cost to less than 2 man-years and produced a system that is completely understood by two programmers.

The low cost of programming makes it acceptable to throw away awkward programs and rewrite them. We did this several times: An early 6-pass compiler was never released (although it worked perfectly) because we found its structure too complicated. The first operating system written in Concurrent Pascal (called *Deamy*) was used only to evaluate the expressive power of the language and was never built. The second one (called *Pilot*) was used for several months but was too slow.

From a manufacturer's point of view it seems both realistic and attractive to replace a huge ineffective "general-purpose" operating system with a range of small, efficient systems for special purposes.

The kernel, the operating system, and the compilers were tested very systematically initially and appear to be correct.

In an excellent paper, Stoy and Strachey [1972] recommend that one should learn to build good operating systems for single users before trying to satisfy many users simultaneously. I have found this to be very good advice. I have also tried to follow the advice of Lampson [1974] and make both the high- and low-level abstractions available to the user programmer.

5.2 JOB INTERFACE

The following describes the interface between user programs and the Solo operating system.

Solo enables a single user to develop and execute Sequential Pascal programs on a PDP 11/45 computer. A Sequential Pascal program is stored in compiled form on disk and invoked by a user command from console. A sequential program interacts with the Solo system by means of procedures implemented within the operating system. These *interface procedures* and their parameter types are declared in a *prefix* to the user's program. The prefix enables the Pascal compiler to make complete type checking of calls to the operating system. No hardware mechanisms are used to supplement the compile-time checking of job interactions with run-time checking.

The system can put the prefix automatically in front of user programs before they are compiled. This makes it impossible to violate the system interface conventions. The interface can be modified by editing and recompilation of the Solo operating system (the latter taking about 2.5 min). The use of an interface declaration during compilation seems to be a very simple solution to the nontrivial problem of how to confine a user program to a well-defined set of interactions with an operating system.

This section explains the standard interface to the Solo system and gives an example of its use by a Sequential Pascal program. The implementation of the interface procedures within the Solo system is explained later. One of the interface procedures allows Pascal programs to call one another recursively and pass parameters among themselves. This makes it possible to use Sequential Pascal as a job control language.

Program Parameters

In the Solo system a Sequential Pascal program can be called either by the operating system itself or by another Pascal program. The caller passes a list of parameters to the program. They can be booleans, integers, identifiers, pointers, or niltypes. The program parameters are declared in a prefix to the user's program text

```
const idlength = 12;
type identifier = array (.1..idlength.) of char;

type argtag =
    (niltype, booltype, inttype, idtype, ptrtype);

type pointer = @ anytype;

type argtype = record
                case tag: argtag of
                    niltype, booltype: (bool: boolean);
                    inttype: (int: integer);
                    idtype: (id: identifier);
                    ptrtype: (ptr: pointer)
              end;

const maxarg = 10;
type arglist = array (.1..maxarg.) of argtype;

program p(var param: arglist);

"user program text follows here"
```

The programmer can refer to a program parameter as follows

```
param(.2.)
```

The user calls a program by writing its name and parameters on the console, for example

```
copy(cards, tape)
```

This causes the system to call the program *copy* with the two identifiers *cards* and *tape* as parameters as explained in Section 5.1. The system always extends the parameters specified by the user with a boolean. It is used by the program to indicate whether it succeeded in doing its job. So the copy program has access to three parameters

ok:	boolean;	"param(.1.)"
source:	identifier;	"param(.2.)"
destination:	identifier;	"param(.3.)"

(The rest of the parameters are niltypes.)

A program must check that its parameters are of the right types to detect a meaningless call, such as

$$copy(15, true)$$

This can be done as follows

```
var source: argtype;

source:= param(.2.);
with source do
if tag <> idtype then help
```

where *help* is a procedure within the program that tells the user how to call it correctly.

A program can return parameter values to its caller before it terminates, for example

```
var ok: boolean;

param(.1.).bool:= ok;
```

Catalog Lookup

A Sequential Pascal program can call a set of procedures implemented within the Solo operating system. These interface procedures and their parameter types are declared in the program prefix. As an example, the procedure

```
procedure lookup(id: identifier; var attr: fileattr;
                 var found: boolean)
```

enables a program to call the operating system to look up a file in the disk catalog. Since the procedure is implemented within the operating system it is only necessary to declare its name and parameters in the prefix to user programs.

Lookup returns a boolean, telling whether the file was *found* in the catalog. If it was, it also returns the *attributes* of the file. These attributes are defined by type definitions in the program prefix

```
type filekind =
     (empty, scratch, ascii, seqcode, concode);

type fileattr = record
                     kind: filekind;
                     addr: integer;
                     protected: boolean;
                     notused: array (.1..5.) of integer
                end
```

The file attributes define what *kind* of file it is as well as the disk *address* and *protection* status. There are four kinds of files: *scratch, ascii* text, *sequential code*, and *concurrent code.*

As an example, the copy program will look up the name of its source file to check that it is an ascii file stored on disk or produced by a sequential input program

```
var source: argtype; attr: fileattr; found: boolean;

with source do
if tag <> idtype then help else
begin
   lookup(id, attr, found);
   if not found then
     error('source file unknown(:10:)') else
   case attr.kind of
     scratch, concode:
       error('source kind must be ascii or seqcode (:10:)');
     ascii, seqcode:
   end;
end
```

[The (:10:) denotes the ascii character number 10 = newline.]

Input/Output Streams

A program starts its input/output by sending the names of the source and destination files to the input and output processes. This is done by means of an interface procedure

procedure writearg(s: argseq; arg: argtype)

where

type argseq = (inp, out)

It can be used as follows

var source, dest: argtype;

writearg(inp, source)
writearg(out, dest)

After this the program can read and write its data character by character by calling the interface procedures

procedure read(**var** c: char)
procedure write(c: char)

So the main loop of the copy program could be written this way

var c: char;

repeat
  read(c); write(c);
until c = em

where *em* is the end of medium character.

The read and write procedures are convenient for text processing, but somewhat slow for simple copying. So the copy program transmits its data page by page by calling the interface procedures

> **procedure** readpage(**var** block: **univ** page; **var** eof: boolean)
> **procedure** writepage(block: **univ** page; eof: boolean)

where

> **const** pagelength = 512;
> **type** page = **array** (.1..pagelength.) **of** char;

(The key word *universal* makes it possible to use these procedures to transmit any data type that can be stored on a page, and not just a textstring.)

A file produced by a process must be terminated by an empty page and a boolean *eof* = *true*. This leads to the following loop in the copy program

> **var** block: page; eof: boolean;
>
> **repeat**
>   readpage(block, eof);
>   writepage(block, eof);
> **until** eof

At the end of the file, the program must receive a boolean from the input and output processes to see whether transmission errors occurred during the input/output. These booleans are received by calling the interface procedure

> **procedure** readarg(s: argseq; **var** arg: argtype)

For example

> **var** ok: boolean; arg: argtype;
>
> readarg(inp, arg);
> **if not** arg.bool **then** ok:= false;
> readarg(out, arg);
> **if not** arg.bool **then** ok:= false;

Operator Communication

A program communicates with the operator's console by means of the interface procedures

```
procedure accept(var c: char)
procedure display(c: char)
```

These can, for example, be used to implement the following procedure within a user program

```
procedure writetext(text: line);
var i: integer; c: char;
begin
   i:= 0;
   repeat
      i:= i + 1;
      c:= text(.i.);
      display(c);
   until c = nl;
end
```

where

```
const nl = '(:10:)';
```

```
const linelength = 132;
type line = array (.1..linelength.) of char;
```

A program identifies itself once and for all by calling the interface procedure

```
procedure identify(header: line)
```

For example

```
identify('copy:(:10:)')
```

causes the Solo system to prefix input/output requests on the console with the name of the copy program. If the copy program writes the message

> writetext('source file unknown(:10:)')

it will be displayed as

> copy:
> source file unknown

to the operator. If a program communicates several times with the operator without being interrupted by another one it is only identified once on the terminal.

Program Calls

A Sequential Pascal program can call another Pascal program by means of the interface procedure.

> **procedure** run(id: identifier; **var** param: arglist;
>   **var** line: integer; **var** result: progresult)

The program is identified by its name in the disk catalog. The caller passes it a list of arguments. Upon return the caller is informed about where and how the program terminated (by means of a line number and a program result)

> **type** progresult =
>   (terminated, overflow, pointererror, rangeerror,
>   varianterror, heaplimit, stacklimit, codelimit,
>   timelimit, callerror)

If the copy program, for example, is called to output a file to disk, it will call a file program to enter the new file in the disk catalog. This is done as follows

```
var dest: argtype; length: integer;
    where: (nowhere, ondisk, elsewhere);

procedure savefile;
var line: integer; result: progresult;
    list: arglist;
begin
  with list(.1.) do
  begin tag:= booltype; bool:= false end;
  with list(.2.) do
  begin tag:= idtype;
     if where = nowhere then id:= 'create    '
                        else id:= 'replace   ';
  end;
  with list(.3.) do
  begin tag:= idtype; id:= dest.id end;
  with list(.4.) do
  begin tag:= inttype; int:= length end;
  with list(.5.) do
  begin tag:= idtype; id:= 'ascii     ' end;
  with list(.6.) do
  begin tag:= booltype; bool:= false end;
  run('file      ', list, line, result);
  if (result <> terminated) or not list(.1.).bool
     then error('destination file lost(:10:)');
end
```

This has the same effect as the console command

file(create, dest, length, ascii, false)

(The boolean *false* is the protection status of the new file.)

The ability of Pascal programs to call other Pascal programs and pass parameters to them makes it possible to use Pascal as a job control language. In this example, the copy program controls the execution of the file program.

Disk Files

A program can access a disk file sequentially by sending its name to the input process which then transmits its contents to the job process.

A program can also make random access to a disk file by means of the interface procedures.

> **procedure** open(f: file; id: identifier; **var** found: boolean)
> **procedure** close(f: file)
> **procedure** get(f: file; p: integer; **var** block: **univ** page)
> **procedure** put(f: file; p: integer; block: **univ** page)
> **function** length(f: file): integer

where

$$\text{type file} = 1..2$$

Open makes a file with a given name accessible (if it is found on disk). *Close* makes it inaccessible again. *Get* and *put* transfer page number p of file number f to and from core. (File pages are numbered 1, 2, . . ., length.) *Length* defines the number of pages in a file.

Direct Input/Output

The lowest level of input/output is defined by two interface procedures

> **procedure** iotransfer(device: iodevice; **var** param: ioparam;
>   **var** block: **univ** page)
> **procedure** iomove(device: iodevice; **var** param: ioparam)

where

> **type** iodevice = (typedevice, diskdevice, tapedevice,
>   printdevice, carddevice);
> **type** iooperation = (input, output, move, control);
> **type** ioarg = (writeeof, rewind, upspace, backspace);
> **type** ioresult = (complete, intervention, transmission,
>   failure, endfile, endmedium, startmedium);
> **type** ioparam = **record**
>   operation: iooperation;
>   status: ioresult;
>   arg: ioarg
>   **end**

These are the elementary input/output operations discussed in Section 4.1.

Heap Allocation

The interface procedures

$$\text{procedure mark(var top: integer)}$$
$$\text{procedure release(top: integer)}$$

return the current top address of the heap and reset it to a given value as explained in Chapter 8.

Task Kind

The interface function

$$\text{function task: taskkind}$$

where

$$\text{type taskkind = (inputtask, jobtask, outputtask)}$$

tells a program whether it is being executed by the input process, the job process, or the output process.

The Complete Prefix

```
const nl = '(:10:)'; ff = '(:12:)';
      cr = '(:13:)'; em = '(:25:)';

const pagelength = 512;
type page = array (.1..pagelength.) of char;

const linelength = 132;
type line = array (.1..linelength.) of char;

const idlength = 12;
type identifier = array (.1..idlength.) of char;
```

```
type file = 1..2;

type filekind = (empty, scratch, ascii, seqcode, concode);

type fileattr = record
                kind: filekind;
                addr: integer;
                protected: boolean;
                notused: array (.1..5.) of integer
            end;

type iodevice = (typedevice, diskdevice, tapedevice,
                printdevice, carddevice);

type iooperation = (input, output, move, control);

type ioarg = (writeeof, rewind, upspace, backspace);

type ioresult = (complete, intervention, transmission,
                failure, endfile, endmedium, startmedium);

type ioparam = record
                operation: iooperation;
                status: ioresult;
                arg: ioarg
            end;

type taskkind = (inputtask, jobtask, outputtask);

type argtag = (niltype, booltype, inttype, idtype, ptrtype);

type pointer = @ boolean;

type argtype = record
                case tag: argtag of
                   niltype, booltype: (bool: boolean);
                   inttype: (int: integer);
                   idtype: (id: identifier);
                   ptrtype: (ptr: pointer)
               end;

const maxarg = 10;
type arglist = array (.1..maxarg.) of argtype;
```

```
type argseq = (inp, out);

type progresult = (terminated, overflow, pointererror,
                   rangeerror, varianterror, heaplimit,
                   stacklimit, codelimit, timelimit,
                   callerror);

procedure read(var c: char);
procedure write(c: char);

procedure open(f: file; id: identifier; var found: boolean);
procedure close(f: file);
procedure get(f: file; p: integer; var block: univ page);
procedure put(f: file; p: integer; block: univ page);
function length(f: file): integer;

procedure mark(var top: integer);
procedure release(top: integer);

procedure identify(header: line);
procedure accept(var c: char);
procedure display(c: char);

procedure readpage(var block: univ page; var eof: boolean);
procedure writepage(block: univ page; eof: boolean);

procedure readline(var text: univ line);
procedure writeline(text: univ line);

procedure readarg(s: argseq; var arg: argtype);
procedure writearg(s: argseq; arg: argtype);

procedure lookup(id: identifier; var attr: fileattr;
                 var found: boolean);

procedure iotransfer(device: iodevice; var param: ioparam;
                     var block: univ page);
procedure iomove(device: iodevice; var param: ioparam);

function task: taskkind;
```

```
procedure run(id: identifier; var param: arglist;
              var line: integer; var result: progresult);

program p(var param: arglist);
```

The compiler regards the prefix as being the first part of a Sequential Pascal program. The input, job, and output processes use the same prefix (but the procedures *readline* and *writeline* have no effect within the job process).

A Sequential Program: Copy

This is an example of a complete program that uses the prefix to interact with the operating system. The program copies a text file from a source medium (console, cards, disk, or tape) to a destination medium (console, printer, disk, or tape).

```
var source, dest: argtype; ok: boolean;
    where: (nowhere, ondisk, elsewhere);
    length: integer;

procedure writetext(text: line);
var i: integer; c: char;
begin
  i:= 0;
  repeat
    i:= i + 1;
    c:= text(.i.);
    display(c);
  until c = nl;
end;

procedure error(text: line);
begin
  writetext(text);
  ok:= false;
end;
```

```
procedure help;
begin
  if ok then
  begin
    writetext('try again(:10:)');
    writetext('   copy(source, destination: identifier) (:10:)');
    ok:= false;
  end;
end;

procedure savefile;
var line: integer; result: progresult;
    list: arglist;
begin
  with list(.1.) do
  begin tag:= booltype; bool:= false end;
  with list(.2.) do
  begin tag:= idtype;
    if where = nowhere then id:= 'create   '
                       else id:= 'replace  ';
  end;
  with list(.3.) do
  begin tag:= idtype; id:= dest.id end;
  with list(.4.) do
  begin tag:= inttype; int:= length end;
  with list(.5.) do
  begin tag:= idtype; id:= 'ascii    ' end;
  with list(.6.) do
  begin tag:= booltype; bool:= false end;
  run('file    ', list, line, result);
  if (result <> terminated) or not list(.1.).bool then
    error('destination file lost(:10:)');
end;
```

```
procedure checkarg;
var attr: fileattr; found: boolean;
begin
  source:= param(.2.);
  with source do
  if tag <> idtype then help else
  begin
    lookup(id, attr, found);
    if not found then
      error('source file unknown(:10:)') else
    case attr.kind of
      scratch, concode:
        error('source kind must be ascii or seqcode (:10:)');
      ascii, seqcode:
    end;
  end;
  dest:= param(.3.);
  with dest do
  if tag <> idtype then help else
  begin
    lookup(id, attr, found);
    if not found then where:= nowhere else
    if attr.kind = seqcode then where:= elsewhere else
    if attr.protected then
      error('destination file protected (:10:)') else
      where:= ondisk;
  end;
end;


procedure initio;
var arg: argtype;
begin
  writearg(inp, source);
  if where = elsewhere then writearg(out, dest) else
  begin
    with arg do
    begin tag:= idtype; id:= 'next     ' end;
    writearg(out, arg);
  end;
end;
```

```
procedure checkio;
var arg: argtype;
begin
   readarg(inp, arg);
   if not arg.bool then ok:= false;
   if where <> elsewhere then
   begin readarg(out, arg); length:= arg.int end;
   readarg(out, arg);
   if not arg.bool then ok:= false;
   if (where <> elsewhere) & ok then savefile;
end;

procedure copytext;
var block: page; eof: boolean;
begin
   repeat
     readpage(block, eof);
     writepage(block, eof);
   until eof;
end;

procedure initialize;
begin
   identify('copy:(:10:)');
   ok:= (task = jobtask);
   checkarg;
end;

procedure terminate;
begin
   with param(.1.) do
   begin tag:= booltype; bool:= ok end;
end;

begin
   initialize;
   if ok then
   begin
     initio;
     copytext;
     checkio;
   end;
   terminate;
end.
```

The copy program initializes itself by checking its arguments. If they are ok it starts concurrent input/output, copies the file, and checks the input/output for transmission errors.

Conclusion

The Sequential Pascal compiler assumes that the interface procedures and their parameter types are declared exactly the same way in the prefix and within the operating system. Since the compiler has no way of checking whether the prefix is correct it must be handled with some care.

In developing the Solo system, we found it sufficient to maintain the prefix as a standard card deck that was put in front of all the programs before they were stored on disk. The prefix is now kept on disk as a separate text file. It can be put in front of a program file by means of a concatenation program called from the console

concat(prefix, source, dest)

As long as the informal use of a single prefix causes no problems for system programmers, I see no reason to handle it by more complicated, automatic mechanisms. But, for general use, it is, of course, much safer and more convenient to let the system automatically put a prefix in front of all user programs before compilation. The *job stream* system described in Chapter 6 does just that.

Since the compiler refuses to accept further interface definitions after the key word *program*, a user cannot change a prefix by adding his own declarations to it. In many cases, a much smaller prefix than the one described here will be used. As an example, the job stream system will compile and execute programs with input from cards and output on a line printer. A compiled program needs only a prefix defining five procedures for reading and writing of text and numbers.

The use of a prefix to check interactions between an operating system and its jobs illustrates a persistent theme in the Concurrent Pascal project: *Program relationships that remain unchanged for long periods of time can be verified once and for all at compile time.* The verification of system invariants at compile time contributes to program reliability by detecting errors *before* systems are put into operation. It also increases program efficiency by removing the need for complicated hardware protection mechanisms.

5.3   PROCESSES, MONITORS, AND CLASSES

This is a description of the program structure of the Solo operating system.

The main idea of Concurrent Pascal is to divide the global data structures of an operating system into small parts and define the meaningful operations on each of them. In Solo, for example, there is a data structure, called a *resource*, which is used to give concurrent processes exclusive access to a disk. This data structure can only be accessed by means of two procedures that *request* and *release* access to the disk. The programmer specifies that these are the only operations one can perform on a resource, and the compiler checks that this rule is obeyed in the rest of the system. This approach to program reliability has been called *resource protection at compile time* [Brinch Hansen, 1973b].

The combination of a data structure and the operations used to access it is called an *abstract data type*. It is abstract because the rest of the system only needs to know what operations one can perform on it but can ignore the details of how they are carried out. A Concurrent Pascal program is constructed from three kinds of abstract data types: processes, monitors, and classes. *Processes* perform concurrent operations on data structures. They use *monitors* to synchronize themselves and exhange data. They access private data structures by means of *classes*. Chapters 2 and 4 are an overview of these concepts and their use in concurrent programming.

The following is a complete, annotated program listing of the Solo system. It also explains how the system was tested systematically.

Program Structure

Solo consists of a hierarchy of *program layers*, each of which controls a particular kind of computer resource, and a set of concurrent processes that use these resources (Fig. 5.5).

Resource management controls the scheduling of the operator's console and the disk among concurrent processes.

Console management lets processes communicate with the operator after they have gained access to the console.

Disk management gives processes access to disk files and a catalog describing them.

Program management fetches program files from disk into core on demand from processes that wish to execute them.

Buffer management transmits data among processes.

These facilities are used by seven concurrent processes:

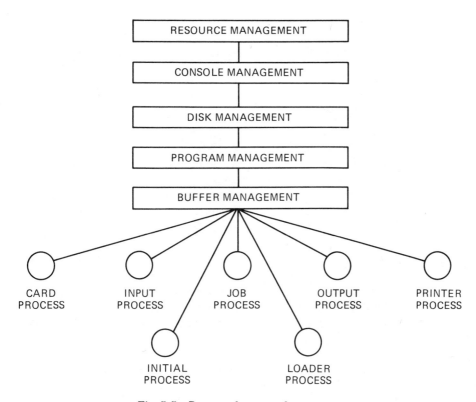

Fig. 5.5 Program layers and processes

A *job process* executes Pascal programs upon request from the operator.

Two *input/output processes* produce and consume the data of the job process.

A *card process* feeds punched cards to the input process which then removes trailing blanks from them and packs the text into blocks.

A *printer process* prints lines that are unpacked from blocks and sent to it by the output process.

A *loader process* preempts and reinitializes the operating system when the operator pushes the bell key on the console.

An *initial process* starts up the rest of the system after system loading.

The term *program layer* is only used as a convenient way of explaining the gross division of labor within the system. It is not represented by the language notation of Concurrent Pascal.

Abstract Data Types

Each program layer consists of one or more abstract data types (monitors and classes).

Resource management

A *fifo* class implements a first-in, first-out queue that is used to maintain multiprocess queues and message buffers.

A *resource* monitor gives processes exclusive access to a computer resource. It is used to control disk access.

A *typewriter resource* monitor gives processes exclusive access to a console and tells them whether they need to identify themselves to the operator.

Console management

A *typewriter* class transmits a single line between a process and a console (but does not give the process exclusive access to it).

A *terminal* class gives a process the illusion that it has its own private console by giving the process exclusive access to the operator for input or output of a single line.

A *terminal stream* makes a terminal look character oriented.

Disk management

A *disk* class can access a page anywhere on disk (but does not give a process exclusive access to it). It uses a terminal to report disk failure.

A *disk file* class can access any page belonging to a particular file. The file pages, which may be scattered on disk, are addressed indirectly through a page map. The disk address of the page map identifies the file. It uses a disk to access the map and its pages.

A *disk table* class makes a disk catalog of files look like an array of entries, some of which describe files, and some of which are empty. The entries are identified by numeric indices. The class uses a disk file to access the catalog page by page.

A *disk catalog* monitor can look up files in a catalog by means of their names. It uses a resource to get exclusive access to the disk and a disk table to scan the catalog.

A *data file* class gives a process access to a named disk file. It uses a resource, a disk catalog, and a disk file to access the disk.

Program management

A *program file* class can load a named disk file into core when a process wishes to execute it. It uses a resource, a disk catalog, and a disk file to do this.

A *program stack* monitor keeps track of nested program calls within a process.

Buffer management

The *buffer* monitors transmit various kinds of messages between processes: arguments (enumerations or identifiers), lines, and pages.

The following defines the purpose, specification, and implementation of each of these abstract data types.

Input/Output

The data types below are used in elementary input/output operations. They define the identifiers of peripheral devices, input/output operations and their results, as well as the data types to be transferred (printer lines and disk pages). They are similar to the input/output types used in the pipeline program (Section 4.1).

```
type iodevice = (typedevice, diskdevice, tapedevice,
             printdevice, carddevice);

type iooperation = (input, output, move, control);

type ioarg = (writeeof, rewind, upspace, backspace);

type ioresult = (complete, intervention, transmission,
             failure, endfile, endmedium, startmedium);

type ioparam = record
               operation: iooperation;
               status: ioresult;
               arg: ioarg
           end;

const nl = '(:10:)'; ff = '(:12:)';
      cr = '(:13:)'; em = '(:25:)';
```

const linelength = 132;
type line = array (.1..linelength.) of char;

const pagelength = 512;
type page = array (.1..pagelength.) of char;

Fifo Queue

A fifo keeps track of the length and the head and tail indices of an array used as a first-in, first-out queue (but does not contain the queue elements themselves).

The access rights and routines of a fifo are:

type fifo = class(limit: integer)
A fifo is initialized with a constant that defines its range of queue indices 1..limit.

function arrival: integer
Returns the index of the next queue element in which an arrival can take place.

function departure: integer
Returns the index of the next queue element from which a departure can take place.

function empty: boolean
Defines whether the queue is empty (arrivals = departures).

function full: boolean
Defines whether the queue is full (arrivals = departures + limit).

A user of a fifo queue must ensure that the length of the queue remains within its physical limit

$$0 \leqslant \text{arrivals} - \text{departures} \leqslant \text{limit}$$

IMPLEMENTATION:

A fifo queue is represented by its limit, head, tail, and length. The Concurrent Pascal compiler will ensure that these variables are accessed only by the routines of the class. In general, a class variable can be accessed only by calling one of the routine entries associated with it. The statement at the end of the class is executed when an instance of a fifo queue is declared and initialized.

```
type fifo =
class(limit: integer);

var head, tail, length: integer;

function entry arrival: integer;
begin
    arrival:= tail;
    tail:= tail mod limit + 1;
    length:= length + 1;
end;

function entry departure: integer;
begin
    departure:= head;
    head:= head mod limit + 1;
    length:= length - 1;
end;

function entry empty: boolean;
begin empty:= (length = 0) end;

function entry full: boolean;
begin full:= (length = limit) end;

begin head:= 1; tail:= 1; length:= 0 end;
```

Resource

A resource gives processes exclusive access to a computer resource (but does not perform any operations on the resource itself).

type resource = monitor

procedure request
Gives the calling process exclusive access to the resource.

procedure release
Makes the resource available for other processes.

A user of a resource must request it before using it and must release it afterwards. If the resource is released within a finite time it will also become available to any process requesting it within a finite time. In short, the resource scheduling is fair.

IMPLEMENTATION:

A resource is represented by its state (free or used) and a queue of processes waiting for it. The multiprocess queue is represented by two data structures: an array of single process queues and a fifo to keep track of the queue indices.

The initial statement of the monitor sets the resource state to *free* and initializes the fifo variable with a constant defining the total number of processes which can wait in the queue.

The compiler will ensure that the monitor variables can be accessed only by calling the routine entries associated with them. The virtual machine will ensure that at most one process at a time is executing a routine within this monitor. The monitor can delay or continue the execution of a calling process.

A routine associated with a class or monitor is called by mentioning the class or monitor variable followed by the name of the routine. As an example, the call

next.arrival

will perform an *arrival* operation on the fifo variable *next*.

```
const processcount = 7;
type processqueue = array (.1..processcount.) of queue;

type resource =
monitor

var free: boolean; q: processqueue; next: fifo;

procedure entry request;
begin
   if free then free:= false
     else delay(q(.next.arrival.));
end;
```

```
procedure entry release;
begin
  if next.empty then free:= true
    else continue(q(.next.departure.));
end;

begin free:= true; init next(processcount) end;
```

Typewriter Resource

A typewriter resource gives processes exclusive access to a typewriter console. A calling process supplies its own identification and is told whether it needs to display it to the operator.

type typeresource = monitor

procedure request(text: line; var changed: boolean)
Gives the calling process exclusive access to the resource. The process identifies itself by a text line. A boolean *changed* defines whether this is the same identification that was used in the last call of *request* (in which case there is no need to display it to the operator again).

procedure release
Makes the resource available for other processes.

The resource scheduling is fair, as explained earlier.

IMPLEMENTATION:

```
type typeresource =
monitor

var free: boolean; q: processqueue; next: fifo; header: line;

procedure entry request(text: line; var changed: boolean);
begin
  if free then free:= false
    else delay(q(.next.arrival.));
  changed:= (header <> text);
  header:= text;
end;
```

```
procedure entry release;
begin
  if next.empty then free:= true
    else continue(q(.next.departure.));
end;

begin
  free:= true; header(.1.):= nl;
  init next(processcount);
end;
```

Typewriter

A typewriter can transfer a text line to or from a typewriter console. It does not identify the calling process on the console or give the process exclusive access to it.

type typewriter = class(device: iodevice)
A typewriter is initialized with the identifier of the device it controls.

procedure write(text: line)
Writes a line on the typewriter.

procedure read(var text: line)
Rings the bell on the typewriter and reads a line from it. Single characters or the whole line can be erased and retyped by typing *control c* or *control l*. The typewriter responds to erasure by writing a question mark.

A newline character (NL) terminates the input or output of a line. A line that exceeds 73 characters is forcefully terminated by a newline character.

IMPLEMENTATION:

The standard procedure *io* delays the calling process until the transfer of a single character is completed.

The procedure *writechar* is not a routine entry; it can only be called within the typewriter class.

```
type typewriter =
class(device: iodevice);

const linelimit = 73;
      cancelchar = '(:3:)' "control c";
      cancelline = '(:12:)' "control l";

procedure writechar(x: char);
var param: ioparam; c: char;
begin
  param.operation:= output;
  c:= x;
  io(c, param, device);
end;

procedure entry write(text: line);
var param: ioparam;
    i: integer; c: char;
begin
  param.operation:= output;
  i:= 0;
  repeat
    i:= i + 1; c:= text(.i.);
    io(c, param, device);
  until (c = nl) or (i = linelimit);
  if c <> nl then writechar(nl);
end;
```

```
procedure entry read(var text: line);
const bel = '(:7:)';
var param: ioparam;
    i: integer; c: char;
begin
  writechar(bel);
  param.operation:= input;
  i:= 0;
  repeat
    io(c, param, device);
    if c = cancelline then
    begin
      writechar(nl);
      writechar('?');
      i:= 0;
    end else
    if c = cancelchar then
    begin
      if i > 0 then
      begin
        writechar('?');
        i:= i - 1;
      end;
    end else
    begin i:= i + 1; text(.i.):= c end;
  until (c = nl) or (i = linelimit);
  if c <> nl then
  begin
    writechar(nl);
    text(.linelimit + 1.):= nl;
  end;
end;

begin end;
```

Terminal

A terminal gives a single process exclusive access to a typewriter, identifies the process to the operator, and transfers a line to or from the device.

type terminal = class(access: typeresource)
The terminal uses a typewriter resource to get exclusive access to the device.

procedure read(header: line; var text: line)
Writes a header (if necessary) on the typewriter and reads a text line from it.

procedure write(header, text: line)
Writes a header (if necessary) followed by a text line on the typewriter.

The *header* identifies the calling process. It is only output if it is different from the last header output on the typewriter.

IMPLEMENTATION:

A class or monitor can only call other classes or monitors if they are declared as variables within it or passed as parameters to it during initialization. So a terminal can only call the monitor *access* and the class *unit*. These access rights are checked during compilation.

```
type terminal =
class (access: typeresource);

var unit: typewriter;

procedure entry read(header: line; var text: line);
var changed: boolean;
begin
   access.request(header, changed);
   if changed then unit.write(header);
   unit.read(text);
   access.release;
end;

procedure entry write(header, text: line);
var changed: boolean;
begin
   access.request(header, changed);
   if changed then unit.write(header);
   unit.write(text);
   access.release;
end;

begin init unit(typedevice) end;
```

Terminal Stream

A terminal stream enables a process to identify itself once and for all and then proceed to read and write single characters on a terminal.

type terminalstream = class(operator: terminal)
A terminal stream uses a terminal to input or output a line at a time.

procedure read(var c: char)
Reads a character from the terminal.

procedure write(c: char)
Writes a character on the terminal.

procedure reset(text: line)
Identifies the calling process.

IMPLEMENTATION:

The terminal stream uses two line buffers for input and output.

```
type terminalstream =
class(operator: terminal);

const linelimit = 80;

var header: line; endinput: boolean;
    inp, out: record count: integer; text: line end;

procedure initialize(text: line);
begin
  header:= text;
  endinput:= true;
  out.count:= 0;
end;
```

```
procedure entry read(var c: char);
begin
   with inp do
   begin
      if endinput then
      begin
         operator.read(header, text);
         count:= 0;
      end;
      count:= count + 1;
      c:= text(.count.);
      endinput:= (c = nl);
   end;
end;

procedure entry write(c: char);
begin
   with out do
   begin
      count:= count + 1;
      text(.count.):= c;
      if (c = nl) or (count = linelimit) then
      begin
         operator.write(header, text);
         count:= 0;
      end;
   end;
end;

procedure entry reset(text: line);
begin initialize(text) end;

begin initialize('unidentified:(:10:)') end;
```

Disk

A disk can transfer any page to or from a disk device.

type disk = class(typeuse: typeresource)
A disk uses a typewriter resource to get exclusive access to a terminal to report disk failure.

procedure read(pageaddr: integer; var block: univ page)
Reads a page identified by its absolute disk address.

procedure write(pageaddr: integer; var block: univ page)
Writes a page identified by its absolute page address.

A page is declared as a *universal type* to make it possible to use the disk
to transfer pages of different types (and not just text).

IMPLEMENTATION:

After a disk failure, the disk writes a message to the operator and
repeats the operation when he types a NL character.

```
type disk =
class(typeuse: typeresource);

var operator: terminal;

procedure transfer(command: iooperation;
   pageaddr: univ ioarg; var block: page);
var param: ioparam; response: line;
begin
  with param, operator do
  begin
    operation:= command;
    arg:= pageaddr;
    io(block, param, diskdevice);
    while status <> complete do
    begin
       write('disk:(:10:)', 'error(:10:)');
       read('push return(:10:)', response);
       io(block, param, diskdevice);
    end;
  end;
 end;

   procedure entry read(pageaddr: integer; var block: univ page);
   begin transfer(input, pageaddr, block) end;
```

procedure entry write(pageaddr: integer; **var** block: **univ** page);
begin transfer(output, pageaddr, block) **end**;

begin init operator(typeuse) **end**;

Disk file

A disk file enables a process to access a disk file consisting of a fixed number of pages ($\leqslant$ 255). The disk file is identified by the absolute disk address of a page map that defines the length of the file and the disk addresses of its pages. From the point of view of a calling process the pages of a file are numbered 1, 2, . . ., length.

type diskfile = class(typeuse: typeresource)
A disk file uses a typewriter resource to get exclusive access to the operator after a disk failure. Initially, the file is closed (inaccessible).

procedure open(mapaddr: integer)
Makes a disk file with a given page map accessible.

procedure close
Makes the disk file inaccessible.

function length: integer
Returns the length of the disk file (in pages). The length of a closed file is zero.

procedure read(pageno: integer; var block: univ page)
Reads a page with a given number from the disk file.

procedure write(pageno: integer; var block: univ page)
Writes a page with a given number on the disk file.

A user of a file must *open* it before using it and *close* it afterwards. *Read* and *write* have no effect if the file is closed or if the page number is outside the range 1..length.

IMPLEMENTATION:

The variable *length* is prefixed with the word *entry*. This means that its value can be used directly outside the class. It can, however, only be changed within the class. So a *variable entry* is similar to a function entry. Variable entries can only be used within classes.

```
const maplength = 255;
type filemap = record
                 filelength: integer;
                 pageset: array (.1..maplength.) of integer
              end;

type diskfile =
class(typeuse: typeresource);

var unit: disk; map: filemap; opened: boolean;

entry length: integer;

function includes(pageno: integer): boolean;
begin
  includes:= opened &
    (1 <= pageno) & (pageno <= length);
end;

procedure entry open(mapaddr: integer);
begin
  unit.read(mapaddr, map);
  length:= map.filelength;
  opened:= true;
end;

procedure entry close;
begin
  length:= 0;
  opened:= false;
end;

procedure entry read(pageno: integer; var block: univ page);
begin
  if includes(pageno) then
    unit.read(map.pageset(.pageno.), block);
end;

procedure entry write(pageno: integer; var block: univ page);
begin
  if includes(pageno) then
    unit.write(map.pageset(.pageno.), block);
end;
```

```
begin
   init unit(typeuse);
   length:= 0;
   opened:= false;
end;
```

Catalog Structure

The disk contains a catalog of all files. The data types below define the structure of the catalog.

The catalog is itself a file defined by a page map stored at the *catalog address*. Every *catalog page* contains a fixed number of catalog entries. A *catalog entry* describes a file by its *identifier, attributes*, and hash *key*. The *search length* defines the number of files that have a hash key equal to the index of this entry. It is used to limit the search for a nonexisting file name.

The attributes of a file are its *kind* (empty, scratch, ascii, sequential or concurrent code), the *address* of its page map, and a boolean defining whether it is *protected* against accidental deletion or overwriting. The latter is checked by all system programs operating on the disk, but not by the operating system. Solo provides a mechanism for protection, but does not enforce it.

```
const idlength = 12;
type identifier = array (.1..idlength.) of char;

type filekind = (empty, scratch, ascii, seqcode, concode);

type fileattr = record
                  kind: filekind;
                  addr: integer;
                  protected: boolean;
                  notused: array (.1..5.) of integer
                end;

type catentry = record
                  id: identifier;
                  attr: fileattr;
                  key, searchlength: integer
                end;

const catpagelength = 16;
type catpage = array (.1..catpagelength.) of catentry;

const cataddr = 154;
```

Disk Table

A disk table makes a disk catalog look like an array of catalog entries identified by numeric indices 1, 2, . . . , length.

type disktable =
class(typeuse: typeresource; cataddr: integer)
A disk table uses a typewriter resource to get exclusive access to the operator after a disk failure and a catalog address to locate a catalog on disk.

function length: integer
Defines the number of entries in the catalog.

procedure read(i: integer; var elem: catentry)
Reads entry number *i* in the catalog. If the entry number is outside the range 1..length the contents of the entry are undefined.

IMPLEMENTATION:

A disk table stores the most recently used catalog page to make a sequential search of the catalog fast.

```
type disktable =
class(typeuse: typeresource; cataddr: integer);

var file: diskfile; pageno: integer; block: catpage;

entry length: integer;

procedure entry read(i: integer; var elem: catentry);
var index: integer;
begin
   index:= (i – 1) div catpagelength + 1;
   if pageno <> index then
   begin
      pageno:= index;
      file.read(pageno, block);
   end;
   elem:= block(.(i – 1) mod catpagelength + 1.);
end;
```

```
  begin
    init file(typeuse);
    file.open(cataddr);
    length:= file.length * catpagelength;
    pageno:= 0;
  end;
```

Disk Catalog

The disk catalog describes all disk files by means of a set of named entries that can be looked up by processes.

type diskcatalog =
monitor(typeuse: typeresource; diskuse: resource; cataddr: integer)
A disk catalog uses a resource to get exclusive access to the disk during a catalog lookup and a typewriter to get exclusive access to the operator after a disk failure. It uses a catalog address to locate the catalog on disk.

procedure lookup(id: identifier; var attr: fileattr; var found: boolean)
Searches for a catalog entry describing a file with a given identifier and indicates whether it found it. If so, it also returns the file attributes.

IMPLEMENTATION:

A disk catalog uses a disk table to make a cyclical search for an identifier. The initial catalog entry is selected by hashing. The search stops when the identifier is found or when there are no more entries with the same hash key. The disk catalog has exclusive access to the disk during the lookup to prevent competing processes from causing disk arm movement.

```
    type diskcatalog =
    monitor(typeuse: typeresource; diskuse: resource;
            cataddr: integer);

    var table: disktable;
```

```
function hash(id: identifier): integer;
var key, i: integer; c: char;
begin
  key:= 1; i:= 0;
  repeat
    i:= i + 1; c:= id(.i.);
    if c <> ' ' then
      key:= key * ord(c) mod table.length + 1;
  until (c = ' ') or (i = idlength);
  hash:= key;
end;


procedure entry lookup(id: identifier; var attr: fileattr;
                              var found: boolean);
var key, more, index: integer; elem: catentry;
begin
  diskuse.request;
  key:= hash(id);
  table.read(key, elem);
  more:= elem.searchlength;
  index:= key; found:= false;
  while not found & (more > 0) do
  begin
    table.read(index, elem);
    if elem.id = id then
    begin attr:= elem.attr; found:= true end
    else
    begin
      if elem.key = key then more:= more - 1;
      index:= index mod table.length + 1;
    end;
  end;
  diskuse.release;
end;


begin init table(typeuse, cataddr) end;
```

Data File

A data file enables a process to access a disk file by means of its name in a disk catalog. The pages of a data file are numbered 1, 2, ..., length.

type datafile =
class(typeuse: typeresource; diskuse: resource; catalog: diskcatalog)
A data file uses a resource to get exclusive access to the disk during a page transfer and a typewriter resource to get exclusive access to the operator after disk failure. It uses a catalog to look up the file. Initially the data file is inaccessible (closed).

procedure open(id: identifier; var found: boolean)
Makes a file with a given identifier accessible if it is found in the catalog.

procedure close
Makes the file inaccessible.

procedure read(pageno: integer; var block: univ page)
Reads a page with a given number from the file. It has no effect if the file is closed or if the page number is outside the range 1..length.

procedure write(pageno: integer; var block: univ page)
Writes a page with a given number on the file. It has no effect if the file is closed or if the page number is outside the range 1..length.

function length: integer
Defines the number of pages in the file. The length of a closed file is zero.

A user of a data file must open it before using it and close it afterwards. If a process needs exclusive access to a data file while using it, this must be ensured at higher levels of programming.

IMPLEMENTATION:

```
type datafile =
class(typeuse: typeresource; diskuse: resource;
        catalog: diskcatalog);

var file: diskfile; opened: boolean;

entry length: integer;
```

```
procedure entry open(id: identifier; var found: boolean);
var attr: fileattr;
begin
  catalog.lookup(id, attr, found);
  if found then
  begin
    diskuse.request;
    file.open(attr.addr);
    length:= file.length;
    diskuse.release;
  end;
  opened:= found;
end;

procedure entry close;
begin
  file.close;
  length:= 0;
  opened:= false;
end;

procedure entry read(pageno: integer; var block: univ page);
begin
  if opened then
  begin
    diskuse.request;
    file.read(pageno, block);
    diskuse.release;
  end;
end;

procedure entry write(pageno: integer; var block: univ page);
begin
  if opened then
  begin
    diskuse.request;
    file.write(pageno, block);
    diskuse.release;
  end;
end;
```

```
begin
    init file(typeuse);
    length:= 0;
    opened:= false;
end;
```

Program File

A program file can transfer a sequential program from a disk file into core. The program file is identified by its name in a disk catalog.

type progfile =
class(typeuse: typeresource; diskuse: resource; catalog: diskcatalog)
A program file uses a resource to get exclusive access to the disk during program loading and a typewriter resource to get exclusive access to the operator after disk failure. It uses a disk catalog to look up the file.

procedure open(id: identifier; var state: progstate)
Loads a program with a given identifier from disk and returns its state. The *program state* is one of the following: *ready* for execution, *not found*, the disk file is *not sequential code*, or the file is *too big* to be loaded into core.

function store: progstore
Defines the variable in which the program file is stored. A *program store* is an array of disk pages.

IMPLEMENTATION:

A program file has exclusive access to the disk until it has loaded the entire program. This is to prevent competing processes from slowing down program loading by causing disk arm movement.

Solo uses two kinds of program files (*progfile1* and *progfile2*): one for large programs and another one for small ones. They differ only in the dimension of the program store used. The need to repeat the entire class definition to handle arrays of different lengths is an awkward inheritance from Pascal.

```
type progstate = (ready, notfound, notseq, toobig);

const storelength = 40 "(or 8)";
type progstore = array (.1..storelength.) of page;
```

```
type progfile =
class(typeuse: typeresource; diskuse: resource;
      catalog: diskcatalog);

var file: diskfile;

entry store: progstore;

procedure entry open(id: identifier; var state: progstate);
var attr: fileattr; found: boolean; pageno: integer;
begin
   catalog.lookup(id, attr, found);
   with diskuse, file, attr do
   if not found then
     state:= notfound else
   if kind <> seqcode then
     state:= notseq else
   begin
     request;
     open(addr);
     if length <= storelength then
     begin
       for pageno:= 1 to length do
          read(pageno, store(.pageno.));
        state:= ready;
     end else
        state:= toobig;
     close;
     release;
   end;
end;

begin init file(typeuse) end;
```

Program Stack

A program stack maintains a last-in, first-out list of identifiers of programs that have called one another. It enables a process to keep track of nested calls of sequential programs.

type progstack = monitor
For historical reasons a program stack was defined as a monitor. In the present version of the system it might as well have been a class.

function space: boolean
Tells whether there is more space in the program stack.

function any: boolean
Defines whether the stack contains any identifiers.

procedure push(id: identifier)
Puts an identifier on top of the stack. It has no effect if the stack is full.

procedure pop(var line, result: univ integer)
Removes a program identifier from the top of the stack and defines the line number at which the program terminated as well as its result. The result either indicates normal termination or one of several run-time errors as explained in the Concurrent Pascal report (Chapter 8).

procedure get(var id: identifier)
Defines the identifier stored in the top of the stack (without removing it). It has no effect if the stack is empty.

IMPLEMENTATION:

A program stack measures the extent of the heap of the calling process before pushing a program identifier on the stack. If a pop operation shows abnormal termination, the heap is reset to its original point to prevent the calling process from crashing due to lack of data space.

The standard routines

attribute   setheap

are defined precisely in the Concurrent Pascal report (Chapter 8).

```
type resulttype = (terminated, overflow, pointererror,
                   rangeerror, varianterror, heaplimit,
                   stacklimit, codelimit, timelimit,
                   callerror);

type attrindex = (caller, heaptop, progline, progresult,
                  runtime);

type progstack =
monitor

const stacklength = 5;
```

```
var stack: array (.1..stacklength.) of
          record
              progid: identifier;
              heapaddr: integer
          end;
     top: 0..stacklength;

function entry space: boolean;
begin space:= (top < stacklength) end;

function entry any: boolean;
begin any:= (top > 0) end;

procedure entry push(id: identifier);
begin
   if top < stacklength then
   begin
     top:= top + 1;
     with stack(.top.) do
     begin
        progid:= id;
        heapaddr:= attribute(heaptop);
     end;
   end;
end;

procedure entry pop(var line, result: univ integer);
const terminated = 0;
begin
   line:= attribute(progline);
   result:= attribute(progresult);
   if result <> terminated then
     setheap(stack(.top.).heapaddr);
   top:= top - 1;
end;

procedure entry  get(var id: identifier);
begin
   if top > 0 then id:= stack(.top.).progid;
end;

begin top:= 0 end;
```

Page Buffer

A page buffer transmits a sequence of data pages from one process to another. Each sequence is terminated by an end of file mark.

type pagebuffer = monitor

procedure read(var text: page; var eof: boolean)
Receives a message consisting of a text page and an end of file indication.

procedure write(text: page; eof: boolean)
Sends a message consisting of a text page and an end of file indication.

If the end of file is true then the text page is empty.

IMPLEMENTATION:

A page buffer stores a single message at a time. It will delay the sending process as long as the buffer is full and the receiving process until it becomes full ($0 \leqslant$ writes – reads $\leqslant 1$).

Solo also implements buffers for transmission of *arguments* (enumerations and identifiers) and *lines*. They are similar to the page buffer (but use no end of file marks). The need to duplicate the routines for each message type is an inconvenience caused by the fixed data types of Pascal.

```
type pagebuffer =
monitor

var buffer: page; last, full: boolean;
    sender, receiver: queue;

procedure entry read(var text: page; var eof: boolean);
begin
  if not full then delay(receiver);
  text:= buffer; eof:= last; full:= false;
  continue(sender);
end;
```

```
procedure entry write(text: page; eof: boolean);
begin
   if full then delay(sender);
   buffer:= text; last:= eof; full:= true;
   continue(receiver);
end;

begin full:= false end;
```

Character Stream

A character stream enables a process to communicate with another process character by character.

type charstream = class(buffer: pagebuffer)
A character stream uses a page buffer to transmit one page of characters at a time from one process to another.

procedure initread
Opens a character stream for reading.

procedure initwrite
Opens a character stream for writing.

procedure read(var c: char)
Reads the next character from the stream. The effect is undefined if the stream is not open for reading.

procedure write(c: char)
Writes the next character in the stream. The effect is undefined if the stream is not open for writing.

A sending process must open its stream for writing before using it. The last character transmitted in a sequence should be an end of medium (EM).
A receiving process must open its stream for reading before using it.

IMPLEMENTATION:

```
type charstream =
class(buffer: pagebuffer);

var text: page; count: integer; eof: boolean;
```

```
procedure entry read(var c: char);
begin
  if count = pagelength then
  begin
    buffer.read(text, eof);
    count:= 0;
  end;
  count:= count + 1;
  c:= text(.count.);
  if c = em then
  begin
    while not eof do buffer.read(text, eof);
    count:= pagelength;
  end;
end;

procedure entry initread;
begin count:= pagelength end;

procedure entry write(c: char);
begin
  count:= count + 1;
  text(.count.):= c;
  if (count = pagelength) or (c = em) then
  begin
    buffer.write(text, false); count:= 0;
    if c = em then buffer.write(text, true);
  end;
end;

procedure entry initwrite;
begin count:= 0 end;

begin end;
```

Tasks and Arguments

The following data types are used by several processes

```
type taskkind = (inputtask, jobtask, outputtask);

type argtag = (niltype, booltype, inttype,
               idtype, ptrtype);
```

```
type argtype = record
              tag: argtag;
              arg: identifier
          end;

const maxarg = 10;
type arglist = array (.1..maxarg.) of argtype;

type argseq = (inp, out);
```

The *task kind* defines whether a process is performing an input task, a job task, or an output task. It is used by sequential programs to determine whether they have been called by the right kind of process. As an example, a program that controls card reader input can only be called by an input process.

A process that executes a sequential program passes a list of *arguments* to it. A program argument consists of a tag field defining its type (boolean, integer, identifier, or pointer) and another field defining its value. (Since Concurrent Pascal does not include the *variant records* of Sequential Pascal one can only represent a program argument by the largest one of its variants — an identifier.)

A job process is connected to an input process and an output process by two *argument buffers* called its *input* and *output sequences*.

Job Process

A job process executes Sequential Pascal programs that can call one another recursively. Initially, it executes a program called *do*. A job process also implements the interface between sequential programs and the Solo operating system defined in Section 5.2.

```
type jobprocess =
process(typeuse: typeresource; diskuse: resource;
        catalog: diskcatalog; inbuffer, outbuffer: pagebuffer;
        inrequest, inresponse, outrequest, outresponse: argbuffer;
        stack: progstack);
```

"program data space = " + 16000
A job process needs access to the operator's console, the disk, and its catalog. It is connected to an input and an output process by two page buffers and four argument buffers as explained in Section 5.1. It uses a program stack to handle nested calls of sequential programs.

It requires a data space of 16000 bytes for user programs and a code space of 20000 bytes. This enables the Pascal compiler to compile itself.

IMPLEMENTATION:

The private variables of a job process give it access to a terminal stream, two character streams for input and output, and two data files. It uses a large program file to store the currently executed program. These variables are inaccessible to other processes.

The job process contains a declaration of a *sequential program* that defines the types of its arguments and the variable in which its code is stored (the latter is inaccessible to the program). It also defines a list of *interface routines* that can be called by a program. These routines are implemented within the job process. They are defined in Section 5.2.

Before a job process can *call* a sequential program it must load it from disk into a program store and push its identifier onto a program stack. After termination of the program, the job process pops its identifier, line number, and result from the program stack, reloads the previous program from disk and returns to it.

A process can only interact with other processes by calling routines within monitors that are passed as parameters to it during initialization (such as the catalog declared at the beginning of a job process). These access rights are checked at compile time.

```
type jobprocess =
process(typeuse: typeresource; diskuse: resource;
        catalog: diskcatalog; inbuffer, outbuffer: pagebuffer;
        inrequest, inresponse, outrequest, outresponse:
        argbuffer; stack: progstack);

"program data space = " + 16000

const maxfile = 2;
type file = 1..maxfile;

var operator: terminal; opstream: terminalstream;

    instream, outstream: charstream;

    files: array (.file.) of datafile;

    code: progfile "(large)";
```

```
program job(var param: arglist; store: progstore);
entry read, write, open, close, get, put, length,
    mark, release, identify, accept, display, readpage,
    writepage, readline, writeline, readarg, writearg,
    lookup, iotransfer, iomove, task, run;

procedure call(id: identifier; var param: arglist;
               var line: integer; var result: resulttype);
var state: progstate; lastid: identifier;
begin
  with code, stack do
  begin
    line:= 0;
    open(id, state);
    if (state = ready) & space then
    begin
      push(id);
      job(param, store);
      pop(line, result);
    end else
    if state = toobig then result:= codelimit
                  else result:= callerror;
    if any then
    begin get(lastid); open(lastid, state) end;
  end;
end;

procedure entry read(var c: char);
begin instream.read(c) end;

procedure entry write(c: char);
begin outstream.write(c) end;

procedure entry open(f: file; id: identifier;
                     var found: boolean);
begin files(.f.).open(id, found) end;

procedure entry close(f: file);
begin files(.f.).close end;

procedure entry get(f: file; p: integer; var block: page);
begin files(.f.).read(p, block) end;
```

```
procedure entry put(f: file; p: integer; var block: page);
begin files(.f.).write(p, block) end;

function entry length(f: file): integer;
begin length:= files(.f.).length end;

procedure entry mark(var top: integer);
begin top:= attribute(heaptop) end;

procedure entry release(top: integer);
begin setheap(top) end;

procedure entry identify(header: text);
begin opstream.reset(header) end;

procedure entry accept(var c: char);
begin opstream.read(c) end;

procedure entry display(c: char);
begin opstream.write(c) end;

procedure entry readpage(var block: page; var eof: boolean);
begin inbuffer.read(block, eof) end;

procedure entry writepage(block: page; eof: boolean);
begin outbuffer.write(block, eof) end;

procedure entry readline(var text: line);
begin end;

procedure entry writeline(text: line);
begin end;

procedure entry readarg(s: argseq; var arg: argtype);
begin
    if s = inp then inresponse.read(arg)
             else outresponse.read(arg);
end;

procedure entry writearg(s: argseq; arg: argtype);
begin
    if s = inp then inrequest.write(arg)
             else outrequest.write(arg);
end;
```

```
procedure entry lookup(id: identifier; var attr: fileattr;
                        var found: boolean);
begin catalog.lookup(id, attr, found) end;

procedure entry iotransfer(device: iodevice;
          var param: ioparam; var block: page);
begin
  if device = diskdevice then
  begin
    diskuse.request;
    io(block, param, device);
    diskuse.release;
  end else
    io(block, param, device);
end;

procedure entry iomove(device: iodevice; var param: ioparam);
begin io(param, param, device) end;

function entry task: taskkind;
begin task:= jobtask end;

procedure entry run(id: identifier; var param: arglist;
                    var line: integer; var result: resulttype);
begin call(id, param, line, result) end;

procedure initialize;
var i: integer; param: arglist;
    line: integer; result: resulttype;
begin
  init operator(typeuse), opstream(operator),
    instream(inbuffer), outstream(outbuffer);
  instream.initread; outstream.initwrite;
  for i:= 1 to maxfile do
    init files(.i.)(typeuse, diskuse, catalog);
  init code(typeuse, diskuse, catalog);
  with param(.2.) do
  begin tag:= idtype; arg:= 'console   ' end;
  call('do     ', param, line, result);
  operator.write('jobprocess:(:10:)', 'terminated (:10:)');
end;

begin initialize end;
```

IO Process

An io process executes Sequential Pascal programs that produce or consume data for a job process. It also implements the interface between these programs and the Solo operating system.

type ioprocess =
process(typeuse: typeresource; diskuse: resource;
catalog: diskcatalog; slowio: linebuffer;
buffer: pagebuffer; request, response: argbuffer;
stack: progstack; iotask: taskkind);

"program data space = " +2000
An io process needs access to the operator, the disk, and the catalog. It is connected to a card reader (or a line printer) by a line buffer and to a job process by a page buffer and two argument buffers. It uses a program stack to handle nested calls of sequential programs.

It requires a data space of 2000 bytes for input/output programs and a code space of 4000 bytes.

Initially, it executes a program called *io.*

IMPLEMENTATION:

The implementation details are similar to a job process.

```
type ioprocess =
process(typeuse: typeresource; diskuse: resource;
        catalog: diskcatalog; slowio: linebuffer;
        buffer: pagebuffer; request, response: argbuffer;
        stack: progstack; iotask: taskkind);

"program data space = " +2000

type file = 1..1;

var operator: terminal; opstream: terminalstream;

    iostream: charstream; iofile: datafile;

    code: progfile "(small)";
```

```
program driver(var param: arglist; store: progstore);
entry read, write, open, close, get, put, length,
    mark, release, identify, accept, display, readpage,
    writepage, readline, writeline, readarg, writearg,
    lookup, iotransfer, iomove, task, run;

procedure call(id: identifier; var param: arglist;
                        var line: integer; var result: resulttype);
var state: progstate; lastid: identifier;
begin
  with code, stack do
  begin
    line:= 0;
    open(id, state);
    if (state = ready) & space then
    begin
        push(id);
        driver(param, store);
        pop(line, result);
    end else
    if state = toobig then result:= codelimit
                    else result:= callerror;
    if any then
    begin get(lastid); open(lastid, state) end;
  end;
end;

procedure entry read(var c: char);
begin iostream.read(c) end;

procedure entry write(c: char);
begin iostream.write(c) end;

procedure entry open(f: file; id: identifier;
                        var found: boolean);
begin iofile.open(id, found) end;

procedure entry close(f: file);
begin iofile.close end;

procedure entry get(f: file; p: integer; var block: page);
begin iofile.read(p, block) end;
```

```
procedure entry put(f: file; p: integer; var block: page);
begin iofile.write(p, block) end;

function entry length(f: file): integer;
begin length:= iofile.length end;

procedure entry mark(var top: integer);
begin top:= attribute(heaptop) end;

procedure entry release(top: integer);
begin setheap(top) end;

procedure entry identify(header: line);
begin opstream.reset(header) end;

procedure entry accept(var c: char);
begin opstream.read(c) end;

procedure entry display(c: char);
begin opstream.write(c) end;

procedure entry readpage(var block: page; var eof: boolean);
begin buffer.read(block, eof) end;

procedure entry writepage(block: page; eof: boolean);
begin buffer.write(block, eof) end;

procedure entry readline(var text: line);
begin slowio.read(text) end;

procedure entry writeline(text: line);
begin slowio.write(text) end;

procedure entry readarg(s: argseq; var arg: argtype);
begin request.read(arg) end;

procedure entry writearg(s: argseq; arg: argtype);
begin response.write(arg) end;

procedure entry lookup(id: identifier; var attr: fileattr;
                       var found: boolean);
begin catalog.lookup(id, attr, found) end;
```

```
procedure entry iotransfer(device: iodevice;
        var param: ioparam; var block: page);
begin
  if device = diskdevice then
  begin
    diskuse.request;
    io(block, param, device);
    diskuse.release;
  end else
    io(block, param, device);
end;

procedure entry iomove(device: iodevice; var param: ioparam);
begin io(param, param, device) end;

function entry task: taskkind;
begin task:= iotask end;

procedure entry run(id: identifier; var param: arglist;
                    var line: integer; var result: resulttype);
begin call(id, param, line, result) end;

procedure initialize;
var param: arglist; line: integer; result: resulttype;
begin
  init operator(typeuse), opstream(operator),
    iostream(buffer),
    iofile(typeuse, diskuse, catalog),
    code(typeuse, diskuse, catalog);
  if iotask = inputtask then iostream.initwrite
                      else iostream.initread;
  call('io      ', param, line, result);
  operator.write('ioprocess: (:10:)', 'terminated (:10:)');
end;

begin initialize end;
```

Card Process

A card process transmits cards from a card reader through a line buffer to an input process.

type cardprocess =
process(typeuse: typeresource; buffer: linebuffer)
A card process can access the operator to report device failure and a line buffer to transmit data. It is assumed that the card reader is controlled only by a single card process. As long as the card reader is turned off or is empty the card process waits. It begins to read cards as soon as they are available in the reader. After a transmission error the card process writes a message to the operator and continues the input of cards.

IMPLEMENTATION:

The standard procedure

wait

delays the card process for 1 sec. This reduces the processor time spent waiting for operation intervention.

```
type cardprocess =
process(typeuse: typeresource; buffer: linebuffer);

var operator: terminal; text: line;
     param: ioparam; ok: boolean;
```

```
begin
  init operator(typeuse);
  param.operation:= input;
  cycle
    repeat
      io(text, param, carddevice);
      case param.status of
        complete:
          ok:= true;
        intervention:
          begin ok:= false; wait end;
        transmission, failure:
          begin
            operator.write('cards: (:10:)', 'error(:10:)');
            ok:= false;
          end
      end
    until ok;
    buffer.write(text);
  end;
end;
```

Printer Process

A printer process transmits lines from an output process to a line printer.

type printerprocess =
process(typeuse: typeresource; buffer: linebuffer)
A printer process can access the operator to report device failure and a line buffer to receive data. It is assumed that the line printer is controlled only by a single printer process. After a printer failure the printer writes a message to the operator and repeats the output of the current line until it is successful.

IMPLEMENTATION:

```
type printerprocess =
process(typeuse: typeresource; buffer: linebuffer);

var operator: terminal; param: ioparam; text: line;
```

```
begin
  init operator(typeuse);
  param.operation:= output;
  cycle
    buffer.read(text);
    io(text, param, printdevice);
    if param.status <> complete then
    begin
      operator.write('printer: (:10:)', 'inspect(:10:)');
      repeat
        wait;
        io(text, param, printdevice);
      until param.status = complete;
    end;
  end;
end;
```

Loader Process

A loader process preempts the operating system and reinitializes it when the operator pushes the BEL key ('control g') on the console.

type loaderprocess =
process(diskuse: resource)
A loader process needs access to the disk to be able to reload the system.

IMPLEMENTATION:

A *control* operation on the *typewriter* delays the calling process until the operator pushes the BEL key (Chapter 8).

The Solo operating system is stored on consecutive disk pages starting at the *Solo address*. It is loaded by means of a *control* operation on the disk as defined in the Concurrent Pascal report (Chapter 8). Consecutive disk pages are used to make the system kernel unaware of the structure of a particular filing system (such as the one used by Solo). The disk contains a sequential program *start* that can copy the Solo system from a concurrent code file into the consecutive disk segment defined above.

```
type loaderprocess =
process(diskuse: resource);

const soloaddr = 24;
var param: ioparam;
```

```
procedure initialize(pageno: univ ioarg);
begin
  with param do
  begin
    operation:= control;
    arg:= pageno;
  end;
end;

begin
  initialize(soloaddr);
  "await bel signal"
  io(param, param, typedevice);
  "reload solo system"
  diskuse.request;
  io(param, param, diskdevice);
  diskuse.release;
end;
```

Initial Process

The initial process initializes all other processes and monitors and defines their access rights to one another. After initialization the operating system consists of a fixed set of components: a card process, an input process, a job process, an output process, a printer process, and a loader process. They have access to an operator, a disk, and a catalog of files. Process communication takes place by means of two page buffers, two line buffers, and four argument buffers (see Fig. 5.1).

When a process, such as the initial process, terminates its execution, its variables continue to exist (because they may be used by other processes).

IMPLEMENTATION:

```
var typeuse: typeresource;
    diskuse: resource; catalog: diskcatalog;
    inbuffer, outbuffer: pagebuffer;
    cardbuffer, printerbuffer: linebuffer;
    inrequest, inresponse, outrequest, outresponse: argbuffer;
    instack, outstack, jobstack: progstack;
    reader: cardprocess; writer: printerprocess;
    producer, consumer: ioprocess; master: jobprocess;
    watchdog: loaderprocess;
```

```
    begin
      init typeuse, diskuse,
        catalog(typeuse, diskuse, cataddr),
        inbuffer, outbuffer,
        cardbuffer, printerbuffer,
        inrequest, inresponse, outrequest, outresponse,
        instack, outstack, jobstack,
        reader(typeuse, cardbuffer),
        writer(typeuse, printerbuffer),
        producer(typeuse, diskuse, catalog, cardbuffer,
            inbuffer, inrequest, inresponse, instack, inputtask),
        consumer(typeuse, diskuse, catalog, printerbuffer,
            outbuffer, outrequest, outresponse, outstack, outputtask),
        master(typeuse, diskuse, catalog, inbuffer, outbuffer,
            inrequest, inresponse, outrequest, outresponse,
            jobstack),
        watchdog(diskuse);
    end.
```

Conclusion

The Solo system consists of 22 line printer pages of Concurrent Pascal text divided into 23 component types (10 classes, 7 monitors, and 6 processes). A typical component type is less than one page long and can be studied in isolation as an (almost) independent piece of program. All program components called by a given component are explicitly declared within that component (either as permanent variables or as parameters to it). To understand a component it is only necessary to know *what* other components called by it do, but *how* they do it in detail is irrelevant.

The entire system can be studied component by component as one would read a book. In that sense, Concurrent Pascal supports *abstraction* and *hierarchical structuring* of concurrent programs very nicely.

It took 4 *compilations* to remove the formal programming errors from the Solo system. It was then *tested* systematically from the bottom up by adding one component type at a time and trying it by means of short test processes. The whole program was tested in 27 runs (or about 1 run per component type). This revealed 7 errors in the test processes and 2 trivial ones in the system itself. Later, about one third of it was rewritten to speed up program loading. This took about 1 week. It was then compiled and put into operation in 1 day and has worked ever since.

I can only suggest two plausible explanations for this unusual testing experience. It seems to be vital that the compiler prevents new components from destroying old ones (since old components cannot call new ones, and new ones can only call old ones through routines that have already been tested). This strict checking of hierarchical access rights makes it possible for a large system to evolve gradually through a sequence of intermediate, stable subsystems.

I am also convinced now that the use of abstract data types which hide implementation details within a fixed set of routines encourages a clarity of design that makes programs practically correct before they are even tested. The slight inconvenience of strict type checking is of minor importance compared to the advantages of instant program reliability.

Although Solo is a concurrent program of only 1300 lines it does implement a virtual machine that is very convenient to use for program development. The availability of cheap microprocessors will put increasing pressure on software designers to develop special-purpose operating systems at very low cost. Concurrent Pascal is one example of a programming tool that may make this possible.

5.4 DISK SCHEDULING

In allocating program files on a slow disk an operating system designer is faced with a dilemma: He can place a program on consecutive disk pages and make loading of it fast. But at the same time file allocation (or deletion) becomes painfully slow (since files must be compacted from time to time).

Or he can place a program on scattered pages (linked in some way) and make file allocation fast. But program loading will now be slowed down considerably (because random references to the disk require more disk revolutions than sequential references do).

This section describes an algorithm that combines the best features of consecutive and nonconsecutive disk allocation: fast sequential access and fast allocation. The algorithm tries to place a file on consecutive pages (but will scatter them somewhat if necessary). It then rearranges these pages to minimize rotational delay during a sequential scan of the file. Since this is done once and for all *before* a program is compiled and stored in a file it is called *disk scheduling at compile time*.

A Numerical Example

The Solo system for the PDP 11/45 computer uses a disk with 200 cylinders each holding 24 pages (distributed on two surfaces). The disk is slow

disk revolution	45 msec
head movement	10 – 90 msec
page transfer	4 msec

During a compilation of a Pascal program, 20 system programs of altogether 300 pages are loaded from disk. If a file is allocated on consecutive pages program loading will take about 3 sec per compilation. But file allocation can take up to 3 min.

If the pages of a file are scattered randomly over the disk, file allocation will only take a second or so, but compiler loading will now last 16 sec.

The algorithm suggested here is a compromise between these extremes: It makes it possible to allocate a file in a few seconds and load the compiler in 5 sec.

Disk Allocation

In the Solo system, the pages allocated to a single file are addressed indirectly through a *page map* (Fig. 5.6). This map makes the pages appear to be consecutive to the user but allows the operating system to place them anywhere on disk.

The disk allocation algorithm takes advantage of the following knowledge about program files

(1)   A program file consists of a fixed set of disk pages throughout its lifetime (that is, until recompilation).

(2)   It is always loaded sequentially in a single operation (since demand paging is not used).

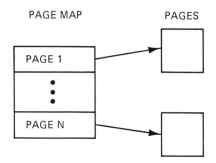

PAGE MAP   PAGES

PAGE 1

PAGE N

Fig. 5.6   A disk file

These assumptions make it possible to simulate program loading at compile time and schedule a fast sequence of page transfers once and for all. The algorithm tries to place a file consecutively on neighboring cylinders (but will make gaps between page segments whenever this is necessary to skip existing files). It then rearranges the page addresses within the page map to minimize the number of disk revolutions and head movements needed to load the file.

Since one cannot always place a file on consecutive pages the problem cannot be solved by formatting the entire disk once. It must be done piecemeal each time a file is allocated because only then the set of available pages is known.

Figure 5.7 illustrates the scheduling algorithm for the simple case of a file placed on 16 consecutive pages, A to P, on two neighboring cylinders.

The algorithm selects page A as the page map of the new file. Now the rotational gap between two neighboring pages is only 0.5 msec. This is too little to allow the Solo system to start another page transfer. To avoid losing a complete disk revolution the algorithm therefore skips page B and makes C the first page of the file. It continues to select every second page and put it in the page map. After two (simulated) disk revolutions all pages on the first cylinder have been placed in the page map. (It takes four revolutions if one considers that a cylinder is placed on two surfaces).

The disk head is now positioned after page H on cylinder 1 (corresponding to page P on cylinder 2). The algorithm knows that a cylinder shift takes enough time to move the disk head to page L. So this becomes the next page in the map, and the scheduling now proceeds as before, selecting every

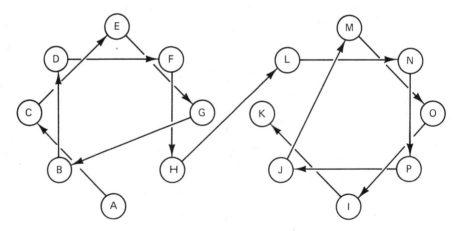

Fig. 5.7   Disk scheduling

PAGE NO	PAGE ADDRESS		PAGE NO	PAGE ADDRESS
1	C		9	N
2	E		10	P
3	G		11	J
4	B		12	M
5	D		13	O
6	F		14	I
7	H		15	K
8	L			

Fig. 5.8   Final page map

second page during two (or four) simulated revolutions. Figure 5.8 shows the final page map.

When a file does not consist of consecutive pages the algorithm will allocate a page and search for the nearest page following the next one on the same cylinder until that cylinder is exhausted.

It is, of course, essential in a multiprogramming system to give a process *exclusive access* to the disk during program loading. Otherwise, competing processes could interrupt the fast loading sequence by disk arm movement. Since program loading is an indivisible operation of finite duration, there is no danger of processes monopolizing the disk (provided program loading is handled by the operating system).

The Multiscan Algorithm

The following is an abstract version of the disk scheduling algorithm. It scans the original page map cylinder by cylinder and rearranges it. In doing so it keeps track of the set of pages allocated within the current *cylinder* and the current *position* of the disk head.

Initially the disk head is positioned at the page map itself. When the algorithm switches to another cylinder it uses a function *distance to cylinder* to compute how far the disk turns while the head moves to that cylinder. It then removes one page at a time from the cylinder, puts it in the new page map, and searches for the nearest page following the next one.

The algorithm performs quite well even when a file consists of many disjoint page segments scattered over a number of cylinders. In one extreme case, a file of 255 pages (11 cylinders) was broken into 47 pieces scattered over a distance of 50 cylinders (due to a flaw in the initial allocation algorithm). The scheduling algorithm nevertheless made it possible to load this file in 82 disk revolutions (which is 50 per cent of the best performance obtainable on the given disk).

```
const cylinder_length = 24 "pages";
      sector_increment = 2 "pages";

type page_index = 0..23;

var pages: set of page_index;
    size: 0..cylinder_length;
    position: page_index;

begin
  position:= initial_position;
  for every_cylinder_of_file do
  begin
    pages:= all_pages_on_cylinder;
    size:= number_of_pages_on_cylinder;
    position:= position + distance_to_cylinder;
    for size downto 1 do
    begin
      while not (position in pages) do
        position:= (position + 1) mod cylinder_length;
      pages:= pages - (.position.);
      put_position_in_page_map;
      position:=
        (position + sector_increment) mod cylinder_length;
    end;
  end;
end;
```

Conclusion

The use of a special disk scheduling algorithm for a frequent case (program loading) illustrates a sound principle of operating system design: *The best operating systems are always highly specialized programs that take full advantage of the expected usage of the computer resources* [Brinch Hansen, 1973b].

By comparison, a more "general" disk scheduling algorithm, such as the scan algorithm [Hoare, 1974], will have negligible effect in this case simply because its only assumption about disk usage is the worst possible one of unrestricted competition among concurrent processes.

The problem also illustrates a common temptation for software designers: to make a theory of optimization out of a complicated device instead of suggesting a simpler one. (The generation of excellent code for computers with complicated instruction sets is another example of this).

5.5 LIST OF SOLO COMPONENTS

Arglist type, 81
Argseq type, 128
Argtag type, 81
Argtype, 81
Attrindex type, 123

Cardprocess, 136
Catentry type, 115
Catpage type, 115
Charstream class, 126
Copy program, 93

Datafile class, 118
Diskcatalog monitor, 117
Disk class, 111
Diskfile class, 113
Disktable class, 116

Fifo class, 102
Fileattr type, 115
Filekind type, 115
Filemap type, 114

Identifier type, 115
Initial process, 140
Ioarg type, 101
Iodevice type, 101
Iooperation type, 101
Ioparam type, 101

Ioprocess, 133
Ioresult type, 101

Jobprocess, 128

Line type, 102
Loaderprocess, 139

Multiscan algorithm, 145

Pagebuffer monitor, 125
Page type, 102
Prefix, 90
Printerprocess, 138
Processqueue type, 104
Progfile class, 121
Progresult type, 87
Progstack monitor, 122
Progstate type, 121
Progstore type, 121

Resource monitor, 103
Resulttype, 123

Taskkind type, 127
Terminal class, 108
Terminalstream class, 110
Typeresource monitor, 105
Typewriter class, 106

6

THE JOB STREAM SYSTEM

The operating system called *job stream* compiles and executes a stream of user programs input from a card reader and output on a line printer. Job stream is written in Concurrent Pascal and user programs are written in Sequential Pascal.

This chapter has another theme besides describing a particular kind of operating system. It illustrates how one can build a system to achieve the best possible *performance* on a given machine and predict its speed *before* constructing it.

6.1 FUNCTION AND PERFORMANCE

The system gives informal access and fast response to short jobs such as the ones written by students in an introductory course on programming.

A *job* is a card deck consisting of a Sequential Pascal program and its input data terminated by an *end of file* card. The latter is a card containing the character # followed by 79 blanks.

The system is run by the users themselves. To run a job a user places a card deck in the reader and pushes a button. When the cards have been read the user removes them and proceeds to a printer where the output appears shortly.

The output of a job consists of a program listing followed by compiler error messages or program results.

To avoid confusion at the printer, jobs are processed in their order of arrival (*first-come, first-served*).

To ensure fast response, a user is limited to at most 1 min of compilation and execution time per job.

The *interface* between a user program and the operating system is defined by a piece of text called the *job prefix* (Section 5.2).

const nl = '(:10:)'; ff = '(:12:)'; em = '(:25:)';

const linelength = 132;
type line = **array** (.1..linelength.) **of** char;

procedure read(**var** c: char);
procedure write(c: char);
procedure readint(**var** value: integer);
procedure writeint(value, length: integer);
procedure writetext(text: line);

program job;

The prefix lists the operating system procedures that user programs may call

read(c)	Inputs a character c (if any). Returns the character EM if a job has no more input data.
write(c)	Outputs a character c. After an EM further output of a job is ignored.
readint(value)	Inputs an integer value (if any). Returns the value 0 if a job has no more numeric input.
writeint(value, length)	Outputs an integer with a given length (in characters).
writetext(text)	Outputs a text string terminated by the character #. The latter is not output.

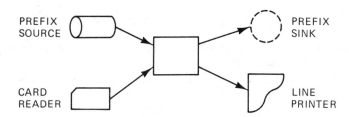

PREFIX SOURCE

PREFIX SINK

CARD READER

LINE PRINTER

Fig. 6.1   Job input/output

The system automatically puts the prefix in front of a user program before it is compiled and removes it again before it is printed (Fig. 6.1).

The system is designed for one purpose only: to execute short jobs as fast as possible. The decision to emphasize performance rather than functional scope is, of course, meaningless unless one can estimate in advance how fast a proposed system will be. The following describes how the system structure evolved from performance estimates.

Most student jobs have few input data and produce little or no output during testing. So the system will mainly be reading, compiling, and printing program text. For the purpose of predicting performance we will assume that a typical *student program* consists of 100 lines of 25 characters each.

The *card reader* and *line printer* can transfer 1000 and 600 lines/min (corresponding to 60 and 100 msec/line). The user needs about 10 sec to insert a card deck and remove a printer listing.

The *compiler* speed is 240 char/sec (or about 100 msec/line) (Chapter 9). Compiler loading from disk takes 5 sec (Chapter 5). The compiler needs another 2 sec to scan a job prefix of say 20 lines.

So a job must be processed in turn by three system components with the following service times

card reader:	10 sec/job + 0.06 sec/line
compiler:	7 sec/job + 0.1 sec/line
line printer:	10 sec/job + 0.1 sec/line

The simplest (and slowest) system would be one in which input, compilation, and output of a job take place strictly one at a time. In such a system the total service time would be

sequential system: 27 sec/job + 0.26 sec/line

or 53 sec for a program of 100 lines.

To reduce service time below this upper bound we must let input, compilation, and output take place simultaneously (Fig. 6.2). In a con-

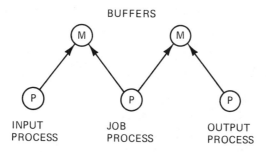

Fig. 6.2 Concurrent system

current system the line printer sets a lower limit on service time.

concurrent system: 10 sec/job + 0.1 sec/line

or 20 sec for 100 lines.

Let us assume that a user needs 5 min after a compilation to correct trivial program errors before resubmitting a job. Now if a single user only needs 20 sec of service time every 300 sec there will be practically no waiting time as long as the system is shared by no more than $(300 + 20)/20 = 16$ people at a time. If more people use it simultaneously each additional user will delay the others by 20 sec. So with 31 active users the response time at the machine will be about 5 min.

So far we have derived the main *process structure* by examining the desired *average behavior* of the system. To achieve the predicted performance it is essential that the line printer can operate continuously at top speed. The main problem of doing this is that the compiler produces its output text in short bursts followed by long pauses.

So we must now look at the *buffers* connecting the processes and make sure that they are able to absorb temporary *speed variations* within the system.

The compiler scans 100 lines of program text and outputs it in 4 sec. It then uses another 13 sec to check the program text before outputting error messages or code. Since it takes the printer 10 sec to output the program text, the buffer connecting the job and output processes must be large and fast enough to absorb 100 lines (or 2500 characters) in 4 sec.

Similarly, to use the card reader continuously we need a large buffer between the input and job processes.

Since user jobs may vary in length both buffers should be large enough to absorb up to one minute of text input/output. A buffer of 600 lines (15,000 characters) is too large to keep in the core store of the available computer. So *we must use the disk to buffer input/output.*

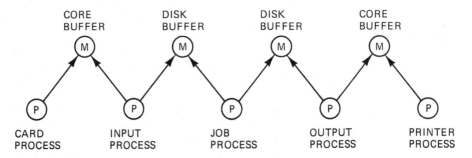

Fig. 6.3   Final process structure

Each disk transfer (of about 20 lines) made by the output process will delay it by about 100 msec. This will slow the line printer down by 5 msec/line (or 5 per cent). To reduce rotational delay, the job process has exclusive access to the disk while it is loading the compiler (Section 5.4). These long disk transfers will occasionally slow the output process and the printer down even more.

To enable the card reader and line printer to continue at full speed during disk transfers we will introduce two more processes (Fig. 6.3).

The *card process* reads cards and transmits them through a buffer in core store to an input process.

The *input process* puts a prefix in front of each job, packs the text into blocks, and sends it through a disk buffer to a job process.

The *job process* compiles and executes programs sending their output through another disk buffer to an output process.

The *output process* removes the prefix from each job, splits the rest of the text into lines, and transmits them through another buffer in core store to a printer process.

The *printer process* receives lines and prints them.

Each core buffer must be large enough to absorb text input/output while a program is being loaded from the disk. Since this takes at most 1 sec, a buffer capacity of 10 lines (250 characters) is sufficient.

This completes the design of the system structure from performance considerations. However crude this performance estimate may seem it turned out to be accurate. When the system was finished it ran short jobs continuously at the speed of the line printer.

To choose a system structure that makes performance prediction trivial is one of the main goals of engineering design. In the job stream system the use of suitable buffers made it possible to ignore the detailed dynamic behavior of concurrent processes and describe them in terms of their average properties only.

6.2 SEQUENTIAL PROGRAMS AND FILES

The job stream system uses the disk to store its own system programs and the temporary data of user jobs. Since users cannot store programs and data permanently on the disk, the job stream system can consider itself the owner of the disk. It can therefore use the file system developed for the Solo operating system (Chapter 5).

The *disk files* used by job stream are called

> jobstream
> jobinput
> jobservice
> joboutput
> jobprefix
> job
> jobbuffer1
> jobbuffer2

Job stream is a concurrent program that is started by giving the command

> start(jobstream)

to the Solo system (Section 5.1). Job stream returns to the Solo system when the BEL key is pushed on the teletype.

The input, job, and output processes of job stream execute three sequential programs called *job input, job service,* and *job output.*

The *job prefix* is a text file described earlier. The generated code is stored temporarily in the *job* file.

Job buffers 1 and 2 are the disk buffers used for input/output of user text.

In addition, the job process uses the *Sequential Pascal compiler.* It consists of seven programs (*spass1* to *spass7*) which use two scratch files (*temp1* and *temp2*). The compiler is described in Chapter 9.

We will now look at each of the job stream programs mentioned above.

Job Input

Job input is a Sequential Pascal program that adds the prefix to user programs and copies them from cards to disk

```
begin
    initprefix; initblank;
    repeat
        copyprefix;
        copycards;
    until false;
end.
```

The input program can call four operating system routines (defined in its own *prefix*)

prefixlength	Defines the length of the job prefix (in disk pages).
readprefix(pageno, block)	Reads a given disk page from the job prefix.
readline(text)	Receives a line from the card process.
writestream(block)	Sends a disk page to the job process.

The variables used to output text to the disk are the current disk page and its length as well as the length of the last page of the prefix file (both in characters)

```
var block: page; blocklength, initlength: integer;
```

Initially, the input program scans the last page of the job prefix to define its length (excluding the final EM character)

```
procedure initprefix;
begin
    readprefix(prefixlength, block);
    initlength:= 0;
    while block(.initlength + 1.) <> em do
        initlength:= initlength + 1;
end
```

The following procedure puts the prefix in front of a job

```
procedure copyprefix;
var pageno: integer;
begin
    for pageno:= 1 to prefixlength – 1 do
    begin
        readprefix(pageno, block);
        writestream(block);
    end;
    readprefix(prefixlength, block);
    blocklength:= initlength;
end
```

The beginning of the job text will be copied from cards into the last page of the prefix before it is transmitted to the job process.

The variables used to input text from the card reader are the current input line and its length (in characters)

```
var card: line; cardlength: integer;
```

The program packs input lines into disk pages and sends them to the job process

```
procedure copycards;
var blockspace, i: integer;
begin
  repeat
    readcard;
    blockspace:= pagelength – blocklength;
    if blockspace < cardlength then
    begin
      for i:= 1 to blockspace do
        block(.blocklength + i.):= card(.i.);
      writestream(block);
      blocklength:= cardlength – blockspace;
      for i:= 1 to blocklength do
        block(.i.):= card(.blockspace + i.);
    end else
    begin
      for i:= 1 to cardlength do
        block(.blocklength + i.):= card(.i.);
      blocklength:= blocklength + cardlength;
    end
  until block(.blocklength.) = em;
  writestream(block);
  blocklength:= 0;
end
```

After receiving a line from the card process the input process eliminates trailing blanks from it and terminates it with a NL character.

A job deck is terminated by a card consisting of the character # only. It is converted into an EM character

```
procedure readcard;
begin
  readline(card);
  cardlength:= cardlimit(card, blank);
  if cardlength > 0 then
    while card(.cardlength.) = ' ' do
      cardlength:= cardlength - 1;
  if (cardlength = 1) & (card(.1.) = '#')
    then card(.1.):= em else
    begin
      cardlength:= cardlength + 1;
      card(.cardlength.):= nl;
    end;
end
```

The program uses a blank line to eliminate trailing blanks fast

```
var blank: line;

procedure initblank;
var charno: integer;
begin
  for charno:= 1 to linelength do
    blank(.charno.):= ' ';
end
```

where a line is defined as

```
const linelength = 132;
type line = array (.1..linelength.) of char;
```

About 55 characters of each line are trailing blanks [Hartmann, 1975]. They can be scanned character by character by a simple loop

```
while (card(.cardlength.) = ' ') & (cardlength > 1) do
  cardlength:= cardlength - 1;
```

But this takes about 10 per cent of the processor time (10 msec/line). This overhead can be reduced by an order of magnitude by comparing longer strings of input text directly with blanks. The input program tries to eliminate first 40 blanks at once, then 20, and finally 10.

To be able to access character strings within a line directly, the program uses an alternative type definition of a line

```
type headtype = array (.1..2, 1..2, 1..2, 1..10.) of char;
     tailtype = array (.1..52.) of char;
     image = record head: headtype; tail: tailtype end;
```

The first 80 characters of a line *image* (the line *head*) are now accessible as an array of strings of lengths 40, 20, and 10. An image is scanned as follows

```
function cardlimit(card, blank: univ image): integer;
var i, j, k: integer;
begin
  if card.head(.2.) <> blank.head(.2.)
    then i:= 2 else i:= 1;
  if card.head(.i, 2.) <> blank.head(.i, 2.)
    then j:= 2 else j:= 1;
  if card.head(.i, j, 2.) <> blank.head(.i, j, 2.)
    then k:= 2 else
  if card.head(.i, j, 1.) <> blank.head(.i, j, 1.)
    then k:= 1 else k:= 0;
  cardlimit:= (((i – 1)*2 + (j – 1))*2 + k)*10;
end
```

The rest of the input program must still be able to do fast scanning, character by character, of the beginning of a line to be able to copy it into a disk page. The use of the key word *univ* makes it possible to call the function *card limit* with arguments that are declared elsewhere to be of type *line* (and not of type *image*) (Section 3.7)

$$cardlength:= cardlimit(card, blank)$$

Job Service

Job service is a Sequential Pascal program that compiles and executes user jobs. The service program calls seven compiler passes one at a time and executes the generated code (if it is correct)

```
        begin
            initialize;
            if ok then callpass(pass1);
            if ok then callpass(pass2);
            if ok then callpass(pass3);
            if ok then callpass(pass4);
            if ok then callpass(pass5);
            if ok then callpass(pass6);
            if ok then open(2, job, ok);
            if ok then callpass(pass7);
            if ok then calljob;
            terminate;
        end.
```

The service program can call the following operating system routines (defined in its own *prefix*)

read(c)	Input and output of text buffered on
write(c)	disk as defined in Section 6.1.
writeint(value, length)	
writetext(text)	
open(fileno, identifier, found)	Input and output of compiler scratch
close(fileno)	files as defined in Section 5.2.
get(fileno, pageno, block)	
put(fileno, pageno, block)	
length(fileno)	
runpass(identifier, param, lineno, result)	Calls a compiler pass with a given identifier and a parameter list. Defines where and how the pass terminated.
runjob(lineno, result)	Calls a compiled job and defines where and how it terminated.

The types of the *parameters* and *results* of programs are defined in Chapter 5.
The service program uses the following file identifiers

```
        const temp1 = 'temp1    '; temp2 = 'temp2    ';
              pass1  = 'spass1   '; pass2  = 'spass2   ';
              pass3  = 'spass3   '; pass4  = 'spass4   ';
              pass5  = 'spass5   '; pass6  = 'spass6   ';
              pass7  = 'spass7   '; job    = 'job      ';
```

and two variables

var ok: boolean; list: arglist;

One is a boolean defining whether compilation was successful; the other is a parameter list for the compiler passes.

The compiler uses three parameters: a boolean defining whether compilation was successful, a pointer to a symbol table constructed by one pass for another, and an integer defining the length of the generated code (if any).

The service program starts compilation by opening the scratch files and initializing the compiler parameters

```
procedure initialize;
begin
    open(1, temp1, ok);
    if ok then open(2, temp2, ok);
    with list(.1.) do
    begin tag:= booltype; bool:= false end;
    with list(.2.) do
    begin tag:= ptrtype; ptr:= nil end;
    with list(.3.) do
    begin tag:= inttype; int:= 0 end;
end
```

It then calls the seven passes one at a time using the following procedure

```
procedure callpass(id: identifier);
var lineno: integer; result: progresult;
begin
    runpass(id, list, lineno, result);
    if result <> terminated
        then writeerror(id, lineno, result)
        else ok:= list(.1.).bool;
end
```

After a successful compilation the user program is executed

```
procedure calljob;
var lineno: integer; result: progresult;
begin
   runjob(lineno, result);
   if result <> terminated then
      writeerror(job, lineno, result);
end
```

The service program terminates a job by closing the scratch files

```
procedure terminate;
begin close(1); close(2) end
```

If the compiler or user program fails or exceeds the time limit of 1 min the service program writes a message of the form

spass3: line 1215 stack limit

or

job: line 58 pointer error

```
procedure writeerror(id: identifier;
   lineno: integer; result: progresult);
begin
   write(nl);
   writeid(id);
   writetext(': line #');
   writeint(lineno, 4);
   write(' ');
   writeresult(result);
   write(nl);
   ok:= (result = terminated);
end;
```

```
procedure writeresult(result: progresult);
begin
  case result of
    terminated:  writetext('terminated #');
    overflow:    writetext('overflow #');
    pointererror: writetext('pointer error#');
    rangeerror:  writetext('range error#');
    varianterror: writetext('variant error#');
    heaplimit:   writetext('heap limit #');
    stacklimit:  writetext('stack limit#');
    codelimit:   writetext('code limit #');
    timelimit:   writetext('time limit #');
    callerror:   writetext('system error #')
  end;
end;


procedure writeid(id: identifier);
var charno: integer;
begin
  for charno:= 1 to idlength do
    if id(.charno.) <> ' ' then
      write(id(.charno.));
end;
```

Job Output

Job output is a Sequential Pascal program that removes the prefix from user jobs and copies them from the disk to the printer

```
begin
  initprefix; initline;
  repeat
    skipprefix;
    printfile;
  until false;
end.
```

The output program can call four operating system routines (defined by its own *prefix*)

prefixlength   Defines the length of the job prefix file (in disk pages).

readprefix(pageno, block)	Reads a given disk page from the job prefix file.
readstream(block)	Receives a disk page from the job process.
writeline(text)	Sends a line to the printer process.

The variables used to input text from the disk are the current disk page and its length (in characters)

$$\textbf{var } block: page; \; blocklength: integer;$$

The compiler adds a line number of 5 characters to each line of the program text (including the prefix). The prefix (as output by the compiler) is defined by its length (in disk pages) and the length of its last disk page (in characters)

$$\textbf{var } prefixpages, \; initlength: integer;$$

Initially, the output program scans the prefix file (as stored on the disk) to define its length (as output by the compiler)

```
procedure initprefix;
var c: char;
    pageno, charno, chars: integer;
begin
  chars:= 0;
  for pageno:= 1 to prefixlength do
  begin
    readprefix(pageno, block);
    charno:= 0;
    repeat
      charno:= charno + 1;
      c:= block(.charno.);
      if c = nl then
        chars:= chars + 5;
    until (charno = pagelength)
      or (c = em);
    chars:= chars + charno;
  end;
  prefixpages:=
    (chars + pagelength - 1) div pagelength;
  initlength:= (chars - 1) mod pagelength;
end
```

The following procedure skips the prefix in front of a job

```
procedure skipprefix;
var pageno: integer;
begin
  for pageno:= 1 to prefixpages do
    readstream(block);
  blocklength:= initlength;
end
```

The job text begins on the last disk page of the prefix.
A job file is printed as follows

```
procedure printfile;
var endfile: boolean;
begin
  endfile:= false;
  repeat printpage(endfile)
  until endfile;
end
```

A printed page consists of a blank line followed by at most 60 lines of text

```
            const firstline = 2; lastline = 61;

            procedure printpage(var endfile: boolean);
            var lineno: integer; endpage: boolean;
            begin
               endpage:= false;
               for lineno:= 1 to firstline - 1 do
                  printchar(nl);
               lineno:= firstline - 1;
               repeat
                  lineno:= lineno + 1;
                  printline(endpage, endfile);
               until (lineno = lastline)
                     or endpage;
               printchar(ff);
            end
```

A printed line consists of a left margin of 23 blanks followed by at most 86 characters and terminated by a control character (CR, NL, or FF)

```
            const firstchar = 24; lastchar = 109;

            var image: line; controlchar: set of char;
```

The line image is initialized as follows

```
            procedure initline;
            var charno: integer;
            begin
               for charno:= 1 to firstchar - 1 do
                  image(.charno.):= ' ';
               image(.lastchar + 1.):= nl;
               controlchar:= (.cr, nl, ff, em.);
            end
```

and output as shown below

```
procedure printline(var endpage, endfile: boolean);
var charno: integer; c: char;
begin
  charno:= firstchar – 1;
  repeat
    if blocklength = pagelength then
    begin
      readstream(block);
      blocklength:= 0;
    end;
    blocklength:= blocklength + 1;
    c:= block(.blocklength.);
    charno:= charno + 1;
    image(.charno.):= c;
  until (c in controlchar)
      or (charno = lastchar);
  if c = ff then
  begin writeline(image); endpage:= true end
  else
  if c = em then
  begin endpage:= true; endfile:= true end
  else
    writeline(image);
end
```

The following procedure outputs a blank line terminated by a NL or FF character

```
procedure printchar(c: char);
begin
  image(.firstchar.):= c;
  writeline(image);
end
```

6.3 CONCURRENT PROGRAM

Job stream is a Concurrent Pascal program consisting of 24 *abstract data types*

	class	fifo
	monitor	resource
	monitor	typeresource
	class	typewriter
	class	terminal
	class	disk
	class	diskfile
	class	disktable
	monitor	diskcatalog
	process	loaderprocess
	class	datafile
*	monitor	pagebuffer
*	class	inputstream
*	class	outputstream
	class	progfile
*	monitor	progtimer
*	process	clockprocess
*	monitor	linebuffer
	process	cardprocess
*	process	inputprocess
*	process	jobprocess
*	process	outputprocess
	process	printerprocess
*	process	initial process

Of these components, 14 are taken from the Solo system (Section 5.3). The other 10 (marked *) are new and will be described in the sequel.

The job stream uses two line buffers (in core store) and two page buffers (on disk) as shown in Fig. 6.3. The following defines the function and implementation of these buffers.

Page Buffer

A page buffer transmits data pages from one process to another. It is stored on disk as a data file.

type pagebuffer =
monitor(typeuse: typeresource; diskuse: resource; catalog: diskcatalog)
A page buffer needs access to a teletype, a disk, and a catalog. Initially, the buffer is inaccessible (closed).

procedure read(var block: page)
Receives a page from the buffer. It has no effect if the buffer is closed.

procedure write(block: page)
Sends a page through the buffer. It has no effect if the buffer is closed.

procedure open(id: identifier)
Makes a disk file with a given identifier accessible as a page buffer (if it is found in the disk catalog). It has no effect if the buffer already has been opened.

IMPLEMENTATION:

A page buffer is represented by two data structures: a *data file* on disk and a *fifo* that keeps track of the indices of its first and last pages. The buffer delays receiving and sending processes as long as it is empty and full, respectively.

```
type pagebuffer =
monitor(typeuse: typeresource; diskuse: resource;
        catalog: diskcatalog);

var opened: boolean;
    buffer: datafile; next: fifo;
    sender, receiver: queue;

procedure entry read(var block: page);
begin
  with buffer, next do
  if opened then
  begin
    if empty then delay(receiver);
    read(departure, block);
    continue(sender);
  end;
end;

procedure entry write(var block: page);
begin
  with buffer, next do
  if opened then
  begin
    if full then delay(sender);
    write(arrival, block);
    continue(receiver);
  end;
end;
```

```
procedure entry open(id: identifier);
begin
   with buffer do
   if not opened then
   begin
      open(id, opened);
      init next(length);
   end;
end;

begin
   init buffer(typeuse, diskuse, catalog);
   opened:= false;
end;
```

Input Stream

An input stream enables a process to receive text sequences character by character from another process. Each sequence is terminated by an EM character.

type inputstream = class(buffer: pagebuffer)
An input stream uses a page buffer to transmit one page of characters at a time from one process to another. Initially, the stream is inaccessible.

procedure read(var c: char)
Gets the next character from the present sequence (if any). After an EM character the stream becomes inaccessible. Further reads will return EMs until the stream is made accessible for input of the next sequence.

procedure next
Makes the stream accessible for input of the next sequence.

IMPLEMENTATION:

```
type inputstream =
class(buffer: pagebuffer);

var text: page; count: integer;
    more: boolean;
```

```
procedure entry read(var c: char);
begin
  if more then
  begin
    if count = pagelength then
    begin
      buffer.read(text);
      count:= 0;
    end;
    count:= count + 1;
    c:= text(.count.);
    more:= (c <> em);
  end else
    c:= em;
end;

procedure entry next;
begin
  more:= true;
  buffer.read(text);
  count:= 0;
end;

begin more:= false end;
```

Output Stream

An output stream enables a process to send text sequences character by character to another process. Each sequence is terminated by an EM character.

type outputstream = class(buffer: pagebuffer)
An output stream uses a page buffer to transmit one page of characters at a time from one process to another. Initially, the stream is inaccessible.

procedure write(c: char)
Puts the next character into the present sequence. After an EM character the stream becomes inaccessible. Further writes have no effect until the stream is made accessible again for output of the next sequence.

procedure next
Makes the stream accessible for output of the next sequence.

IMPLEMENTATION:

```
type outputstream =
class(buffer: pagebuffer);

var text: page; count: integer;
    more: boolean;

procedure entry write(c: char);
begin
  if more then
  begin
    count:= count + 1;
    text(.count.):= c;
    if (count = pagelength) or (c = em) then
    begin
      buffer.write(text);
      count:= 0;
      more:= (c <> em)
    end;
  end;
end;

procedure entry next;
begin more:= true; count:= 0 end;

begin more:= false end;
```

Line Buffer

A line buffer has the same function as in the Solo system (Section 5.3), but is implemented differently in the job stream system.

IMPLEMENTATION:

The buffer is represented by an array of lines and a fifo that keeps track of the indices of its first and last lines.

```
type linebuffer =
monitor
```

```
const maxline = 20;
type lines = array (.1..maxline.) of line;

var buffer: lines; next: fifo;
    sender, receiver: queue;

procedure entry read(var text: line);
begin
  with next do
  begin
    if empty then delay(receiver);
    text:= buffer(.departure.);
    continue(sender);
  end;
end;

procedure entry write(text: line);
begin
  with next do
  begin
    if full then delay(sender);
    buffer(.arrival.):= text;
    continue(receiver);
  end;
end;

begin init next(maxline) end;
```

Preemption

A user job is preempted if its compilation and execution time exceeds a certain limit. In the Solo system, which only serves a single user at a time, a job is preempted simply by restarting the whole operating system (Section 5.3).

The job stream system, however, is serving several users at the same time by outputting one job while another job is being compiled and a third one is being input. So one must take care that preemption of one job does not interrupt the input and output of other jobs; otherwise, data stored temporarily in core store could be lost. Figure 6.4 shows how this is done.

At the beginning of a job the *job process* calls a monitor (called a *program timer*) and defines its time limit. The job process also calls the program timer before and after executing a compiler pass or user program.

PROGTIMER

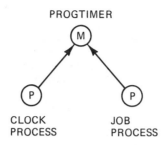

CLOCK
PROCESS

JOB
PROCESS

Fig. 6.4   Program preemption

A *clock process* calls the program timer every second to check whether the job process is executing a program that should be preempted. In that case, the program timer forces the program to terminate and return to the point where it was called by the job process.

Program Timer

A program timer enables a job process to limit the real time during which a user job is being compiled and executed. (Notice that it limits the *real time* of the service phase and *not* the *processor time*. This is accurate enough as long as the rest of the operating system activities consume a reasonably small and constant fraction of processor time.)

type progtimer = monitor
Initially the job process is not executing a preemptible program.

procedure limit(maxtime: integer)
Defines the time limit of a job in seconds.

procedure tick
Assumes that 1 sec has passed and checks whether the job process is executing a program that should be preempted.

procedure enterprog
Marks the beginning of a preemptible program executed as part of the present job.

procedure endprog
Marks the end of a preemptible program executed as part of the present job.

IMPLEMENTATION:

The identity of the job process is defined by the standard function

attribute(caller)

```
type progtimer =
monitor

var who, timeleft: integer; running: boolean;

procedure entry limit(maxtime: integer);
begin
   who:= attribute(caller);
   timeleft:= maxtime;
end;

procedure entry tick;
begin
   timeleft:= timeleft – 1;
   if (timeleft <= 0) & running then
   begin
      stop(who, timelimit);
      running:= false;
   end;
end;

procedure entry enterprog;
begin running:= true end;

procedure entry endprog;
begin running:= false; start end;

begin timeleft:= 0; running:= false end;
```

The standard procedure

stop(who, timelimit)

causes the virtual machine to terminate the sequential program executed by
the job process with the result *timelimit*. If stop is called while a sequential

program is executing an operating system routine then preemption is delayed until the routine call has been completed.

The standard procedure

start

prevents preemption of the next sequential program to be called by the
job process (until another stop operation is executed).

These standard procedures are defined precisely in the Concurrent
Pascal report (Chapter 8).

Clock Process

A clock process calls a program timer every second to check whether a
sequential program should be preempted.

type clockprocess = process(timer: progtimer)
A clock process must have access to a program timer.

IMPLEMENTATION:

The standard procedure

wait

delays the clock process until the next second signal is produced by the
machine.

```
type clockprocess =
process(timer: progtimer);

begin
  cycle
    wait; timer.tick;
  end;
end;
```

Input Process

An input process executes a sequential program *job input* which produces data for a job process.

type inputprocess =
process(typeuse: typeresource; diskuse: resource;
*   catalog: diskcatalog; inbuffer: linebuffer;*
*   outbuffer: pagebuffer);*

"program data space = " + 1000
An input process needs access to a teletype, a disk, and a catalog. It is connected to a card reader by a line buffer and to a job process by a page buffer.

It uses a data space of 1000 bytes for the job input program and a code space of 2000 bytes.

IMPLEMENTATION:

Initially, the process opens the job prefix file and calls the job input program.

```
type inputprocess =
process(typeuse: typeresource; diskuse: resource;
        catalog: diskcatalog; inbuffer: linebuffer;
        outbuffer: pagebuffer);

"program data space = " + 1000

var operator: terminal; prefix: datafile;

    code: progfile "(small)";

program driver(store: progstore);
entry prefixlength, readprefix,
    readline, writestream;

function entry prefixlength: integer;
begin prefixlength:= prefix.length end;

procedure entry readprefix(pageno: integer;
                              var block: page);
begin prefix.read(pageno, block) end;

procedure entry readline(var text: line);
begin inbuffer.read(text) end;

procedure entry writestream(var block: page);
begin outbuffer.write(block) end;
```

```
procedure initialize;
var found: boolean; state: progstate;
begin
   init operator(typeuse),
       prefix(typeuse, diskuse, catalog),
       code(typeuse, diskuse, catalog);
   prefix.open(jobprefix, found);
   code.open(jobinput, state);
   if state = ready then driver(code.store);
   operator.write('job input: (:10:)',
                  'terminated (:10:)');
end;

begin initialize end;
```

Job Process

A job process executes a sequential program *job service* which in turn compiles and executes user programs.

type jobprocess =
process(typeuse: typeresource; diskuse: resource;
*   catalog: diskcatalog; inbuffer, outbuffer: pagebuffer;*
*   timer: progtimer);*

"program data space = " + 16000
A job process needs access to a teletype, a disk, and a catalog. It is connected to an input and an output process by two page buffers. It uses a program timer to preempt user jobs that exceed their time limit.

It uses a data space of 16000 bytes and a code space of 20000 bytes for Sequential Pascal programs.

IMPLEMENTATION:

A user job is processed as follows: First, its input and output sequences are made accessible. (This delays the job process until input data are available.) Then the time limit of the job is set to 60 sec and the job service program is called.

The job service program compiles and executes the user program before returning to the job process. (If the user program fails to terminate the program timer stops it.)

Finally, the job process skips the rest of the job input data (if any) and completes its output by an EM character (unless that has already been done). The job process is now ready to process the next job.

Notice the use of different program declarations and prefixes to give different access rights to different sequential programs executed by the same process (in this case, the job service program, the compiler passes, and the user programs).

Notice also that compiler passes and user programs are made preemptible by calling the program timer before and after their execution. The job service program, however, is not preemptible since it must be able to output a termination message to the user.

```
type jobprocess =
process(typeuse: typeresource; diskuse: resource;
        catalog: diskcatalog; inbuffer, outbuffer:
        pagebuffer; timer: progtimer);

"program data space = " + 16000

const maxfile = 2;
type file = 1..maxfile;

var instream: inputstream; outstream: outputstream;

    files: array (.file.) of datafile;

    code: progfile "(large)";

    digits, sign, numeric: set of char;
    mininteger: integer;

program pascal(store: progstore);
entry read, write, writeint, writetext,
    open, close, get, put, length,
    runpass, runjob;

program pass(var param: arglist; store: progstore);
entry read, write, open, close, get, put, length,
    mark, release;

program user(store: progstore);
entry read, write, readint, writeint, writetext;

procedure entry read(var c: char);
begin instream.read(c) end;
```

```
procedure entry write(c: char);
begin outstream.write(c) end;

procedure entry readint(var value: integer);
var positive, overflow: boolean;
    c: char; digit: integer;
begin
   with instream do
   begin
      repeat read(c) until c in numeric;
      if c in sign then
      begin positive:= (c = '+'); read (c) end
      else positive:= true;
      overflow:= false; value:= 0;
      while not overflow & (c in digits) do
      begin
         digit:= ord(c) - ord('0');
         if  value < (mininteger + digit) div 10
            then overflow:= true
            else value:= 10*value - digit;
         read(c);
      end;
      while c in digits do read(c);
      if positive then
         if value = mininteger then overflow:= true
                               else  value:= - value;
   end;
   if overflow then stop(attribute(caller), rangeerror);
end;
```

```
procedure entry writeint(value, length: integer);
var number: array (.1..6.) of char;
    digits, remainder, i: integer;
begin
  with outstream do
  begin
    remainder:= value; digits:= 0;
    repeat
      digits:= digits + 1;
      number(.digits.):=
        chr(abs(remainder mod 10) + ord('0'));
      remainder:= remainder div 10;
    until remainder = 0;
    for i:= 1 to length - digits - 1 do
      write(' ');
    if value < 0 then write('-') else write(' ');
    for i:= digits downto 1 do
      write(number(.i.));
  end;
end;

procedure entry writetext(text: line);
var charno: integer; c: char;
begin
  with outstream do
  begin
    charno:= 1; c:= text(.1.);
    while (c <> '#') & (charno < linelength) do
    begin
      write(c); charno:= charno + 1;
      c:= text(.charno.);
    end;
  end;
end;

procedure entry open(fileno: file; id: identifier;
                     var found: boolean);
begin files(.fileno.).open(id, found) end;

procedure entry close(fileno: file);
begin files(.fileno.).close end;
```

```
procedure entry get(fileno: file; pageno: integer;
                           var block: page);
begin files(.fileno.).read(pageno, block) end;

procedure entry put(fileno: file; pageno: integer;
                           var block: page);
begin files(.fileno.).write(pageno, block) end;

function entry length(fileno: file): integer;
begin length:= files(.fileno.).length end;

procedure entry mark(var top: integer);
begin top:= attribute(heaptop) end;

procedure entry release(top: integer);
begin setheap(top) end;

procedure entry runpass(id: identifier; var param: arglist;
                             var line, result: univ integer);
const terminated = 0;
var state: progstate; heapaddr: integer;
begin
   with code, timer do
   begin
      open(id, state);
      enterprog;
      heapaddr:= attribute(heaptop);
      pass(param, store);
      line:= attribute(progline);
      result:= attribute(progresult);
      if result <> terminated then setheap(heapaddr);
      endprog;
      open(jobservice, state);
   end;
end;
```

```
procedure entry runjob(var line, result: univ integer);
var state: progstate; heapaddr: integer;
begin
   with code, timer do
   begin
      open(job, state);
      enterprog;
      heapaddr:= attribute(heaptop);
      user(store);
      line:= attribute(progline);
      result:= attribute(progresult);
      setheap(heapaddr);
      endprog;
      open(jobservice, state);
   end;
end;


procedure nextjob;
const maxtime = 60 "seconds";
var state: progstate; heapaddr: integer; c: char;
begin
   with code, timer do
   begin
      instream.next; outstream.next;
      limit(maxtime);
      open(jobservice, state);
      heapaddr:= attribute(heaptop);
      pascal(store);
      setheap(heapaddr);
      repeat instream.read(c) until c = em;
      with outstream do
      begin write(nl); write(em) end;
   end;
end;
```

```
procedure initialize;
var f: file;
begin
   init instream(inbuffer), outstream(outbuffer);
   for f:= 1 to maxfile do
      init files(.f.)(typeuse, diskuse, catalog);
   init code(typeuse, diskuse, catalog);
   digits:= (.'0', '1', '2', '3', '4',
                '5', '6', '7', '8', '9'.);
   sign:= (.'+', '-'.);
   numeric:= digits or sign or (.em.);
   mininteger:= -32767 - 1;
end;

begin
   initialize;
   cycle nextjob end;
end;
```

Output Process

An output process executes a sequential program *job output* that consumes data for a job process.

type outputprocess =
process(typeuse: typeresource; diskuse: resource;
*   catalog: diskcatalog; inbuffer: pagebuffer;*
*   outbuffer: linebuffer);*

"program data space = " +1000
An output process needs access to a teletype, a disk, and a catalog. It is connected to a job process by a page buffer and to a line printer by a line buffer.

It uses a data space of 1000 bytes for the job output program and a code space of 2000 bytes.

IMPLEMENTATION:

Initially, the process opens the job prefix file and calls the job output program.

```
type outputprocess =
process(typeuse: typeresource; diskuse: resource;
        catalog: diskcatalog; inbuffer: pagebuffer;
        outbuffer: linebuffer);

"program data space = " +1000

var operator: terminal; prefix: datafile;

   code: progfile "(small)";

program driver(store: progstore);
entry prefixlength, readprefix,
   readstream, writeline;

function entry prefixlength: integer;
begin prefixlength:= prefix.length end;

procedure entry readprefix(pageno: integer;
                                var block: page);
begin prefix.read(pageno, block) end;

procedure entry readstream(var block: page);
begin inbuffer.read(block) end;

procedure entry writeline(text: line);
begin outbuffer.write(text) end;

procedure initialize;
var found: boolean; state: progstate;
begin
   init operator(typeuse),
      prefix(typeuse, diskuse, catalog),
      code(typeuse, diskuse, catalog);
   prefix.open(jobprefix, found);
   code.open(joboutput, state);
   if state = ready then driver(code.store);
   operator.write('job output:(:10:)',
                     'terminated (:10:)');
end;

begin initialize end;
```

Initial Process

The initial process checks whether the disk contains all the job stream files. It then initializes the other processes and monitors defining their access rights to one another.

IMPLEMENTATION:

```
var diskuse: resource;
    typeuse: typeresource;
    operator: terminal;
    catalog: diskcatalog;
    watchdog: loaderprocess;
    inbuffer, outbuffer: pagebuffer;
    timer: progtimer;
    clock: clockprocess;
    cardbuffer, printerbuffer: linebuffer;
    reader: cardprocess;
    producer: inputprocess;
    master: jobprocess;
    consumer: outputprocess;
    writer: printerprocess;

function exists(file: identifier;
                kind: filekind): boolean;
var attr: fileattr; found: boolean;
begin
    catalog.lookup(file, attr, found);
    exists:= found & (attr.kind = kind);
end;
```

```
begin
   init diskuse, typeuse, operator(typeuse),
      catalog(typeuse, diskuse, cataddr),
      watchdog(diskuse);
   if exists(jobprefix, ascii) &
      exists(jobinput, seqcode) &
      exists(jobservice, seqcode) &
      exists(joboutput, seqcode) &
      exists(job, seqcode) &
      exists(jobbuffer1, scratch) &
      exists(jobbuffer2, scratch) &
      exists(temp1, scratch) &
      exists(temp2, scratch) then
   begin
      init inbuffer(typeuse, diskuse, catalog),
         outbuffer(typeuse, diskuse, catalog);
      inbuffer.open(jobbuffer1);
      outbuffer.open(jobbuffer2);
      init timer, clock(timer),
         cardbuffer, printerbuffer,
         reader(typeuse, cardbuffer),
         producer(typeuse, diskuse, catalog,
            cardbuffer, inbuffer),
         master(typeuse, diskuse, catalog,
            inbuffer, outbuffer, timer),
         consumer(typeuse, diskuse, catalog,
            outbuffer, printerbuffer),
         writer(typeuse, printerbuffer);
   end else
      operator.write('job stream:(:10:)',
                     'files missing(:10:)');
end.
```

6.4   FINAL REMARKS

The job stream system consists of 1800 lines of program text

Program	Lines	K Words
job stream	1360	4
job input	130	1
job service	160	1
job output	150	1
	1800	7

700 lines of the job stream system were taken directly from the Solo system. So the total programming effort was only 1100 lines.

The job stream system requires 38 K words of core store for programs and data

kernel	4 K words
operating system	16 K words
user program	18 K words
core store	38 K words

I designed, programmed, and tested the job stream system in 10 days. It was *tested* in the following steps

(1)   The job input, service, and output programs were tested under the Solo system (using a slight modification of the interface routines).

(2)   The job stream program was derived from the Solo program (using page buffers in the core store) and tested by compiling small programs.

(3)   Job preemption was turned on and tested on an endless user program.

(4)   Page buffers were moved from the core store to the disk.

(5)   Line buffers were changed from a single to several line slots.

In summary, the Solo and job stream systems have shown that *it is possible to design operating system components that can be used in different operating systems.* Testing is, of course, simplified considerably when one operating system is derived from another by gradual replacement of program components.

6.5 LIST OF JOB STREAM COMPONENTS

Arglist type, 81
Attrindex type, 123

Cardprocess, 136
Clockprocess, 175

Datafile class, 118
Diskcatalog monitor, 117
Disk class, 111
Diskfile class, 113
Disktable class, 116

Fifo class, 102
Fileattr type, 115
Filekind type, 115

Identifier type, 115
Image type, 158
Initial process, 185
Inputprocess, 175
Inputstream class, 169

Jobinput prefix, 154

7

A REAL-TIME SCHEDULER

This chapter describes a simple real-time scheduler for process control applications in which a fixed number of concurrent tasks are carried out periodically with frequencies chosen by a human operator.

The real-time scheduler is inspired by an existing process control system [Brinch Hansen, 1967]. It is written in Concurrent Pascal.

The design of any nontrivial program begins with an attempt to define the purpose of the program and its gross structure. It is then written as a sequence of program components which can be tested systematically, one at a time. This is a description of each of these development phases: design, programming, and testing.

7.1 PURPOSE AND DESIGN

A creative programmer will try to use a particular application as an inspiration to look for program structures that can be used in a class of similar applications. And that is what we will try to do here.

A Process Control Application

The application that inspired this concurrent program was a small process control system built by Peter Kraft and myself in 1967 for an ammonia nitrate plant.

The plant is operated manually under supervision of an RC4000 computer with 4 K words of core store (Fig. 7.1). The computer uses an analog to digital converter to measure more than 500 temperatures, pressures, and flow rates. About 150 digital inputs register single pulses from kilowatt-hour meters and bag filling devices as well as the state of alarm contacts in the plant. A digital output register controls a light panel that shows the operator in which part of the plant alarm conditions exist.

Regular alarm and data logging reports are printed on two typewriters. The operator uses a third typewriter to communicate with the computer. During normal operation, digital pulses are input every second and accumulated in a table. Analog flow values are measured every 5 min and accumulated in another table.

The state of all alarm contacts is examined every 5 min also. At the same time analog values are scanned and checked against alarm limits.

Every hour, a log report is printed as a snapshot of how the plant operates. Every 8 hours another report is printed showing the consumption of electricity and production of ammonia nitrate during this period. It also includes the total flow of materials, such as natural gas, steam, ammonia, and nitric acid.

When a section of the plant is being started up after repair the operator may want some of these tasks carried out more frequently. So the computer system makes it possible to specify for each task when it should be started and how often it should be repeated.

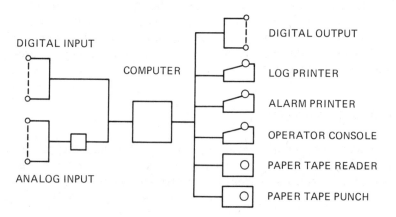

Fig. 7.1 Process control application

Task Scheduling

From this specific description of a single application we can now start looking for a more general characterization of the real-time scheduling required.

We have a single computer that must perform a number of more or less independent tasks, each having its own real-time requirements. The tasks are executed cyclically with periods chosen by an operator. This means that one task cannot make assumptions about the relative speed of other tasks. So conceptually we must regard them as *concurrent processes* coordinated by a *real-time scheduler* (Fig. 7.2).

Now the *task processes* will clearly be different in each application, but we can try to write a real-time scheduler that can be used in many applications of this kind. This scheduler should enable the operator to do three things

(1)   Tell the system what time it is

$$\text{time}(16{:}27{:}18)$$

in hours, minutes, and seconds.

(2)   Say when a task should be executed for the first time

$$\text{start}(\log, 18{:}35{:}00)$$

and how often it should be repeated

$$\text{period}(\log, 1{:}00{:}00)$$

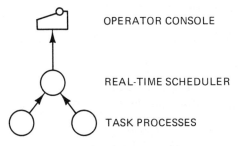

OPERATOR CONSOLE

REAL-TIME SCHEDULER

TASK PROCESSES

Fig. 7.2   Task scheduling

(3)   Stop further execution of a task

$$stop(log)$$

The scheduler must know the names and real-time requirements of the tasks, but need not know what they do.

Program Structure

Having extracted the essence of the problem, we must then break the real-time scheduler down into components that are so small that they can be programmed and tested separately.

How does one invent program structure? I do it by drawing pictures of it from different viewpoints over and over again until a simple and convincing pattern emerges. Perhaps, there are more systematic ways of inventing structure — I don't know. But I do recognize a good program when I find one.

A good program can be read like a book, from the beginning to the end without turning pages back and forth looking elsewhere for an explanation of what is going on. Its parts are no more than a page long so they can be comprehended at a glance. And each part only interacts with a very small number of other parts. It can therefore be studied in isolation from the rest of the system.

To discover a program structure that comes close to this ideal, I ask myself three questions

(1)   Which activities must take place simultaneously to handle this application?

(2)   What are the major data structures needed to solve the problem on a computer?

(3)   Can these data structures be split into smaller ones by introducing the known requirements one at a time?

The real-time system must be able to do the following things at the same time

keep track of the time
talk to the operator
execute tasks

So we can start by recognizing three kinds of program components: a *clock process*, an *operator process*, and some *task processes* (Fig. 7.3).

TASK   CLOCK   OPERATOR
PROCESS   PROCESS   PROCESS

Fig. 7.3   Concurrent processes

Whenever a process uses a peripheral device or cooperates with another process (by exchanging data or timing signals) we need a data structure to control this interaction. It is fairly easy to identify the following kinds of interactions in the real-time system

(1)   The operator process needs access to a *console* to be able to input commands.

(2)   The operator process needs access to a *time schedule* of all tasks, so that it can change it. The tasks must use this table to await their turn. And the clock process must examine it regularly (say, every second) to resume tasks that are due.

We can therefore extend the picture with a console class and a time schedule monitor (Fig. 7.4). This kind of picture shows which data structures can be used by each process. It is an *access graph* (Section 2.5).

We must now try to find simpler aspects of the problems solved by these main data structures. Let us take the operator's console first. At the lowest level of programming in Concurrent Pascal this device is seen as a combination of a *typewriter* that can input and output one character at a time and a *bell key* used by the operator when he needs the attention of the operator process. To make the typewriter a little easier to use at higher levels of programming, we will add a *terminal* component on top of the typewriter component. It can output textstrings and integers as well as single characters (Fig. 7.5).

So the operator process waits for the operator to push the bell key,

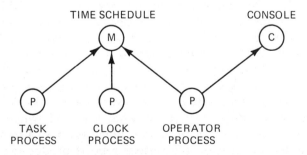

Fig. 7.4   Major data structures

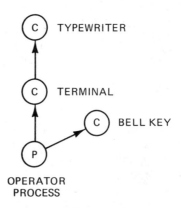

Fig. 7.5   Console components

inputs a command from the terminal, executes it, and responds with a short message on the terminal. It then waits for the bell again and repeats the cycle.

At this point it seems useful to make it possible for several processes to share a single console. So we will add a *resource* monitor that processes must call to get exclusive access to the console. Waiting processes will be served in their order of requesting console access. (But this policy will be hidden inside the resource component and will be easy to modify.)

Figure 7.6 shows this arrangement that gives each process the illusion of having its own private console. This is a useful programming technique for implementing *virtual peripherals* by means of a single, shared device.

Breaking the time schedule down into smaller parts is a little harder. First, we may notice that task processes only need to know that they will be asked to go through a single processing cycle every now and then. But there is no reason why they should worry about how often they are executed. (The operator may indeed change that.)

This insight makes it natural to introduce a simple *task queue* in which a task process can await its turn until it is signalled by another part of the scheduler (Fig. 7.7). In implementing the task queue, we will assume that an attempt to resume a task process before it has completed its last turn will have no effect. (But that too could be changed without influencing the rest of the program.) What we are trying to do is to hide a small number of design decisions within each program component.

Somewhere in the system there is a counter representing the present time. This counter is incremented by one every second thanks to the clock process. The time schedule must know what time it is when it decides to resume a task process. The task processes, however, may also need to know what time it is and print it on the various reports produced by them. The

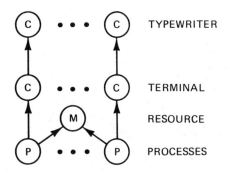

Fig. 7.6   Shared console

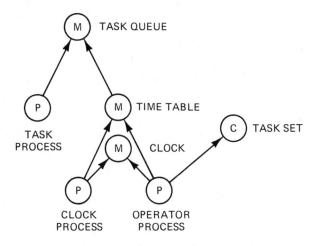

Fig. 7.7   Scheduler components

most practical thing then is to separate a *clock* component defining what time it is from the components that use it. These other components are: The operator process that initializes the clock, the clock process that updates it, and the tasks which print it on their reports. A *timetable* defines the start times and periods of all tasks.

Finally, we may realize that although the operator prefers to identify task processes by names, it may be more convenient elsewhere to represent them by numbers that can be used to look up the timetable and the task queue. This means that the operator process needs a *task set* to convert names to numbers.

Let me summarize what this system does:

A *task process* is a cyclical process that waits in the *task queue* until

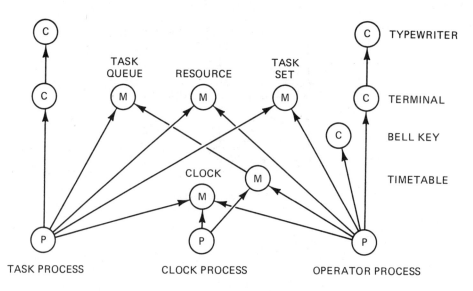

Fig. 7.8 Program structure

it is resumed by a signal from the *timetable*. It then performs its task and waits again. (Although Fig. 7.7 only shows one task process there will be several of them in practice. But they will all use the same task queue.)

The *clock process* is a cyclical process that waits for 1 sec, updates the *clock*, and examines the timetable looking for tasks waiting in the queue to be resumed.

The *operator process* is a cyclical process that waits for a *bell key* signal, inputs a command from the *terminal*, and executes it. The command either sets the clock or changes the time schedule of a task. In the latter case, the operator process looks up its name in the *task set* to see if it exists and what number it has in the timetable and task queue.

This completes the rough definition of program structure. For demonstration purposes, a task process will just print its name and the present time on the console each time it runs. A task therefore needs access both to the clock and the task set.

If we put all program components and their access rights together we get a rather confusing picture (Fig. 7.8). Evidently one should not insist on seeing the whole truth in one picture. Pictures (like program components) are useful only if they show a small part of a hierarchical system.

7.2 PROGRAMMING

So far we have only outlined the purpose of the abstract data structures in a suggestive manner. We will now go through them one at a time and define first what operations one can perform on each data structure and then program them in detail.

Starting with the requirements of the application itself, we outlined a program structure from the *top down* (by first identifying the major data structures and then splitting them into minor ones). We will now work from the *bottom up* to write an executable program for a computer (starting with those program components that do not depend on others).

Input/Output Types

The data types used in elementary input/output operations define the identifiers of peripheral devices, input/output operations, and their results as well as the data types to be transferred (text lines).

```
type iodevice = (typedevice);

type iooperation = (input, output, move, control);

type ioresult = (complete, intervention, transmission,
                 failure);

type ioparam = record
                  operation: iooperation;
                  status: ioresult;
                  arg: integer
               end;

const bel = '(:7:)'; nl = '(:10:)';

const linelength = 72;
type line = array (.1..linelength.) of char;
```

Similar types are used in the Solo operating system (Chapter 5). The details of input/output operations are explained in Chapters 4 and 8 but are not essential for understanding the following.

Typewriter

A typewriter can transfer a single character to or from a typewriter device. It does not give the calling process exclusive access to the device.

type typewriter = class

procedure write(c: char)
Writes a character on the typewriter.

procedure read(var c: char)
Reads a character from the typewriter.

IMPLEMENTATION:

```
type typewriter =
class

procedure entry write(c: char);
var param: ioparam; x: char;
begin
    x:= c; param.operation:= output;
    io(x, param, typedevice);
end;

procedure entry read(var c: char);
var param: ioparam;
begin
    param.operation:= input;
    io(c, param, typedevice);
end;

begin end;
```

Terminal

A terminal can write characters, text strings, and unsigned integers on a typewriter and read characters from it. It does not give the calling process exclusive access to the device.

type terminal = class

procedure write(c: char)
Writes a character on the typewriter.

procedure writetext(text: line)
Writes a text string (terminated by the character #) on the typewriter. The
terminating character is not output.

procedure writeint(int: univ integer)
Writes an unsigned integer on the typewriter. (The integer is of universal
type to make it possible during testing to output boolean values, false and
true, as 0 and 1.)

procedure read(var c: char)
Reads a character from the typewriter.

IMPLEMENTATION:

```
        type terminal =
        class

        var device: typewriter;

        procedure entry write(c: char);
        begin device.write(c) end;

        procedure entry writetext(text: line);
        var i: integer; c: char;
        begin
           i:= 1; c:= text(.1.);
           while c <> '#' do
           begin
              device.write(c);
              i:= i + 1;
              c:= text(.i.);
           end;
        end;
```

```
procedure entry writeint(int: univ integer);
var digits: array (.1..6.) of char;
    rem, length: integer;
begin
  rem:= int; length:= 0;
  repeat
    length:= length + 1;
    digits(.length.):= chr(rem mod 10 + ord('0'));
    rem:= rem div 10;
  until rem = 0;
  for length:= length downto 1 do
    device.write(digits(.length.));
end;

procedure entry read(var c: char);
begin device.read(c) end;

begin init device end;
```

Bell Key

A bell key enables a process to wait until the operator types a BEL character on the typewriter.

type bellkey = class

procedure await
Delays the calling process until the BEL character is pushed.

IMPLEMENTATION:

```
type bellkey =
class

var param: ioparam;

procedure entry await;
begin io(param, param, typedevice) end;

begin param.operation:= control end;
```

Fifo Queue

A fifo keeps track of the length and the head and tail indices of an array used as a first-in, first-out queue (but does not contain the queue elements themselves).

The fifo queue was also used in the Solo system (see Section 5.3). It is used to implement a resource scheduler.

Resource

A resource gives processes exclusive access to a computer resource (but does not perform any operations on the resource itself).

The resource component was taken from the Solo system (Section 5.3) and used with a somewhat larger number of processes

```
const processcount = 10;
type processindex = 1..processcount;
     processqueue = array (.processindex.) of queue;
```

Task Queue

A task queue enables task processes to preempt themselves until re-sumed again. An attempt to resume a task process when it is not waiting in the task queue has no effect.

type taskqueue = monitor
Initially, the task queue is empty.

procedure preempt
Delays the calling process until it is resumed again.

procedure resume(task: processindex)
Continues a given task process if it is waiting in the queue.

IMPLEMENTATION:

Processes are identified by unique integers 1, 2, 3, ... assigned by the virtual machine. A standard function

attribute(caller)

defines the index of the calling process. So task processes need not be aware of their indices.

```
const caller = 0;

type taskqueue =
monitor

var waiting: processqueue;

procedure entry preempt;
begin delay(waiting(.attribute(caller).)) end;

procedure entry resume(task: processindex);
begin continue(waiting(.task.)) end;

begin end;
```

Task Set

A task set associates the names of task processes with their process indices.

type taskset = monitor
Initially, the task set is empty.

procedure include(id: identifier; task: processindex)
Includes a task with a given identifier and process index in the set.

function member(id: identifier): boolean
Defines whether the set includes a task with a given identifier.

function task(id: identifier): processindex
Defines the process index of a task with a given identifier. (Undefined if the task is not in the set.)

procedure me(var id: identifier)
Defines the identifier of the calling process. (Undefined if that process is not in the set).

IMPLEMENTATION:

The task set is represented by an array of identifiers that is looked up by means of the corresponding process indices.

```
const idlength = 12;
type identifier = array (.1..idlength.) of char;

type taskset =
monitor

var table: array (.processindex.) of identifier;

procedure initialize;
var task: processindex;
begin
   for task:= 1 to processcount do
      table(.task.):= '         ';
end;

function index(id: identifier): processindex;
var i, j: processindex;
begin
   i:= 1; j:= processcount;
   while i < j do
      if table(.i.) = id then j:= i
                         else  i:= i + 1;
   index:= i;
end;

procedure entry include(id: identifier; task: processindex);
begin table(.task.):= id end;

function entry member(id: identifier): boolean;
begin member:= (table(.index(id).) = id) end;

function entry task(id: identifier): processindex;
begin task:= index(id) end;

procedure entry me(var id: identifier);
begin id:= table(.attribute(caller).) end;

begin initialize end;
```

Clock

A clock keeps track of real-time.

type clock = monitor
Initially, the time is zero (midnight).

function value: real
Defines the present value of time (in seconds elapsed since midnight).

procedure correct(time: real)
Sets the time to a given value.

procedure tick
Increments time by 1 sec (modulo 24 hours).

IMPLEMENTATION:

Integers on the given machine are not large enough to represent the number of seconds in 24 hours, so time is represented by real values.

```
const onemin =      60.0 "seconds";
      onehour =   3600.0 "seconds";
      halfday = 43200.0 "seconds";
      oneday  = 86400.0 "seconds";

type clock =
monitor

var seconds: real;

function entry value: real;
begin value:= seconds end;

procedure entry correct(time: real);
begin seconds:= time end;

procedure entry tick;
begin
   seconds:= seconds + 1.0;
   if seconds >= oneday then
      seconds:= seconds - oneday;
end;

begin seconds:= 0.0 end;
```

Task Process

A task process performs its task every time it is resumed by the real-time scheduler.

For demonstration purposes, at most three processes should be used. Each task process writes its name and the current time in a separate column on the operator's console when it runs. These task processes can be replaced by others in particular applications.

type taskprocess =
process(typeuse: resource; waiting: taskqueue;
   tasklist: taskset; watch: clock)

A task process needs access to a typewriter resource, a task queue, a task set, and a clock.

IMPLEMENTATION:

```
type taskprocess =
process(typeuse: resource; waiting: taskqueue;
        tasklist: taskset; watch: clock);

var operator: terminal; id: identifier;

procedure writeid(id: identifier);
var i: integer;
begin
  with tasklist, operator do
  begin
    for i:= 1 to (task(id) – 2)*24 do write(' ');
    for i:= 1 to idlength do write(id(.i.));
    write(' '); write(bel);
  end;
end;
```

```
procedure writetime(time: real);
var hour, min, sec: integer; rem: real;
begin
   hour:= trunc(time/onehour);
   rem:= time - conv(hour) * onehour;
   min:= trunc(rem/onemin);
   sec:= trunc(rem - conv(min) * onemin);
   with operator do
   begin
      writeint(hour); write(':');
      writeint(min); write(':');
      writeint(sec); write(nl);
   end;
end;

begin
   init operator; tasklist.me(id);
   cycle
      waiting.preempt;
      typeuse.request;
      writeid(id);
      writetime(watch.value);
      typeuse.release;
   end;
end;
```

Timetable

A timetable holds the start time and period of all tasks. It also schedules the execution of all active tasks. The period of a task cannot exceed 12 hours. An attempt to start a task process before it has completed its last cycle has no effect.

type timetable = monitor(waiting: taskqueue)
A timetable needs access to the task queue in which task processes are waiting to be resumed. Initially, all tasks are inactive.

procedure start(task: processindex; time: real)
Makes a task active and defines its start time.

procedure period(task: processindex; time: real)
Defines the period of a task.

procedure stop(task: processindex)
Makes a task inactive.

procedure examine(time: real)
Examines all active tasks and resumes them if the current time equals or
exceeds their start times. When a task is resumed its start time is incremented by its period (modulo midnight).

IMPLEMENTATION:

```
type taskschedule = record
                        active: boolean;
                        start, period: real
                    end;

type timetable =
monitor(waiting: taskqueue);

var table: array (.processindex.) of taskschedule;

procedure initialize;
var task: processindex;
begin
   for task:= 1 to processcount do
      table(.task.).active:= false;
end;

function reached(time, start: real): boolean;
var diff: real;
begin
   diff:= time – start;
   if abs(diff) >= halfday
      then reached:= (diff < 0.0)
      else  reached:= (diff >= 0.0);
end;

procedure entry start(task: processindex; time: real);
begin
   with table(.task.) do
   begin active:= true; start:= time end;
end;
```

```
procedure entry period(task: processindex; time: real);
begin table(.task.).period:= time end;

procedure entry stop(task: processindex);
begin table(.task.).active:= false end;

procedure entry examine(time: real);
var task: processindex;
begin
   for task:= 1 to processcount do
   with table(.task.) do
   if active then
     if reached(time, start) do
     begin
        waiting.resume(task);
        start:= start + period;
        if start >= oneday then
          start:= start - oneday;
     end;
end;

begin initialize end;
```

Clock Process

A clock process increments a clock every second and examines a time-table of task processes waiting to be resumed.

type clockprocess =
process(watch: clock; schedule: timetable)
A clock process needs access to a clock and a timetable.

IMPLEMENTATION:

The standard procedure

wait

delays the calling process for 1 sec.

```
type clockprocess =
process(watch: clock; schedule: timetable);
```

```
begin
    with watch, schedule do
        cycle wait; tick; examine(value) end;
end;
```

Operator Process

An operator process executes commands input from a typewriter. The human operator must push the BEL key on the typewriter before typing a command. The commands are

start(task, hour:min:sec)
Defines the start time of a task and makes it active.

period(task, hour:min:sec)
Defines the period of a task.

stop(task)
Makes a task inactive.

time(hour:min:sec)
Sets the current time.

The arguments of these commands are of the following types

task: identifier; hour: 0..23; min, sec: 0..59;

```
type operatorprocess =
process(typeuse: resource; tasklist: taskset;
        watch: clock; schedule: timetable)
```
An operator process needs access to a typewriter resource, a task set, a clock, and a timetable.

IMPLEMENTATION:

```
type operatorprocess =
process(typeuse: resource; tasklist: taskset;
        watch: clock; schedule: timetable);

var operator: terminal; bell: bellkey;
    letters, digits: set of char;
    ok: boolean; ch: char; command: identifier;
```

```
procedure help;
begin
  if ok then
  with operator do
  begin
    write(nl);
    writetext('try again (:10:)#');
    writetext('    start(task, hour:min:sec) (:10:)#');
    writetext('    period(task, hour:min:sec) (:10:)#');
    writetext('    stop(task) (:10:)#');
    writetext('    time(hour:min:sec) (:10:)#');
    ok:= false;
  end;
end;

procedure nextchar;
begin
  if ok then
  repeat operator.read(ch) until ch <> ' ';
end;

procedure skipchar(delim: char);
begin
  if ch = delim then nextchar else help;
end;

procedure readint(var int: integer);
const maxint = 32767;
var digit: integer;
begin
  int:= 0;
  if not (ch in digits) then help else
  while (ch in digits) & ok do
  begin
    digit:= ord(ch) - ord('0');
    if int > (maxint - digit) div 10
      then help
      else int:= 10 * int + digit;
    nextchar;
  end;
end;
```

```
procedure readid(var id: identifier);
var length: integer;
begin
  id:= '       ';
  if not (ch in letters) then help else
  begin
    length:= 0;
    while (ch in (letters or digits)) &
          (length < idlength) do
    begin
      length:= length + 1;
      id(.length.):= ch;
      nextchar;
    end;
  end;
end;


procedure readtime(var time: real);
var hour, min, sec: integer;
begin
  readint(hour); skipchar(':');
  readint(min); skipchar(':');
  readint(sec);
  if (hour > 23) or (min > 59) or (sec > 59)
    then help;
  if ok then time:= onehour*conv(hour) +
                    onemin*conv(min) + conv(sec);
end;


procedure start;
var id: identifier; time: real;
begin
  skipchar('('); readid(id);
  skipchar(','); readtime(time);
  skipchar(')');
  if ok then
  with tasklist, schedule, operator do
  if member(id) then start(task(id), time)
    else writetext(' task unknown (:10:)#');
end;
```

```
procedure period;
var id: identifier; time: real;
begin
   skipchar('('); readid(id);
   skipchar(','); readtime(time);
   skipchar(')');
   if ok then
   with tasklist, schedule, operator do
   if member(id) then period(task(id), time)
      else writetext(' task unknown (:10:)#');
end;

procedure stop;
var id: identifier;
begin
   skipchar('('); readid(id);
   skipchar(')');
   if ok then
   with tasklist, schedule, operator do
   if member(id) then stop(task(id))
      else writetext(' task unknown (:10:)#');
end;

procedure correct;
var time: real;
begin
   skipchar('('); readtime(time);
   skipchar(')');
   if ok then watch.correct(time);
end;
```

```
begin
  init operator, bell;
  letters:= (.'a', 'b', 'c', 'd', 'e', 'f', 'g', 'h', 'i',
             'j', 'k', 'l', 'm','n', 'o','p', 'q', 'r',
             's', 't', 'u', 'v', 'w','x','y', 'z', '_'.);
  digits:= (.'0', '1', '2', '3', '4',
            '5', '6', '7', '8', '9'.);
  with typeuse, operator, bell do
  cycle
    await;
    request;
    ok:= true;
    writetext('type command (:7:)(:10:)#');
    nextchar;
    readid(command);
    if command = 'start    ' then start else
    if command = 'period   ' then period else
    if command = 'stop     ' then stop else
    if command = 'time     ' then correct
                               else help;

    write(nl);
    release;
  end;
end;
```

Initial Process

The initial process initializes all other processes and monitors and defines their access rights to one another.

For demonstration purposes, three task processes (called *scan*, *flow*, and *log*) are used.

IMPLEMENTATION:

```
var typeuse: resource; waiting: taskqueue;
    tasklist: taskset; watch: clock;
    scan, flow, log: taskprocess;
    schedule: timetable;
    clockpulse: clockprocess;
    operator: operatorprocess;
```

```
begin
   init typeuse, waiting, tasklist, watch;
   with tasklist do
   begin
      include('scan      ', 2);
      init scan(typeuse, waiting, tasklist, watch);
      include('flow      ', 3);
      init flow(typeuse, waiting, tasklist, watch);
      include('log       ', 4);
      init log(typeuse, waiting, tasklist, watch);
   end;
   init schedule(waiting),
      clockpulse(watch, schedule),
      operator(typeuse, tasklist, watch, schedule);
end.
```

7.3 TESTING

In my experience it is not difficult to make a large program very reliable by testing it. But you must know before writing the program how you intend to test it. Otherwise, there is no guarantee that the structure of the program will make stepwise testing possible and easy.

The least one can do is to make sure that all statements of a program are executed at least once. In addition, one can use insight into the nature of the problem to select certain extreme test cases.

Since a program may be modified later one should be able to repeat test cases to see if the rest of it still works. So test cases must be well documented and reproducible.

If a program is written in an abstract language it should be possible also to understand its behavior during testing in machine-independent terms.

This attitude to program testing clearly rules out spontaneous keyboard artistry and octal dumping. It also makes a special "debugging" program completely unnecessary. During 12 years of programming in industry and universities I have never used these traditional techniques for testing compilers and operating systems.

Systematic techniques for testing compilers and system kernels are described in Naur [1963] and Brinch Hansen [1973a]. The following describes a simple method for testing an operating system consisting of a hierarchy of abstract data types (classes, monitors, and processes). The real-time scheduler is used as an example. It was tested from the bottom up by adding one component at a time and replacing the initial process by a test process that calls the top component and prints test results. The same method was used to test the Solo operating system.

During testing the Concurrent Pascal compiler checks that new (untested) components do not make old (tested) components fail. The controlled access to existing components makes the source of most programming errors obvious.

The following is a list of all test cases used for the real-time scheduler and of the output produced by them.

Typewriter Test

The typewriter is tested by an initial process that reads characters and writes them back.

```
var device: typewriter; c: char;
begin
  init device;
  with device do
  cycle read(c); write(c) end;
end.
```

TEST OUTPUT:

                                 aabbcc ...

Terminal Test

The terminal is tested by an initial process that outputs a text string, copies a character, and writes the smallest and largest unsigned integers.

```
var operator: terminal; c: char;
begin
  init operator;
  with operator do
  begin
    writetext('type a character #');
    read(c); write(c); write(nl);
    writeint(0); write(nl);
    writeint(32767); write(nl);
  end;
end.
```

TEST OUTPUT:

> type a character xx
> 0
> 32767

Bell Key Test

The bell key is tested by a cyclical process that prints a message every time the BEL key is pushed on the typewriter.

```
var operator: terminal; bell: bellkey;
begin
    init operator, bell;
    with operator, bell do
    cycle await; writetext('here i am (:10:)#') end;
end.
```

TEST OUTPUT:

> here i am
> here i am
> . . .

Fifo Queue Test

A fifo queue with a limit of two elements is tested by a cyclical process that fills the queue with arrivals and empties it again by departures. After each operation three integers are printed. They define the queue index of the arrival (or departure) and specify whether the queue is empty or full. (The latter two are boolean values represented by false = 0 and true = 1.)

```
var next: fifo; operator: terminal;
```

```
procedure writestate(index: integer);
begin
    with next, operator do
    begin
        writeint(index); write(' ');
        writeint(empty); write(' ');
        writeint(full); write(nl);
    end;
end;

begin
    init next(2), operator;
    writestate(0);
    with next, operator do
    cycle
        writestate(arrival);
        writestate(arrival);
        writestate(departure);
        writestate(departure);
    end;
end.
```

TEST OUTPUT:

Queue index	Empty	Full
0	1	0
1	0	0
2	0	1
1	0	0
2	1	0
. . .		

Resource Test

An initial process requests a resource, writes a message, and releases it again. This tests the case in which the resource is free when requested and becomes free again upon release.

Afterwards three cyclical processes *a*, *b*, and *c* compete for the resource. This tests the case in which the resource is busy when requested and becomes busy again upon release.

```
type userprocess =
process(me: char; typeuse: resource);

var operator: terminal;

begin
  init operator;
  with typeuse, operator do
  cycle
    request;
    write(me); write(nl);
    release;
    wait;
  end;
end;

var typeuse: resource; operator: terminal;
    user: userprocess;
begin
  init typeuse, operator;
  with typeuse, operator do
  begin
    request;
    writetext('ready (:10:)#');
    release;
  end;
  init user('a', typeuse),
    user('b', typeuse), user('c', typeuse);
end.
```

TEST OUTPUT:

```
                ready
                a
                b
                c
                . . .
```

Task Queue Test

The task queue is tested by means of three task processes *a*, *b*, and *c*, scheduled alternately in alphabetic and reverse order by an initial process.

```
type userprocess =
process(me: char; typeuse: resource;
        waiting: taskqueue);

var operator: terminal;

begin
  init operator;
  with typeuse, waiting, operator do
  cycle
    preempt;
    request; write(me); write(nl); release;
  end;
end;

var typeuse: resource; waiting: taskqueue;
    user: userprocess; task: processindex;
begin
  init typeuse, waiting,
    user('a', typeuse, waiting),
    user('b', typeuse, waiting),
    user('c', typeuse, waiting);
  with waiting do
  cycle
    for task:= 2 to 4 do
    begin wait; resume(task) end;
    for task:= 4 downto 2 do
    begin wait; resume(task) end;
  end;
end.
```

TEST OUTPUT:

```
  ┌──→   a
  │      b
  │      c
  │      c
  │      b
  │      a
  └──    . . .
```

Task Set Test

A task set is tested by an initial process that enters three process names in the set. It prints for each name whether it is in the set before and after its inclusion. It also prints its task index. Finally, the initial process tests whether it can retrieve its own name from the set.

```
var operator: terminal; tasklist: taskset;
    id: identifier;

procedure test(id: identifier; who: processindex);
begin
  with operator, tasklist do
  begin
    writeint(member(id)); write(' ');
    include(id, who);
    writeint(member(id)); write(' ');
    writeint(task(id)); write(nl);
  end;
end;

begin
  init operator, tasklist;
  test('initial    ', 1);
  test('scan       ', 2);
  test('flow       ', 3);
  with operator, tasklist do
  begin
    me(id);
    if id = 'initial    '
      then writetext('ok(:10:)#')
      else  writetext('trouble (:10:)#');
  end;
end.
```

TEST OUTPUT:

Member before	Member after	Task index
0	1	1
0	1	2
0	1	3
ok		

Clock Test

The clock is tested by an initial process that prints its initial value, sets it to 1 min before midnight, and makes it tick for 2 min. (This is also a test of the procedure *writetime* used by a task process.)

```
var operator: terminal; watch: clock; sec: integer;

procedure writetime(time: real);
var hour, min, sec: integer; rem: real;
begin
   hour:= trunc(time/onehour);
   rem:= time - conv(hour) * onehour;
   min:= trunc(rem/onemin);
   sec:= trunc(rem - conv(min) * onemin);
   with operator do
   begin
      writeint(hour); write(':');
      writeint(min); write(':');
      writeint(sec); write(nl);
   end;
end;

begin
   init operator, watch;
   with watch do
   begin
      writetime(value);
      correct(onehour*23.0 + onemin*59.0 + 0.0);
      writetime(value);
      for sec:= 1 to 120 do
      begin tick; writetime(value) end;
   end;
end.
```

TEST OUTPUT:

```
0:0:0
23:59:0
23:59:1
...
23:59:59
0:0:0
0:0:1
...
0:0:59
0:1:0
```

Task Process Test

A task process is tested by an initial process that resumes the task every second.

```
var bell: bellkey; typeuse: resource;
    waiting: taskqueue; tasklist: taskset;
    watch: clock; task: taskprocess;

begin
    init bell, typeuse, waiting, tasklist, watch;
    tasklist.include('task      ', 2);
    init task(typeuse, watch, waiting, tasklist);
    with watch, waiting, bell do
    cycle await; tick; resume(2) end;
end.
```

TEST OUTPUT:

```
task           0:0:1
task           0:0:2
task           0:0:3
. . .
```

Timetable and Clock Process Test

The timetable and clock process are tested by means of three task processes *a*, *b*, and *c*, which start after 10, 15, and 20 sec and run every 5, 9, and 13 sec. Process *a* stops after 25, *b* after 30, and *c* after 35 sec.

```
var typeuse: resource; waiting: taskqueue;
    tasklist: taskset; watch: clock;
    a, b, c: taskprocess; schedule: timetable;
    clockpulse: clockprocess;

begin
    init typeuse, waiting, tasklist, watch,
        schedule(waiting);
    with tasklist do
    begin
        include('a        ', 2);
        include('b        ', 3);
        include('c        ', 4);
        init a(typeuse, watch, waiting, tasklist),
            b(typeuse, watch, waiting, tasklist),
            c(typeuse, watch, waiting, tasklist),
            clockpulse(watch, schedule);
    end;
    with watch, schedule do
    begin
        start(2, 10.0); period(2, 5.0);
        start(3, 15.0); period(3, 9.0);
        start(4, 20.0); period(4, 13.0);
        while value < 25.0 do wait; stop(2);
        while value < 30.0 do wait; stop(3);
        while value < 35.0 do wait; stop(4);
    end;
end.
```

TEST OUTPUT:

a	0:0:10
b	0:0:15
a	0:0:15
c	0:0:20
a	0:0:20
b	0:0:24
a	0:0:25
c	0:0:33

Operator Process Test

The operator process is tested by giving commands to the complete system. These commands contain all possible syntactic and semantic errors. Finally, the system is tested under normal operation.

type the following commands:

```
blah
time
time(
time(zero
time(23
time(23:one
time(23:59
time(23:59:two
time(23:59:59
time(24:59:59)
time(23:60:59)
time(23:59:60)
time(123456789)
stop
stop(
stop(scan
stop(thisistoomuch
stop(a1b2c3d4)
start
start(
start(scan
start(scan,
start(scan, 23:59:59
start(what, 23:59:59)
... similar commands for period ...
time(23:58:00)
start(scan, 23:59:50)
period(scan, 0:0:1)
start(flow, 0:0:5)
period(flow, 0:0:5)
start(log, 0:1:0)
period(log, 0:0:10)
... wait a few minutes ...
stop(scan)
stop(flow)
stop(log)
```

TEST OUTPUT:

A command error makes the operator process print the message

> try again
>> start(task, hour:min:sec)
>> period(task, hour:min:sec)
>> stop(task)
>> time(hour:min:sec)

Under normal operation, a task process prints its name and the time each time it runs, for example

> scan   16:20:38

7.4 FINAL REMARKS

The real-time scheduler and its test cases were written by me in 3 days. It took 3 hours of machine time to test it systematically. Two initial compilations revealed 12 errors. After that 3 more errors were found in 21 test runs (plus 6 errors in the test cases). Writing this description took another couple of days. So the whole program was developed in less than a week. The compiled program is about 4 K words long.

The original real-time scheduler for the ammonia nitrate plant was written in assembly language. It was only half as long, but took half a year to make.

It is interesting to compare the following figures for the Concurrent Pascal program

> program   400 lines
> test cases   200 lines
> manual   600 lines

The test cases are half as long as the program, but fortunately they are trivial to write down.

It is more significant that the description of the program is longer than the program itself. I have come to regard this as normal and would like to make the following suggestion to professional programmers: *One way to improve the quality of programs drastically is to take the view that the main purpose of a programming project is to write a highly readable manual describing a program. The program itself is merely a useful byproduct of this effort.*

7.5   LIST OF REAL-TIME COMPONENTS

LANGUAGE DETAILS

8

CONCURRENT PASCAL REPORT

8.1 INTRODUCTION

This report defines *Concurrent Pascal* — an abstract programming language for structured programming of computer operating systems. It extends the sequential programming language *Pascal* with *concurrent processes*, *monitors*, and *classes*.

The central part of this report is a section on *data types*. It is based on the assumption that data and operations on them are inseparable aspects of computing that should not be dealt with separately. For each data type I define the *constants* that represent its values and the *operators* and *statements* that apply to these values.

Concurrent Pascal has been implemented for the PDP 11/45 computer. Section 8.15 defines the additional restrictions and extensions of this implementation.

Chapters 3–7 contain examples of the language constructs of Concurrent Pascal.

8.2 SYNTAX GRAPHS

The language syntax is defined by means of syntax graphs of the form

while statement

A syntax graph defines the name and syntax of a language construct. *Basic symbols* are represented by capitals and special characters, for example

WHILE   DO   +   ;

Constructs defined by other graphs are represented by their names written in small letters, for example

expr   statement

Correct *sequences* of basic symbols and constructs are represented by arrows.

8.3 CHARACTER SET

Concurrent programs are written in a subset of the ASCII character set

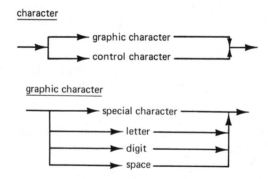

A *graphic character* is a printable character.
The *special characters* are

!	"	#	$	%	&	'	(	)	*	+
,	–	.	/	:	;	<	=	>	?	@

The *letters* are

A	B	C	D	E	F	G	H	I	J	K
L	M	N	O	P	Q	R	S	T	U	V
W	X	Y	Z	_						

The *digits* are

0   1   2   3   4   5   6   7   8   9

control character

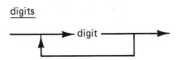

A *control character* is an unprintable character. It is represented by an integer constant called the *ordinal value* of the character (Section 8.16). The ordinal value must be in the range 0..127.

digits

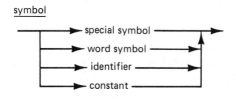

8.4 BASIC SYMBOLS

A program consists of *symbols* and *separators*.

symbol

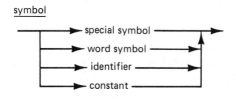

The *special symbols* are

```
+   –   *   /   &   =   <>   <   >   <=   >=
(   )   (.  .)  :=  .   ,   ;   :   '    ..
```

They have fixed meanings (except within string constants and comments).
The *word symbols* are

ARRAY	BEGIN	CASE	CLASS	CONST
CYCLE	DIV	DO	DOWNTO	ELSE
END	ENTRY	FOR	FUNCTION	IF
IN	INIT	MOD	MONITOR	NOT
OF	OR	PROCEDURE	PROCESS	PROGRAM
RECORD	REPEAT	SET	THEN	TO
TYPE	UNIV	UNTIL	VAR	WHILE
WITH				

They have fixed meanings (except within string constants and comments).
Word symbols cannot be used as identifiers.

identifier

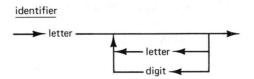

An *identifier* is introduced by a programmer as the name of a constant,
type, variable, or routine.

identifiers

Two constants, identifiers, or word symbols must be separated by at
least one *separator* or special symbol. There may be an arbitrary number of
separators between two symbols, but separators may not occur within
symbols.

separator

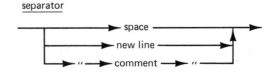

A *comment* is any sequence of graphic characters (except ") enclosed in quotes. It has no effect on the execution of a program.

8.5 BLOCKS

The basic program unit is a *block*.

block

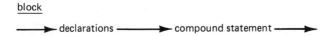

It consists of declarations of computational objects and a compound statement that operates on them.

declarations

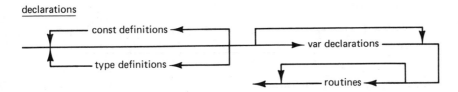

A *declaration* defines a constant, type, variable, or routine and introduces an identifier as its name.

compound statement

A *compound statement* defines a sequence of statements to be executed one at a time from left to right.

8.6 CONSTANTS

A *constant* represents a value that can be used as an operand in an expression.

const definitions

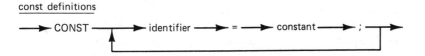

A *constant definition* introduces an identifier as the name of a constant.

constant

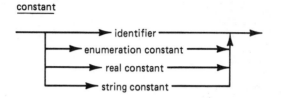

8.7　TYPES

A data *type* defines a set of values which may be assumed by a variable or an expression.

type definitions

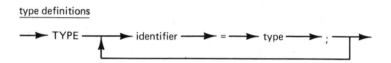

A *type definition* introduces an identifier as the name of a data type. A data type cannot refer to its own type identifier.

type

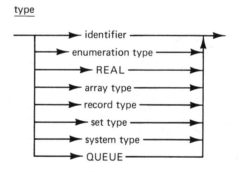

Enumeration types, reals, and queues can only be operated upon as a whole. They are *simple types*.

Arrays, records, sets, and system types are defined in terms of other types. They are *structured types* containing *component types*.

A data type that neither contains system types nor queues is a *passive type*. All other types are *active types*.

An operation can only be performed on two operands if their data types are *compatible* (in the sense defined in Section 8.9).

8.7.1 Enumeration Types

An *enumeration type* consists of a finite, ordered set of values.

enumeration type

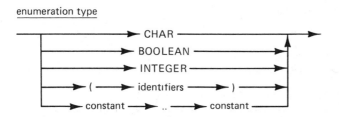

The types *char*, *boolean*, and *integer* are standard enumeration types.

A nonstandard enumeration type is defined by listing the identifiers that denote its values in increasing order.

An enumeration type can also be defined as a *subrange* of another enumeration type by specifying its *min* and *max* values (separated by a double period). The min value must not exceed the max value, and they must be compatible *enumeration constants* (Section 8.9).

enumeration constant

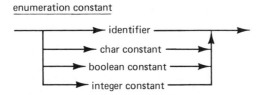

The basic *operators* for enumerations are

:=	(assignment)
<	(less)
=	(equal)
>	(greater)
<=	(less or equal)
<>	(not equal)
>=	(greater or equal)

The result of a *relation* (such as <) is a boolean value.

An enumeration value can be used to *select* one of several statements for execution

case statement

A *case statement* defines an enumeration expression and a set of statements. Each statement is labeled by one or more constants of the same type as the expression. A case statement executes the statement which is labeled with the current value of the expression. (If no such label exists, the effect is unknown.)

labeled statements

The case expression and the *labels* must be of compatible enumeration types, and the labels must be unique.

The following *standard functions* apply to enumerations

succ(x)   The result is the successor value of *x* (if it exists).

pred(x)   The result is the predecessor value of *x* (if it exists).

An enumeration type can be used to execute a statement *repeatedly* for all the enumeration values

for statement

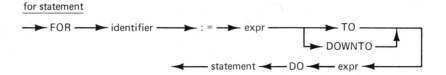

A *for statement* consists of an identifier of a *control variable*, two expressions defining a *subrange*, and a statement to be executed repeatedly for successive values in the subrange.

The control variable can either be incremented from its *min* value *to* its *max* value or be decremented from its *max* value *downto* its *min* value. If the min value is greater than the max value, the statement is not executed. The value of the control variable is undefined after completion of the for statement.

The control variable and the expressions must be of compatible enumeration types. The control variable may not be a constant parameter, a record field, a function identifier, or a variable entry referenced by selection (Sections 8.7.4, 8.8.2, and 8.11). The repeated statement may not change the value of the control variable.

8.7.1.1 Characters

The type *char* is a standard enumeration type. Its values are the set of ASCII characters represented by *char constants*

char constant

The following *standard function* applies to characters

ord(x)   The result (of type integer) is the ordinal value of the character x.

The ordering of characters is defined by their *ordinal values* (Section 8.16).

8.7.1.2 Booleans

The type *boolean* is a standard enumeration type. Its values are represented by *boolean constants*

boolean constant

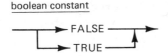

where *false < true*.
The following *operators* are defined for booleans

                               &   (and)
                               or
                               not

The result is a boolean value.
A boolean value can be used to *select* one of two statements for execution. It can also be used to *repeat* the execution of a statement while a condition is true (or until it becomes true).

if statement

An *if statement* defines a boolean expression and two statements. If the expression is true then the first statement is executed, else the second statement is executed. The second statement may be omitted in which case it has no effect.

The expression value must be a boolean.

while statement

A *while statement* defines a boolean expression and a statement. If the expression is false the statement is not executed; otherwise, it is executed repeatedly until the expression becomes false.

The expression value must be a boolean.

repeat statement

A *repeat statement* defines a sequence of statements and a boolean expression. The statements are executed at least once. If the expression is false, they are executed repeatedly until it becomes true.

The expression value must be a boolean.

8.7.1.3　Integers

The type *integer* is a standard enumeration type. Its values are a finite set of successive, whole numbers represented by *integer constants*

integer constant

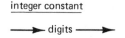

The following *operators* are defined for integers

+	(plus sign or add)
–	(minus sign or subtract)
*	(multiply)
div	(divide)
mod	(modulo)

The result is an integer value.

The following *standard functions* apply to integers

abs(x)   The result (of type integer) is the absolute value of the integer x.

chr(x)   The result (of type char) is the character with the ordinal value x.

conv(x)   The result is the real value corresponding to the integer x.

8.7.2 Reals

The standard type *real* consists of a finite subset of the real numbers represented by *real constants*

real constant

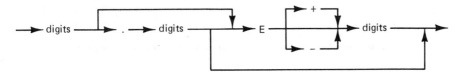

The letter *e* represents the *scale factor* 10.
The following *operators* are defined for reals

:=	(assignment)
<	(less)
=	(equal)
>	(greater)
<=	(less or equal)
<>	(not equal)
>=	(greater or equal)
+	(plus sign or add)
–	(minus sign or subtract)
*	(multiply)
/	(divide)

The result of a *relation* (such as <) is a boolean value. The result of an *arithmetic* operation (such as +) is a real value.
The following *standard functions* apply to reals

abs(x)   The result (of type real) is the abso-
          lute value of the real x.

trunc(x)   The result is the truncated integer
          value corresponding to the real x.

8.7.3 Array Types

An *array* consists of a fixed number of components of the same type. An array component is selected by one or more *index expressions*.

array type

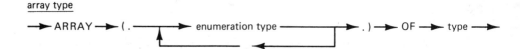

The *index types* must be enumeration types. The *component type* can be any type. The number of index types is called the *dimension* of the array.

array component

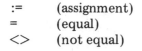

A *component* of an *n*-dimensional array variable is *selected* by means of its variable identifier followed by *n* index expressions (enclosed in brackets and separated by commas).

The number of index expressions must equal the number of index types in the array type definition, and the expressions must be compatible with the corresponding index types.

The basic *operators* for arrays are

$$:=\quad \text{(assignment)}$$
$$=\quad \text{(equal)}$$
$$<>\quad \text{(not equal)}$$

The operands must be passive, compatible arrays. The result of a *relation* (such as =) is a boolean value.

A one-dimensional array of m characters is called a *string type* of *length* m. Its values are the *string constants* of length m

string constant

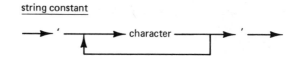

The ordering of characters defines the ordering of strings.

The following *operators* are defined for strings (in addition to those defined for all array types)

$$<\qquad\text{(less)}$$
$$>\qquad\text{(greater)}$$
$$<=\qquad\text{(less or equal)}$$
$$>=\qquad\text{(greater or equal)}$$

The operands must be strings of the same length. The result of a *relation* (such as <) is a boolean value.

8.7.4 Record Types

A *record* consists of a fixed number of components of (possibly) different types

record type

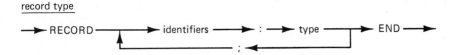

The *components* of a record type are called its *fields*. A field of a record variable is *selected* by means of its variable identifier followed by the field identifier (separated by a period).

record component

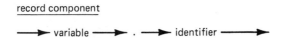

The basic *operators* for records are

$$:=\qquad\text{(assignment)}$$
$$=\qquad\text{(equal)}$$
$$<>\qquad\text{(not equal)}$$

The operands must be passive, compatible records. The result of a *relation* (such as =) is a boolean value.

A *with statement* can be used to operate on the fields of a record variable

with statement

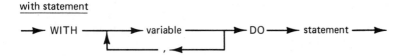

A with statement consists of one or more record variables and a statement. This statement can refer to the record fields by their identifiers only (without qualifying them with the identifiers of the record variables).
The statement

with v1, v2, ... , vn do S

is equivalent to

with v1 do
with v2, ... , vn do S

8.7.5 Set Types

The *set* type of an enumeration type consists of all the subsets that can be formed of the enumeration values

set type

$\longrightarrow$ SET $\longrightarrow$ OF $\longrightarrow$ type $\longrightarrow$

The *component* type of a set type is called its *base type*. It must be an enumeration type.
Set values are constructed as follows

set constructor

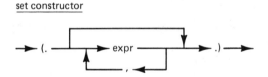

A *set constructor* consists of zero or more expressions enclosed in brackets and separated by commas. It computes the set of these expression values. The *set expressions* must be of compatible enumeration types.
The *empty set* is denoted

(..)

The basic *operators* for sets are

:=	(assignment)
=	(equal)
<>	(not equal)
<=	(contained in)
>=	(contains)
–	(difference)
&	(intersection)
or	(union)

The operands must be compatible sets. The result of a *relation* (such as =) is a boolean value. The result of the other operators is a set value that is compatible with the operands.

in	(membership)

The first operand must be an enumeration type and the second one must be its set type. The result is a boolean value.

8.7.6 System Types

A concurrent program consists of three kinds of *system types*

system type

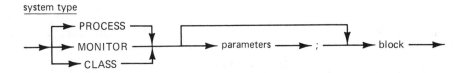

(1)   A *process type* defines a data structure and a sequential statement that can operate on it.

(2)   A *monitor type* defines a data structure and the operations that can be performed on it by concurrent processes. These operations can synchronize processes and exchange data among them.

(3)   A *class type* defines a data structure and the operations that can be performed on it by a single process or monitor. These operations provide controlled access to the data.

A system type consists of the following components:

Parameters that represent constants and other system types on which the system type can operate. They are called the *access rights* of the system type.

Constants, data types, variables, and routines defined within a system type are accessible within it (but generally not outside it). (The variable entries defined in Section 8.8.2 are the only exception to this rule.)

Routine entries defined within a system type are accessible outside it (but not within it). These routines define meaningful operations on the system type that can be performed by other system types.

The *initial statement* of a system type is to be executed when a variable of that type is initialized.

In general, a system type parameter must be a constant parameter of type enumeration, real, set, or monitor (Section 8.11). In addition, a class type can be a parameter of another class type.

A system type can only be defined within another system type (but not within a record type or routine).

A process type can repeat the execution of a set of statements forever by means of a *cycle statement*

cycle statement

8.8 VARIABLES

A *variable* is a named abstract store location that can assume values of a single type. The basic operations on a variable are assignment of a new value to it and a reference to its current value.

var declarations

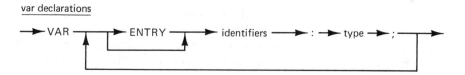

A *variable declaration* defines the identifier and type of a variable. The meaning of a *variable entry* is defined in Section 8.8.2. The declaration

var v1, v2, ... , vn: T;

is equivalent to

$$\textbf{var v1: T; v2: T; ... ; vn: T;}$$

variable

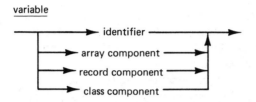

A *variable* is *referenced* by means of its identifier. A *variable component* is selected by means of index expressions or field identifiers (Sections 8.7.3, 8.7.4, and 8.8.2).

assignment

An *assignment* defines the assignment of an expression value to a variable. The variable and the expression must be compatible. The variable must be of passive type. It may not be a constant parameter or a variable entry referenced by selection (Sections 8.7, 8.8.2, and 8.11).

8.8.1 System Components

A variable of system type is called a *system component*. It is either a *process*, a *monitor*, or a *class*.

System components are initialized by means of *init statements*.

init statement

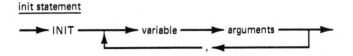

An init statement defines the access rights of a system component (by means of *arguments*), allocates space for its variables, and executes its initial statement.

The statement

$$\textbf{init v1, v2, ... , vn}$$

is equivalent to

$$\text{init } v1; \text{init } v2, \ldots, vn$$

The *initial statement* of a class or monitor is executed as a nameless routine. The initial statement of a process is executed as a sequential process. This process is executed concurrently with all other processes (including the one that initialized it).

The parameters and variables of a system component exist forever after initialization. They are *permanent variables*. A system component must be declared as a permanent variable within a system type. It cannot be declared as a temporary variable within a routine.

A system component can only be initialized once. This must be done in the initial statement of the system type in which it is declared.

8.8.2　Variable Entries

A variable prefixed with the word *entry* is a *variable entry*

$$\textbf{var entry } f\colon T$$

It must be declared as a permanent variable of passive type within a class type.

A class type can refer to one of its own variable entries by means of its identifier *f*

$$f$$

Outside the class type, a variable entry *f* of a class variable *v* can be *selected* either by means of the class identifier *v* followed by the entry identifier *f* (separated by a period)

$$v.f$$

or by means of a *with statement*

$$\textbf{with } v \textbf{ do begin} \ldots f \ldots \textbf{end}$$

A class type can make *assignment* to its variable entries, but outside it they can only be *referenced* (but not changed) by selection. So a variable entry is similar to a *function entry* (Section 8.11).

8.9 EXPRESSIONS

An *expression* defines a computation of a value by application of operators to operands. It is evaluated from left to right using the following *priority rules:*

First, *factors* are evaluated; second, *terms* are evaluated; third, *simple expressions* are evaluated; fourth, complete *expressions* are evaluated.

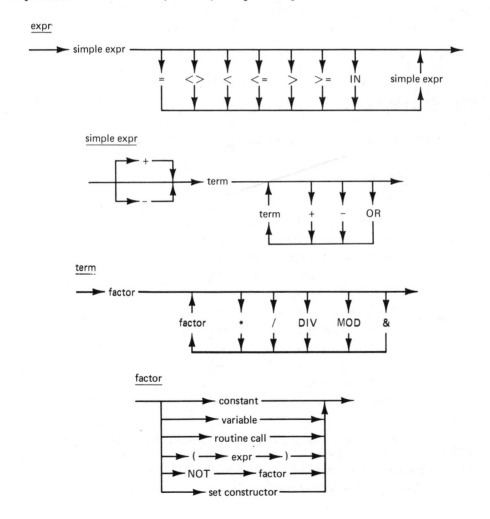

Type Compatibility

An operation can only be performed on two operands if their data types are compatible. They are compatible if one of the following conditions is satisfied

(1) Both types are defined by the same *type definition* or *variable declaration* (Sections 8.7 and 8.8).

(2) Both types are *subranges* of a single enumeration type (Section 8.7.1).

(3) Both types are *strings* of the same length (Section 8.7.3).

(4) Both types are *sets* of compatible base types. The empty set is compatible with any set (Section 8.7.5).

8.10 STATEMENTS

Statements define operations on constants and variables.

statement

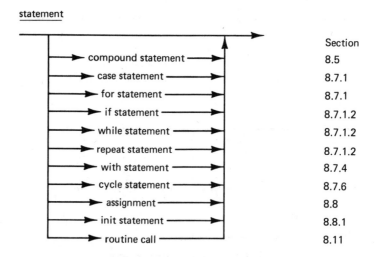

	Section
compound statement	8.5
case statement	8.7.1
for statement	8.7.1
if statement	8.7.1.2
while statement	8.7.1.2
repeat statement	8.7.1.2
with statement	8.7.4
cycle statement	8.7.6
assignment	8.8
init statement	8.8.1
routine call	8.11

Empty statements, assignments, and routine calls cannot be divided into smaller statements. They are *simple statements*. All other statements are *structured statements* formed by combinations of statements.

An *empty statement* has no effect.

8.11 ROUTINES

A *routine* defines a set of parameters and a compound statement that operates on them.

routines

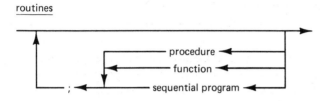

A routine can only be defined within a system type (but not within another routine).

A system component cannot refer to the variables of another system component (except if they are variable entries of a class as defined in Section 8.8.2).

A system component can, however, call *routine entries* defined within other system types. There are four kinds of routine entries

(1) A *process entry* is a routine entry defined within a process type. It can only be called by sequential programs executed by processes of that type (but it cannot be called by system components).

(2) A *monitor entry* is a routine entry defined within a monitor type. It can be called by one or more system components that wish to operate on a monitor of that type. A monitor entry has *exclusive access* to permanent monitor variables while it is being executed. If concurrent processes simultaneously call monitor routines which operate on the same permanent variables, the calls will be executed strictly one at a time.

(3) A *class entry* is a routine entry defined within a class type. It can only be called by one system component. So a class entry also has exclusive access to permanent class variables while it is being executed. But, in contrast to a monitor entry, the exclusive access of a class entry call can be ensured during compilation (and not during execution).

(4) An *initial statement* of a system type is a nameless routine entry called by means of the init statement (Section 8.8.1).

There are three kinds of routines: procedures, functions, and sequential programs.

procedure

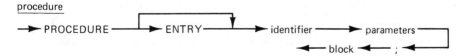

A *procedure* consists of a procedure identifier, a parameter list, and a block to be executed when the procedure is called.

function

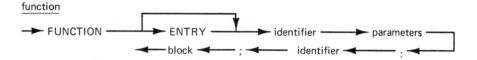

A *function* consists of a function identifier, a parameter list, a function type identifier, and a block to be executed when the function is called.

A function computes a value. The value *e* of a function *f* is defined by an *assignment*

$$f := e$$

within the function block.

The function and its value must be of compatible enumeration types or of type real.

A process that controls the execution of a compiled sequential program is called a *job process*. The process type must include a declaration of the *sequential program*.

sequential program

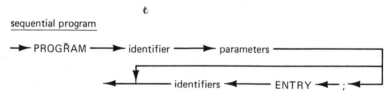

A program declaration consists of a program identifier, a parameter list, and a set of access rights.

Program *parameters* must be of passive types. The rightmost parameter represents the variable in which the code of the sequential program is stored. It cannot be referenced by the sequential program during its execution.

The *access rights* of a program are a list of identifiers of routine entries defined within the job process in which the program is declared. The sequential program may call these routines during its execution.

parameters

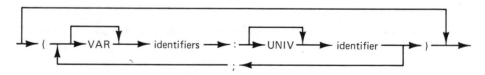

A *parameter list* defines the type of parameters on which a routine can operate. Each parameter is specified by its parameter and type identifiers (separated by a colon).

A *variable parameter* represents a variable to which the routine may assign a value. It is prefixed by the word *var*. The parameter declaration

$$\text{var } v1, v2, \dots , vn: T$$

is equivalent to

$$\text{var } v1: T; \text{var } v2, \dots , vn: T$$

A *constant parameter* represents an expression that is evaluated when the routine is called. Its value cannot be changed by the routine. A constant parameter is *not* prefixed with the word *var*.

The parameter declaration

$$v1, v2, \dots , vn: T$$

is equivalent to

$$v1: T; v2, \dots , vn: T$$

A parameter is of *universal type* if its type identifier is prefixed by the word *univ*. The meaning of universal types will be defined later.

The parameters and variables declared within a routine exist only while it is being executed. They are *temporary variables*.

The *permanent parameters* of a system type define all other system types with which it can *interact*. A system type interacts with another system type when it calls a routine entry defined within the other system type.

Permanent parameters of *system types* must be constant parameters of type enumeration, real, set, or monitor. In addition, a class type can be a parameter of another class type.

Parameters of *routine entries* may not contain queues as components.

Function parameters must be constant.

Program parameters and parameters of *universal type* must be passive (Section 8.7).

Universal Parameters

The prefix *univ* suppresses compatibility checking of parameter and argument types in routine calls (Section 8.9).

An argument of type T1 is compatible with a parameter of universal type T2 if both types are passive and represented by the same number of store locations.

The type checking is only suppressed in routine calls. Inside the given routine the parameter is considered to be of nonuniversal type T2, and outside the routine call the argument is considered to be of nonuniversal type T1.

routine call

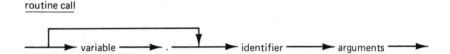

A *routine call* specifies the execution of a routine with a set of arguments. It can be either a *function call*, a *procedure call*, or a *program call*.

A routine that is not prefixed by the word *entry* is a *simple routine*. A system type can call one of its own simple routines by means of its identifier *P* followed by a list of arguments *a1*, ... , *an*

$$P(a1, ... , an)$$

A system type can call a *routine entry* defined within another system type T by qualifying the call with the identifier *v* of a variable of type T

$$v.P(a1, ... , an)$$

or by using a *with statement*

with v do begin ... P(a1, ... , an) ... **end**

A routine may not call itself, and a system type may not call its own routine entries.

A routine call used as a *factor* in an expression must be a function call. A routine call used as a *statement* must be a procedure call (Sections 8.9 and 8.10).

arguments

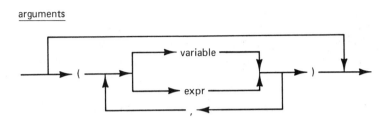

An *argument list* defines the arguments used in a routine call. The number of arguments must equal the number of parameters specified in the routine. The arguments are substituted for the parameters before the routine is executed.

Arguments corresponding to variable and constant parameters must be variables and expressions, respectively. The selection of variable arguments and the evaluation of constant arguments are done once only (before the routine is executed).

The argument types must be compatible with the corresponding parameter types with the following exceptions:

An argument corresponding to a *constant string parameter* may be a string of any length.

An argument corresponding to a *universal parameter* may be of any passive type that occupies the same number of store locations as the parameter type.

8.12   QUEUES

The standard type *queue* may be used within a *monitor* type to delay and resume the execution of a calling process within a routine entry (Sections 8.7.6 and 8.11).

At any time no more than one process can wait in a single queue. A queue is either empty or nonempty. Initially, it is empty.

A variable of type queue can only be declared as a *permanent variable* within a monitor type.

The following *standard function* applies to queues

empty(x)   The result is a boolean value defining whether or not the queue is empty.

The following *standard procedures* are defined for queues

delay(x)   The calling process is delayed in the
                  queue *x* and loses its exclusive access
                  to the given monitor variables. The
                  monitor can now be called by other pro-
                  cesses.

continue(x)   The calling process returns from the
                  monitor routine that performs the con-
                  tinue operation. If another process is
                  waiting in the queue *x* that process
                  will immediately resume its execution
                  of the monitor routine that delayed it.
                  The resumed process now again has ex-
                  clusive access to the monitor variables.

8.13 SCOPE RULES

A *scope* is a region of program text in which an identifier is used with a
single meaning. An identifier must be *introduced* before it is *used*. (The only
exception to this rule is a sequential program declaration within a process
type: It may refer to routine entries defined later in the same process type.
This allows one to call sequential programs recursively.)

A scope is either a system type, a routine, or a with statement. A *system
type* or *routine* introduces identifiers by *declaration;* a *with statement* does
it by *selection* (Sections 8.5, 8.7.4, 8.7.6, 8.8.2, and 8.11).

When a scope is defined within another scope, we have an *outer scope*
and an *inner scope* that are *nested*. An identifier can only be introduced with
one meaning in a scope. It can, however, be introduced with another meaning in an inner scope. In that case, the inner meaning applies in the inner
scope and the outer meaning applies in the outer scope.

System types can be nested, but routines can not. Within a routine, with
statements can be nested. This leads to the following *hierarchy of scopes*

(nested system types
(nonnested routines
(nested with statements)))

A *system type* can use

(1) all constant and type identifiers introduced in its outer scopes.

(2) all identifiers introduced within the system type itself (except its
routine entry identifiers).

A *routine* can use

(1), (2)   defined above and

(3)   all identifiers introduced within the routine itself (except the routine identifier).

A *with statement* can use

(1), (2), (3)   defined above and

(4)   all identifiers introduced by the with statement itself and by its outer with statements.

The phrase "all identifiers introduced in its outer scopes" should be qualified with the phrase "unless these identifiers are used with different meanings in these scopes. In that case, the innermost meaning of each identifier applies in the given scope."

8.14   CONCURRENT PROGRAMS

The outermost scope of a concurrent program is an anonymous, parameterless process type, called the *initial process*.

concurrent program

An instance of this process is automatically initialized after program loading. Its purpose is to initialize other system components.

8.15   PDP 11/45 SYSTEM

This section defines the additional restrictions and extensions of Concurrent Pascal for the PDP 11/45 computer.

8.15.1   Language Restrictions

A nonstandard *enumeration type* cannot consist of more than 128 constant identifiers.
The range of *integers* is –32768..32767.
Integer *case labels* must be in the range 0..127.

The range of *reals* is approximately -10^{38} ..10^{38}. The smallest absolute real value that is nonzero is approximately 10^{-38}. The relative precision of a real is approximately 10^{-16}.

A *string* must contain an even number of characters.

Enumeration types and system types cannot be defined within *record* types.

A *set* of integers can only include members in the range 0..127.

A *process* component can only be declared within the initial process.

The standard procedure *continue* can only be called within a routine entry of a monitor type.

8.15.2 Store Allocation

The compiler determines the store requirements of system components under the assumption that routine calls are not recursive. The scope rules prevent *recursion* within concurrent programs, but not within sequential programs.

The programmer must estimate an *additional data space* needed to execute *sequential programs* within a job process. The data space of a sequential program (in bytes) is defined by an integer constant after the process parameters.

process type

8.15.3 Process Attributes

The *standard function*

$$attribute(x)$$

defines an attribute x of the calling process. The index and value of the attribute are universal enumerations.

The *attribute index x* is of the following type

type attrindex =
(caller, heaptop, progline, progresult, runtime)

The meaning of these attributes is defined in the sequel.
The attribute function can be used to identify the calling process

attribute(caller)	The result is an integer that identifies the calling process. The machine associates consecutive integers 1, 2, ... with processes during their initialization starting with the initial process.

8.15.4   Heap Control

Associated with every process is a *heap* in which *Sequential Pascal programs* can allocate semipermanent data structures (by means of a standard procedure *new* that is not available in Concurrent Pascal).
A process can measure the extent of its heap by means of the standard function *attribute*

attribute(heaptop)	The result is an integer defining the top address of the heap.

The heap top can be reset to a previous value by means of the *standard procedure*

setheap(x)	The top address of the heap is set equal to the integer *x* (defined by a previous call of attribute)

$$x := attribute(heaptop)$$

This crude mechanism is intended mainly to enable a job process to measure the initial extent of its heap before it executes a sequential program, and to reset the heap when the program terminates.

8.15.5   Program Termination

When a *sequential program* terminates, its job process can call the standard function *attribute* to determine the number of the *line* on which the program terminated, and its *result*

attribute(progline)
attribute(progresult)

The line attribute is an integer and the program result is of the following type

$$\textbf{type } resulttype = (\text{terminated, overflow, pointererror,}$$
$$\text{rangeerror, varianterror, heaplimit,}$$
$$\text{stacklimit})$$

The result values have the following meaning

terminated	Correct termination.
overflow	An integer or real is out of range.
pointererror	A variable is referred to by means of a pointer with the value *nil*.
rangeerror	An enumeration value is out of range.
varianterror	A reference to a field of a variant record is incompatible with its tag value.
heaplimit	The heap capacity is exceeded.
stacklimit	The stack capacity is exceeded.

These are the *standard results* of Sequential Pascal programs generated by the machine. A concurrent program may, however, extend the result type with *nonstandard values*, for example

$$\textbf{type } resulttype = (\text{terminated, overflow, pointererror,}$$
$$\text{rangeerror, varianterror, heaplimit,}$$
$$\text{stacklimit, codelimit, timelimit,}$$
$$\text{callerror})$$

Nonstandard program results can be used as arguments to the standard procedure *stop* (defined below).

The following *standard procedures* control *program preemption*

start	Prevents preemption of a sequential program to be executed by the calling process.

stop(x, y)   Preempts a sequential program called by process
               x with the result *y*. The process identity *x* must have
               been defined earlier by a call of attribute

x := attribute(caller)

Start should be called before a sequential program is executed. If *stop*
is called while a sequential program is executing a routine entry within its
job process, preemption is delayed until the routine call has been completed.

8.15.6 Real-Time Control

The *standard routines* for real-time control are

wait   The calling process is delayed until the machine
               produces the next 1-sec signal. (If the waiting is done
               within a monitor this will delay other calls of the
               same monitor.)

realtime   The result is an integer defining the real time (in sec-
               onds) since system initialization.

The standard function *attribute* can be used to define the *run time* of
the calling process

attribute(runtime)   The result is an integer defining the proces-
                     sor time (in seconds) used by the calling
                     process since its initialization. (This is only
                     accurate on a machine with a readable
                     clock.)

8.15.7 Input/Output

Input/output is handled by means of the following *standard procedure*

io(x, y, z)   Peripheral *device z* performs the *operation y* on
               variable x. The calling process is delayed until the
               operation is completed. (If the io is done within a
               monitor, it will delay other calls of the same moni-
               tor.) *x* and *y* are variable parameters of arbitrary

passive types. z is a constant parameter of arbitrary enumeration type.

The machine assumes that the *io device z* and the *io parameter y* are of the following types

> **type** iodevice = (typedevice, diskdevice, tapedevice,
>   printdevice, carddevice)

> **type** ioparam = **record**
>   operation: iooperation;
>   status: ioresult;
>   arg: ioarg
>   **end**

where

> **type** iooperation = (input, output, move, control)

> **type** ioresult = (complete, intervention, transmission,
>   failure, endfile, endmedium, startmedium)

The *io results* have the following meaning

complete	The operation succeeded.
intervention	The operation failed, but can be repeated after manual intervention.
transmission	The operation failed due to a transmission error, but can be repeated immediately.
failure	The operation failed and cannot be repeated until the device has been repaired.
endfile	An end of file mark was reached.
endmedium	An end of medium mark was reached.
startmedium	A start of medium mark was reached.

The types of the *data block x* and the *io argument* within the io parameter *y* vary from device to device.

A concurrent program must ensure that a device is used by no more than one process at a time (wherever this rule applies).

8.15.7.1   Terminal

device name	typedevice
block type	char
input	Inputs a single character and echoes it back as output. The character CR is input as LF and echoed as CR, LF. The character BEL cannot be input (see below).
output	Outputs a single character. The character LF is output as CR, LF.
control	Delays the calling process until the BEL key is depressed. The BEL key can be depressed at any time (whether the terminal is passive, inputting, or outputting); it has no effect unless one or more processes are waiting for it.
result	complete

One or more control operations can be executed simultaneously with a single input/output operation. A BEL signal continues the execution of all processes waiting for it.

8.15.7.2   Disk

device name	diskdevice
block type	**univ array** (.1..512.) **of** char (called a *disk page*)
argument type	0..4799 (called a *page index*)
input	Inputs a disk page with a given page index.
output	Outputs a disk page with a given page index.

control	Starts the execution of a concurrent program stored on consecutive disk pages identified by the first page index.
result	complete, intervention, transmission, or failure

A disk can only perform one operation at a time.

The system uses the following algorithm to convert a *page index* to a physical disk address consisting of a *surface* number, *cylinder* number, and *sector* number

$$\text{surface}:= \text{pageno } \textbf{div } 12 \textbf{ mod } 2;$$
$$\text{cylinder}:= \text{pageno } \textbf{div } 24;$$
$$\text{sector}:= \text{pageno } \textbf{mod } 12;$$

8.15.7.3 Magnetic tape

device name	tapedevice
block type	**univ array** (.1..512.) **of** char (called a *tape block*)
argument type	(writeeof, rewind, upspace, backspace) The argument defines four possible *move* operations.
input	Inputs the next block from tape (if any).
output	Outputs the next block on tape (if there is room for it).
move	Moves the tape as defined by the argument:
	writeeof: outputs an end of file mark (if there is room for it).
	rewind: rewinds the tape.
	upspace: moves the tape forward one block (or file mark), whichever occurs first.
	backspace: moves the tape backwards one block (or file mark), whichever occurs first.

result   complete, intervention, transmission, failure, endfile, endmedium, or startmedium

A tape station can only perform one operation at a time.

8.15.7.4   Line printer

device name   printdevice

block type   **array** (.1..132.) **of** char (called a *printer line*)

output   Outputs a line of 132 characters (or less). A line of less than 132 characters must be terminated by a CR, LF, or FF character.

result   complete or intervention

A line printer can only perform one operation at a time.

8.15.7.5   Card reader

device name   carddevice

block type   **array** (.1..80.) **of** char (called a *punched card*)

input   Inputs a card of 80 characters. Characters that have no graphic representation on a key punch are input as SUB characters.

result   complete, intervention, transmission, or failure

A card reader can only perform one operation at a time.

8.15.8   Compiler Characteristics

The compiler consists of 7 passes. It requires a *code space* of 9 K words and a *data space* of 7 K words. After an initial time of 7 sec the *compilation speed* is 240 char/sec (or about 9–10 lines/sec).

The programmer may prefix a program with compiler *options* enclosed in parentheses and separated by commas

(number, check, test)

The options have the following effect

number
: The generated code will only identify line numbers of the program text at the beginning of routines. (This reduces the code by about 25 per cent, but makes error location more difficult.)

check
: The code will not make range checks of constant enumeration arguments.

test
: The compiler will print the intermediate output of all passes. (This facility is used as a diagnostic aid to locate compiler errors.)

8.15.9 Program Characteristics

Table 8.1 gives the *execution times* of operand references, operators, and statements in μsec (measured on a PDP 11/45 computer with 850 nsec core store). They exceed the figures stated in the computer programming manual by 25 per cent.

TABLE 8.1

	Enumeration	Real	Set (n members)	Structure (n words)
constant c	7	39	53 + 32 n	17
variable v	10	32	46	10
field v.f	27	40	54	18
indexed v(.e.)	40 + e	53 + e	67 + e	31 + e
:=	8	0	0	10 + 5 n
= <>	12	32	67	16 + 6 n
< > <= >=	12	32	74	16 + 11 n
in			31	
succ pred	7			
&	10		82	
or	8		58	
not	10			
+ –	9	38	58	
*	16	45		
div mod /	20	46		
abs	7	17		
conv	21			
trunc		22		

(n iterations)

case e of ... c: S; ... end	$28 + e + S$
for v:= 1 to n do S	$82 + (69 + S)\,n$
if B then S else S	$16 + B + S$
while B do S	$(20 + B + S)\,n$
repeat S until B	$(13 + \overline{B} + S)\,n$
with v do S	$16 + S$
cycle S end	$(7 + S)\,n$
simple routine call (no parameters)	58
process entry call (no parameters)	75
class entry call (no parameters)	80
monitor entry call (no parameters)	200
empty	10
delay, continue (processor switching)	600
clock interrupt (every 17 msec)	900
io	1500

The compiler generates about 5 words of *code* per program line (including line numbers and range checks).

The store requirements of *data* types are

enumeration	1 word(s)
real	4
set	8
string (m characters)	$m/2$

8.16 ASCII CHARACTER SET

TABLE 8.2

0	nul	32		64	@	96	
1	soh	33	!	65	A	97	a
2	stx	34	"	66	B	98	b
3	etx	35	#	67	C	99	c
4	eot	36	$	68	D	100	d
5	enq	37	%	69	E	101	e
6	ack	38	&	70	F	102	f
7	bel	39	'	71	G	103	g
8	bs	40	(	72	H	104	h
9	ht	41	)	73	I	105	i
10	lf	42	*	74	J	106	j
11	vt	43	+	75	K	107	k
12	ff	44	,	76	L	108	l
13	cr	45	–	77	M	109	m
14	so	46	.	78	N	110	n
15	si	47	/	79	O	111	o
16	dle	48	0	80	P	112	p
17	dc1	49	1	81	Q	113	q
18	dc2	50	2	82	R	114	r
19	dc3	51	3	83	S	115	s
20	dc4	52	4	84	T	116	t
21	nak	53	5	85	U	117	u
22	syn	54	6	86	V	118	v
23	etb	55	7	87	W	119	w
24	can	56	8	88	X	120	x
25	em	57	9	89	Y	121	y
26	sub	58	:	90	Z	122	z
27	esc	59	;	91	[	123	{
28	fs	60	<	92	\	124	|
29	gs	61	=	93	]	125	}
30	rs	62	>	94	^	126	⌐
31	us	63	?	95	_	127	del

8.17 INDEX OF REPORT

9

CONCURRENT PASCAL MACHINE

The Concurrent Pascal compiler generates code for a virtual machine that can be simulated by microprogram or machine code on different computers. This chapter describes the implementation of Concurrent Pascal on the PDP 11/45 computer.

9.1 STORE ALLOCATION

We will begin by looking at the allocation of core store among the processes of a concurrent program.

Core Store

A Concurrent Pascal program defines a fixed number of processes. Figure 9.1 shows the core store during the execution of a program. It contains code and data segments. The lengths of these are fixed during compilation.

The *code segments* consist of *virtual code* generated by the Concurrent

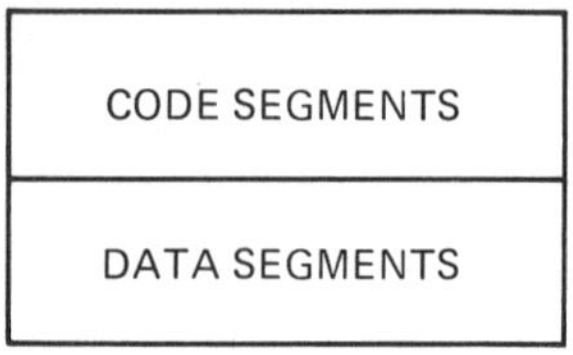

CODE SEGMENTS
DATA SEGMENTS

Fig. 9.1   Core store

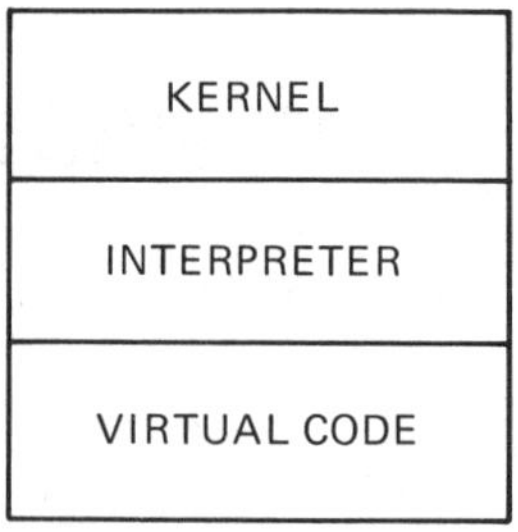

KERNEL
INTERPRETER
VIRTUAL CODE

Fig. 9.2   Code segments

Pascal compiler, an *interpreter* that executes the virtual code, and a *kernel* that schedules the execution of concurrent processes (Fig. 9.2).

The interpreter and kernel are assembly language programs which implement the virtual machine. These two programs of 1 and 3 K words are loaded from disk into core by means of the operator's control panel. They in turn load the virtual code of a Concurrent Pascal program into core and start executing it as a single process, called the *initial process*. The latter can now create a fixed number of *child processes*. The kernel multiplexes the processor among these processes.

Each process has a *data segment* in core (Fig. 9.3). Data segments have fixed lengths determined during compilation. They exist forever during execution. This makes store allocation trivial: segments are allocated contiguously in their order of creation.

The segment length of the initial process and the start address of its code are defined at the beginning of the virtual code. The store requirements and code addresses of child processes are defined by *initprocess* instructions (corresponding to the init statements in the program).

Virtual Store

On the PDP 11/45 computer, the storage space of a process consists of up to 8 segments of at most 4 K words each. These segments can be placed

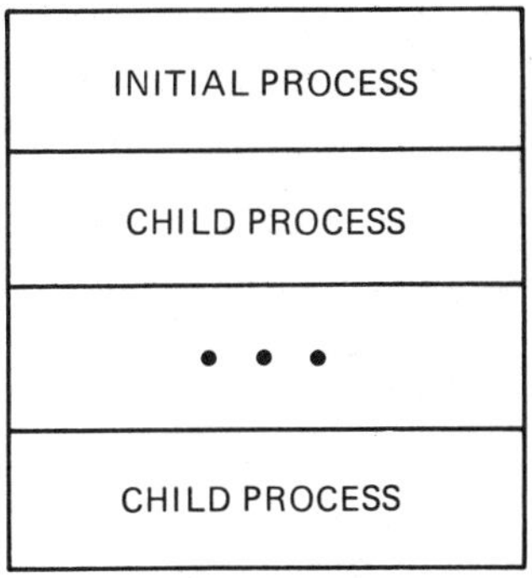

| INITIAL PROCESS |
| CHILD PROCESS |
| • • • |
| CHILD PROCESS |

Fig. 9.3   Data segments

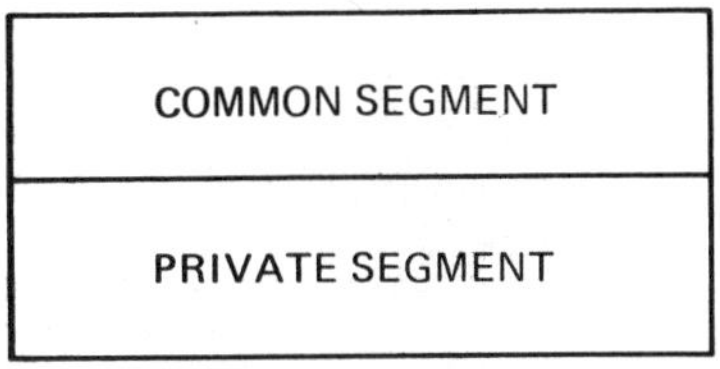

| COMMON SEGMENT |
| PRIVATE SEGMENT |

Fig. 9.4   Virtual store

anywhere in core. An addressing mechanism makes them appear contiguous to the process.

This mechanism is not used by Concurrent Pascal to enforce the access rights of processes. That is done during compilation. It is just a (rather inconvenient) way of extending the addressing capability of a computer with a short word length by letting each process see a part of a larger core store. The addressing mechanism would be unnecessary on a machine that can address the whole store directly.

The *virtual store* of a process gives it access to a *common segment* shared by all processes and to its own data segment (called a *private segment*) (Fig. 9.4).

The common segment consists of the interpreter, the virtual code, and the data segment of the initial process. The latter contains the monitors that processes communicate through (Fig. 9.5).

The initial process has no private data segment. Its data segment is included in the common segment.

Data Segments

A *data segment* contains the stack and heap of a process (Figs. 9.3 and 9.6).

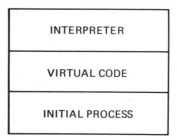

Fig. 9.5 Common segment

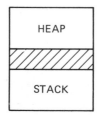

Fig. 9.6 Data segment

The *stack* contains the *permanent variables* (and parameters) of a process as well as its *temporary variables* used within procedures (Fig. 9.7).

The initial process is created by the kernel. It has no parameters. When a child process is created, its parameters are copied from the parent's stack (in the common data segment) into the child's stack (in a private segment).

The *heap* is only accessible to Sequential Pascal programs executed by a Concurrent Pascal process.

Permanent Variables

Figure 9.8 shows the representation of the *permanent variables* and *parameters* of a *class*, *monitor*, or *process*.

A *monitor* contains an address of a data structure called a *gate*. The gate is stored in the kernel. It is used to give a process exclusive access to the monitor. The gate address has no significance for classes and processes.

A process can only operate on one set of permanent variables at a time. They are addressed relative to a *global base* address *g*. When a process is created its global base register points to its own permanent variables. When it calls a monitor (or class) procedure the current base address is pushed onto its stack, and the global base register is used to point to the permanent

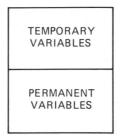

Fig. 9.7   Stack

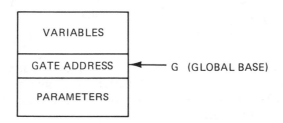

Fig. 9.8   Permanent variables

variables of that monitor (or class). Upon return from the procedure the previous base address is popped from the stack.

Temporary Variables

Figure 9.9 shows the representation of the *parameters*, *variables*, and *temporaries* of a *procedure call*. A *dynamic link* connects the procedure to the context in which it was called.

A process can only operate on one set of temporary variables (and parameters) at a time. They are addressed relative to a *local base* address b. Temporaries are addressed relative to a *stack top s*.

The dynamic link defines the *stack addresses g, b*, and *s* used by a process before a procedure call and a *return address q* in the virtual code. The link also contains the current *line number* within the procedure to facilitate location of run-time errors.

When a process is created its global and local base registers both point to the permanent variables of that process. It is initialized with no temporaries and an empty heap.

When a process calls one of its own procedures, the local base register will point to the temporary variables of that procedure, while its global base address remains unchanged.

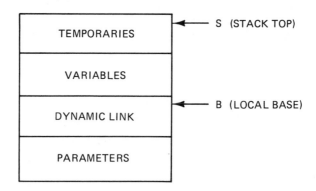

Fig. 9.9   Temporary variables

When a process calls a monitor (or class) procedure, the global base register will point to the permanent variables of that monitor (or class), and the local base register will point to the temporary variables of the monitor (or class) procedure.

Upon return from a procedure its temporary variables are popped from the stack and the previous values of the base registers are reestablished by means of the dynamic link.

Disk Allocation

The disk used by the *Solo* operating system contains 4800 pages of 256 words each. The beginning of the disk contains 5 *contiguous segments*

kernel segment
: The machine code of the kernel and the interpreter (6 K words).

Solo segment
: The virtual code of the Solo operating system (16 K words).

other OS segment
: The virtual code of another operating system (16 K words). It is used by the Sequential Pascal program *start* to execute another Concurrent Pascal program (Section 5.1).

free page list
: The set of free disk pages (0.5 K words). It is used by the Sequential Pascal program *file* to allocate disk files (Section 5.1).

catalog page map   A disk page which defines the length of the
                          disk catalog and the location of its pages
                          (Fig. 5.4).

The first three of these segments are larger than they need to be to permit future expansion of the kernel and the operating systems. The rest of the disk contains *catalog pages* and *disk files*. The organization of these is described in Sections 5.1 and 5.4.

The kernel is loaded from disk into core by means of the operator's control panel. The kernel in turn loads the Solo system from disk and starts it. The operating systems are loaded from a fixed set of consecutive disk pages to make the system kernel unaware of the structure of a particular filing system (such as the one used by Solo).

The sequential program *start* can copy a concurrent program from a disk file into one of the operating system segments and load it by means of a *control* operation on the disk device (Section 8.15.7.2).

Compromises

In implementing Concurrent Pascal I followed one simple guideline: *A computer should only do obvious things and should do them well.* Where compromise was needed I firmly put simplicity first, efficiency second, and generality third. Like any other design rule it needs no justification other than the success it leads to in practice.

It takes strong nerves to follow this advice on a machine that invites a software designer to optimize register usage and use sliding addressing windows. I decided to simplify code generation by ignoring the instruction set and different registers of the PDP 11/45 and simulate a simple stack machine instead.

The virtual addressing mechanism is more difficult to ignore since it determines the amount of core store that can be used by a Concurrent Pascal program. The virtual store of the PDP 11/45 consists of two address spaces: one for machine code and another for data. Since the only machine code executed by a process is an interpreter of 1 K words, it is not worth keeping it in a separate address space. So I let the two address spaces be identical.

Concurrent Pascal makes it possible to check the access rights of processes before they are executed. Consequently, monitor calls can be made almost as fast as simple procedure calls. To gain this efficiency, the virtual code and data of monitors were included in the address of every process. (Otherwise, it would have been necessary to change address spaces and copy parameters back and forth between these spaces during monitor calls.)

However, by putting simplicity and efficiency first, we have undoubted-ly lost generality; a process must divide its address space of 32 K words between its private data and the code and common data of all processes. To avoid fragmentation of the virtual address space, processes have only a single segment in common. This is achieved by the following language re-striction: Only the initial process can create other processes and give them access to common data (Section 8.15.1).

Segmentation of address space can be helpful when it supports the scope rules of a high-level language by associating data segments with pro-cedures and classes. But when it arbitrarily cuts physical store into eight parts, segmentation becomes an obstacle to straightforward language im-plementation.

9.2 CODE INTERPRETATION

The Concurrent Pascal compiler generates code for a virtual machine simulated by machine code on the PDP 11/45 computer. This section describes the *virtual code* which is similar to the one used by Wirth's group for Sequential Pascal [Nori, 1974]. The programming technique used to interpret the virtual code is called *threaded code* [Bell, 1973].

The use of virtual code designed directly to support a high-level language makes code generation straightforward and the compiler portable. (The Sequential Pascal compiler for the PDP 11/45 was moved to another mini-computer in one man-month.)

Virtual Code

We will use a programming example to illustrate the virtual code. The example is a *monitor* that defines a *send* operation on a message *buffer*.

```
type page = array (.1..length.) of integer;

type buffer =
monitor

var contents: page; empty: boolean;
    sender, receiver: queue;
```

```
procedure entry send(message: page);
begin
    if not empty then delay(sender);
    contents:= message;
    empty:= false;
    continue(receiver);
end;
.....
begin ... end
```

(The rest of the monitor can be ignored here.)
　　The virtual code generated for the *send* procedure is

```
          entermonitor(stacklength, paramlength,
                          linenumber, varlength)
      pushglobal(empty)
      not
      falsejump(a)
      globaladdr(sender)
      delay
   a: globaladdr(contents)
      pushlocal(message)
      copystructure(length)
      globaladdr(empty)
      pushconst(false)
      copyword
      globaladdr(receiver)
      continue
      exitmonitor
```

　　An *enter monitor* instruction defines the total amount of *stack* needed by the procedure, the length of its *parameters* and local *variables*, and the number of the program *line* on which it begins.

　　The next instruction *pushes* the *global* variable *empty* onto the stack. The program then performs a *not* operation on it, and *jumps* to the label *a* if the result is *false;* otherwise, it pushes the *address* of the *global* variable *sender* on the stack and performs a *delay* operation on it.

　　After this, the *addresses* of the buffer *contents* and the *message* are pushed onto the stack. (The message parameter is represented by a *local* variable that contains a reference to the actual argument.) A *copy structure* instruction moves the message into the buffer.

This is followed by an *assignment* of the constant *false* to the global variable *empty*. The procedure ends with a *continue* operation on the global variable *receiver* followed by an *exit monitor* instruction.

An instance of a buffer monitor can be declared and used as follows

var channel: buffer; data: page;

..... channel.send(data) .....

This *monitor call* generates the following virtual code

globaladdr(channel)
field(varlength)
globaladdr(data)
call(send)

The base *address* of the *global* variable *channel* is pushed onto the stack and incremented by a *field* instruction to make it point to the gate address that separates the permanent variables of the monitor from its parameters (Fig. 9.8). Then the *address* of the *global* variable *data* is pushed onto the stack, and the monitor procedure *send* is *called*.

Variables are identified by their displacements relative to a local or global base address (Figs. 9.8 and 9.9). Program labels are represented by their displacements relative to a virtual program counter (making the code relocatable).

There are about 50 different virtual instructions. To make the software interpreter fast, the addressing modes (local or global) and the data types (bytes, words, reals, or sets) are encoded into the operation codes. This expands the set of operation codes to 110. A quarter of these are used by Concurrent Pascal only. The rest are common to Sequential and Concurrent Pascal.

This description only tries to explain the overall structure of the virtual code and its interpreter. The interpreter listing, which is stored on the Solo disk, contains a complete definition of all virtual instructions.

The language constructs of Concurrent Pascal and the corresponding virtual code are defined by syntax graphs in the compiler description [Hartmann, 1975].

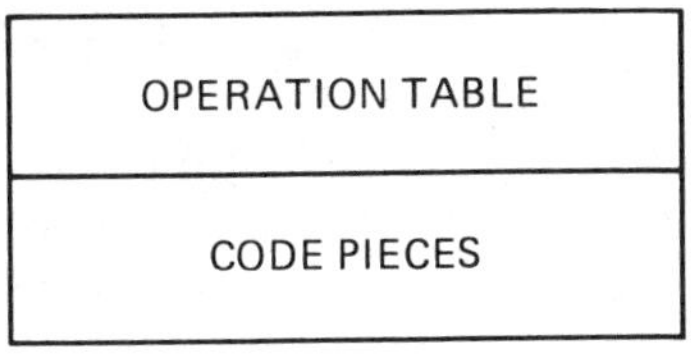

Fig. 9.10　Interpreter

The Interpreter

The *interpreter* is an assembly language program of 1 K words. It consists of *code pieces* that execute virtual instructions and an *operation table* defining the location of these pieces (Fig. 9.10).

A virtual *instruction* consists of an *operation* possibly followed by some *arguments*. The operation and its arguments occupy one machine word each. The interpreter uses a *virtual instruction counter q* to point to the next operation or one of its arguments.

As an example, the virtual instructions

pushconst(false)
copyword

are represented by three machine words

pushconst
false
copyword

Upon entry to the *push constant* code piece in the interpreter, the virtual instruction counter q points to the argument of that instruction (the boolean value *false*). The interpreter executes the push operation as follows

$$s := s - 2; store(s) := store(q); q := q + 2;$$

First, the stack top s is decremented by one word (The PDP 11/45 stack grows from high towards low addresses, and each word in it contains two bytes). Then the argument is moved from its virtual code location *store(q)* to the new stack location *store(s)*. Finally, the virtual instruction counter *q* is incremented by one word (2 bytes). All this is done by a single machine instruction on the PDP 11/45 computer.

The virtual instruction counter now points to the next virtual instruction *copy word*. The interpreter uses the operation code *store(q)* as an index in the operation table (beginning at address zero) to jump to the corresponding code piece

$$\textbf{goto } store(store(q)); q := q + 2;$$

This is also done by a single machine instruction.

Every code piece of the interpreter ends with such a jump to its successor. These three store cycles are the only overhead of interpretation compared to directly executed code. This efficient form of interpretation is called *threaded code* [Bell, 1973]. The execution times for the virtual code on the PDP 11/45 computer are listed in Section 8.15.9.

Registers

The interpreter uses nine registers to execute the virtual code of a process. Three of these are *scratch registers* used during the execution of a single virtual instruction only. The rest have fixed functions throughout the execution of a process (Fig. 9.11).

The *real program counter p* remains within the interpreter. It uses a

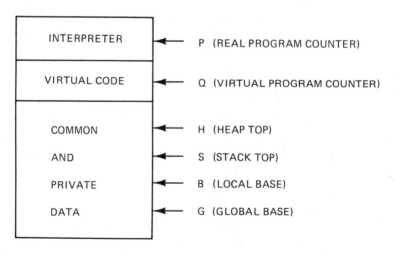

Fig. 9.11   Virtual store and registers

virtual program counter q to point to virtual instructions. The *heap top h* defines the current extent of the heap. (It is stored in a store location within the interpreter instead of a register.) The stack is addressed relative to three registers: a *global base* register *g*, a *local base* register *b*, and a *stack top s* as explained in Section 9.1.

9.3 KERNEL

The kernel of Concurrent Pascal is an assembly language program that multiplexes a PDP 11/45 processor among concurrent processes and gives them exclusive access to monitors.

The kernel was first written in a programming language that resembles Concurrent Pascal. It consists of a collection of data structures representing processes, monitors, and peripherals. Each data structure consists of two parts: One defines how the data are represented in store, the other what operations one can perform on the data. This combination of a data representation and the possible operations on it is called a *class* or an *abstract data type.*

The abstract version of the kernel was translated by hand into assembly language (retaining the abstract version as comments). This programming method has several advantages

(1) A complex program can be programmed as a sequence of small, self-contained components (classes).

(2) These components can be tested one at a time from the bottom up.

(3) If the program only accesses a component through procedures (or macros) associated with it, new (untested) components cannot make old (tested) components fail.

(4) In the rare cases, where it is necessary to use assembly language, one can still use an abstract programming language as a thinking tool, and make the production of assembly code a simple clerical procedure (manual translation).

After an initial test period of 1 month the Concurrent Pascal kernel has been running without problems. One might call this form of programming *reliable machine programming.*

The details of the kernel are simplified somewhat in the following (but most of the simplifications are pointed out). The Solo disk contains a complete kernel listing.

Processor Multiplexing

The computer executes one process at a time. While one process is *running*, other processes must await their turn in a *ready queue*. Every 17 msec the computer switches from one process to another to give the illusion that they are executed simultaneously.

A *process* is represented by a record within the kernel. When a process is *preempted* all *registers* used to interpret its code are stored in its process record (Section 9.2). The register values are restored when the execution of the process is *resumed*

$$\text{type registers} = \textbf{record} \ldots \textbf{end}$$

$$\text{process} = @ \text{ registers}$$

The symbol @ indicates that a *process* is represented by the *address* of the record that contains its *register* values.

A *process queue* is represented by a *sequence* of references to process records

$$\text{type processqueue} = \textbf{sequence of} \text{ process}$$

The only operations on a process queue are

put	Enters a process in the queue.
get	Removes a process from the queue.
any	Tells whether the queue contains anything.
empty	Tells whether the queue is empty.

The *running* process is represented by a class. It contains two permanent variables: The *user* is a reference to the running process; it is *nil* when the processor is idle. In addition, the hardware *registers* are considered part of this class.

Only two operations are defined on the running process: *serve* and *preempted*. They start and stop the execution of a process. The statement at the end of the class is executed when the kernel is initialized. It makes the running process *nil*. (The selection of the initial process for execution is done elsewhere.)

```
var running:
class

var user: process; reg: registers;

procedure serve(p: process);
begin
   user:= p;
   reg:= user@;
end;

function preempted: process;
begin
   user@:= reg;
   preempted:= user;
   user:= nil;
end;

begin user:= nil end
```

The value of the process reference and the record it points to are denoted *user* and *user@*. Although they are not marked with the word *entry* both routines can be called outside the class.

The *ready* queue is represented by another class. In this simplified description, there is only a single queue of *waiting* processes. In practice, we use a three-level queue that gives top priority to processes executing monitor code, middle priority to processes resumed after input/output, and bottom priority to compute-bound processes. Initially the ready queue is empty.

Two operations can be performed on the ready queue: *enter* a process in the queue, and *select* one to be served. An attempt to select a process from an *empty* ready queue causes the processor to *idle* until a peripheral operation has been completed and has entered a process in the ready queue.

```
var ready:
class

var waiting: processqueue;

procedure enter(p: process);
begin waiting.put(p) end;
```

```
procedure select;
begin
   while waiting.empty do idle;
   running.serve(waiting.get);
end;
```

```
begin waiting.initialize end
```

A *clock interrupt* has no effect if the processor is idle; otherwise, it preempts the running process, enters it in the ready queue, and selects another process for execution

```
procedure clockinterrupt;
begin
   if running.user <> nil then
   begin
      ready.enter(running.preempted);
      ready.select;
   end;
end
```

Again, the picture is simplified: The clock will only preempt a process when it has used a reasonable amount of processor time, and it will never interrupt a process inside a monitor procedure (since this could cause the resource controlled by the monitor to remain idle until the execution of the procedure is completed).

The class *running* also contains procedures for process creation. After system loading, the kernel calls a procedure *initparent* that starts execution of the initial process

```
procedure initparent(length: integer);
begin
   new(user);
   virtual.defcommon(length);
   initialize registers;
end
```

The procedure *new* allocates space for a process record in a heap inside the kernel. A procedure *defcommon* within another class *virtual* is then called to define the *length* and location of the common segment used by the initial process and its descendants (Fig. 9.5). Finally, the *registers* are *initialized* with the limits of the stack and the heap within the segment as well as the start address of the process code (Fig. 9.11).

The initial process can, in turn, call a kernel procedure *initchild* to create other processes. (To be more precise, the initial process executes an *initprocess* instruction which causes the interpreter to call the kernel procedure *initchild*.)

> **procedure** initchild(length: integer);
> **begin**
>   ready.enter(preempted);
>   new(user);
>   virtual.defprivate(length);
>   initialize registers;
> **end**

This is similar to the previous procedure, except that the parent is preempted in favor of its child. Again, details have been ignored, such as the accounting of processor time used by processes.

When a *process terminates* its execution, it is preempted forever (but its data segment continues to exist)

> **procedure** endprocess;
> **begin** user:= nil **end**

This leaves the processor idle upon exit from the kernel. To make it busy again, the following statement is always executed upon *kernel exit*

> **if** running.user = nil **then** ready.select

Monitor Implementation

Within the kernel, a monitor variable is represented by a data structure, called a *gate*, which only gives one process at a time access to the monitor. A gate is represented by a boolean defining whether it is *open*, and a queue of processes *waiting* to enter it.

At the beginning and at the end of a monitor procedure a process executes an *enter* and a *leave* operation. (More precisely, these kernel routines are called by the interpreter when it executes the virtual instructions *entermonitor* and *exitmonitor*.)

Enter: If the gate is open, the process enters and closes it; otherwise, the process is preempted to wait outside the gate.

Leave: If nobody is waiting outside the gate, it is left open; otherwise, a single waiting process is resumed (by transferring it to the ready queue).

These are the short-term operations which force processes to enter a monitor one at a time. A monitor can also delay processes for longer periods of time and resume them again by means of *delay* and *continue* operations on single-process queues.

```
type gate =
class

var open: boolean; waiting: processqueue;

procedure enter;
begin
    if open then open:= false
        else waiting.put(running.preempted);
end;

procedure leave;
begin
    if waiting.empty then open:= true
        else ready.enter(waiting.get);
end;

procedure delay(var q: process);
begin q:= running.preempted; leave end;

procedure continue(var q: process);
begin
    if q = nil then leave else
        begin ready.enter(q); q:= nil end;
end;

begin open:=false; waiting.initialize end
```

Delay: Preempts the running process and enters it in a given single-process queue. The monitor can now be entered by another process.

Continue: Forces the running process to leave the monitor and resumes any process that may be waiting in a given single-process queue.

Please, note the distinction between a multiprocess queue which the virtual machine automatically associates with a monitor, and a single-process queue which the programmer declares within a monitor. The former is stored within the kernel while the latter is stored in the common segment (Figs. 9.2 and 9.5).

When a monitor variable is *initialized*, the kernel executes a procedure that allocates its gate in the kernel heap and initializes it

> **procedure** initgate(**var** g: @gate);
> **begin** new(g); g@.initialize **end**

The *gate reference* is stored in the stack of the calling process and passed as a parameter to the kernel each time one of the gate operations is executed (Fig. 9.8).

Details ignored: When a process is resumed within a monitor it will preempt the running process (unless the latter is engaged in nested monitor calls).

It should also be mentioned that all kernel operations are *indivisible* and cannot be interrupted. So conceptually, the *kernel* is a *monitor* used by all processes and peripheral devices.

Peripherals

A peripheral is represented by a class within the kernel. It defines the *device number* of the peripheral and its current *user* process. An *io* statement in Concurrent Pascal is translated into a call of a kernel procedure that *starts* a data transfer and preempts the calling process. An *interrupt* resumes the user process.

Details: The interrupt procedure also returns a status word to the calling process and (usually) gives it priority over the running process.

> **var** peripheral:
> **class**(device: integer);
>
> **var** user: process;
>
> **procedure** start(operation: T);
> **begin**
> 　　startdevice(device, operation);
> 　　user:= running.preempted;
> **end**;

```
procedure interrupt;
begin
  ready.enter(user);
  user:= nil;
end;

begin user:= nil end
```

Only one process at a time can use a peripheral. This must be guaranteed by the operating system written in Concurrent Pascal (and not by the kernel). The main function of the kernel is to make peripherals look uniform with respect to simple input/output operations and their results (Section 8.15.7). It does not perform error recovery.

Notice that *all interrupts are considered to be parameterless routine calls made by the environment of the processor. This combines the conceptual simplicity of the class concept with the fast response needed to keep peripherals busy. This idea could be used in an abstract programming language for real-time applications that require guaranteed, fast response to external events.*

Kernel Classes

The kernel consists of a hierarchy of classes (some of which have already been described):

newcore	Allocates process records and gates in a kernel heap.
processqueue	Implements multiprocess queues.
signal	Implements a queue in which processes can wait until a timing signal is sent.
time	Keeps track of real time.
timer	Measures time intervals.
clock	Delays calling processes for 1 sec.
core	Allocates core store to processes.
virtual	Allocates virtual store to processes.

running	Creates, executes, and preempts processes.
ready	Schedules processes for execution.
gate	Gives processes exclusive access to monitors.
peripherals	Handle simple input/output.

Programming and Testing

The kernel was translated manually line by line into assembly language using the abstract program as comments. A small example is sufficient to illustrate this programming technique

```
gate: .word 1              ; type gate =
                           ; class
open = 0                   ; var open: boolean;
wait = open + .boolean ;       waiting: processqueue;
                           ;
enter:                     ; procedure enter;
    mov gate, r0           ; begin
    dec  (r0)              ;    if open
    beq  1$                ;      then
    clr  (r0)+             ;         open:= false
    mov r0, procq          ;
    jsr  pc, preempt       ;      else
    mov preval, elem       ;         waiting.put(
    jsr  pc, put           ;            running.preempted);
1$: rts  pc                ; end;
```

The kernel was tested, class by class, by *test programs* written in Concurrent Pascal

test 1:	initialization and process creation
test 2:	clock interrupts and processor multiplexing
test 3–4:	monitor gates
test 5:	teletype
test 6:	timer and clock
test 7:	teletype bell key

In test 1, clock interrupts were turned off. In tests 2–6 they were simulated manually by the bell key on the teletype. Test 7 used normal clock
interrupts. The only *test output* used was a message on the teletype every
time a process arrives in a queue or departs from one. This technique for
testing a system kernel is explained elsewhere [Brinch Hansen, 1973a].

   It took 10 test runs to make test 1 work (!) The rest of the tests required 18 runs altogether. Finally, the peripherals were tested by Concurrent Pascal programs in normal operation. After this initial testing (January 1975), the kernel seems to be correct.

Size and Performance

   The kernel classes are of the following *size*

	Words
newcore	560
processqueue	30
signal	40
time	20
timer	10
clock	60
core	40
virtual	160
running	570
ready	130
gate	110
6 peripherals	1020
initialization	160
kernel	2910

The kernel heap in *newcore* has room for 10 process records and 25 monitor
gates. Process creation and termination account for 60 per cent of *running*.
Each *peripheral* is controlled by a class of about 150 words.
   The most critical *execution times* are

empty kernel call	20 μsec
monitor call	200 μsec
delay, continue	600 μsec
clock interrupt	900 μsec

A *monitor call* causes the interpreter to call the kernel twice: at the beginning and at the end of the procedure. The 200 μsec assumes that the process can enter the monitor immediately and continue its execution when it returns from it. This should be compared with the execution time of a simple procedure call (58 μsec).

The figures for *delay* and *continue* (600 μsec) illustrate the cost of switching the processor from one process to another.

9.4 COMPILER

The Concurrent Pascal compiler is written in the programming language Sequential Pascal. Its structure is inspired by the *Gier Algol* and *Siemens Cobol* compilers [Naur, 1963, and Brinch Hansen, 1966]. The compiler is divided into 7 passes. The following describes the overall division of labor among the passes as well as their size and performance. The compiler is described in detail by Hartmann [1975].

Multipass Compilation

Our goal was to make a compiler that can compile operating systems on a minicomputer with at least 16 K words of core store and a slow disk (50 msec/transfer). To fit into a small core store, the compiler is divided into 7 *passes*

> pass 1:   symbol analysis
> pass 2:   syntax analysis
> pass 3:   scope analysis
> pass 4:   declaration analysis
> pass 5:   statement analysis
> pass 6:   code selection
> pass 7:   code assembly

The main efficiency problem is to avoid random references to the slow disk and access it strictly sequentially during compilation. The compiler is loaded one pass at a time. Each pass makes a single sequential scan of the program text and outputs intermediate code on the disk. This becomes the input to the next pass.

So the compiler can be viewed as a pipeline consisting of passes connected by disk buffers. Since the available machine is sequential, only one pass is executed at a time.

A multipass compiler not only makes store allocation and disk access efficient. It also simplifies the programming task considerably. In a one-pass compiler, each procedure performs a variety of compilation tasks

[Wirth, 1971]. This tends to make procedures and symbol tables large and complicated. In a multipass compiler, syntax analysis, semantic analysis, and code generation can be dealt with separately in smaller passes that use simpler data structures tailored to their tasks.

Each pass is essentially a minicompiler that only needs to know the syntax of its input and output languages. The data structures and procedures used by one pass are irrelevant to another. We found it extremely helpful to define the function of each pass by syntax graphs of its expected input and output [Hartmann, 1975].

Intermediate Files

The compiler uses four files: *source text* and *listing, pass input* and *output*. The first two can be stored on any available medium, while the last two are kept on disk. These files are accessed by five procedures implemented within the operating system (Section 5.2)

read	Inputs a character from the source text.
write	Outputs a character on the source listing.
get	Inputs a disk page from the previous pass.
put	Outputs a disk page to the next pass.
length	Defines the length of a disk file in pages.

After each pass, the disk files exchange roles: The output file of the previous pass becomes the input file of the next pass, and the former input file becomes the next output file.

Disk access times are reduced as follows: The pages of the intermediate files are interleaved on the disk. This makes the disk head sweep slowly across both files during a pass instead of moving wildly back and forth between them. The pages which contain the compiler code are arranged on the disk in a manner that minimizes rotational delay during compiler loading (Section 5.4).

A pass can build tables in core store and leave them there for the next pass. This is done by passing a single heap pointer as a parameter from each pass to its successor.

The loading and execution of the passes is controlled by a small Pascal program that also opens and closes all intermediate files (Sections 5.1 and 6.2).

Pass Summary

Symbol analysis scans the program text character by character and converts symbols, identifiers, and numeric constants into unique integers. Identifiers are looked up by hashing. This pass does not distinguish between different uses of the same identifier in different contexts.

Syntax analysis checks the program syntax by means of a set of recursive procedures — one for each language construct [Wirth, 1971]. Syntax errors are handled by erasing part of the program text to make it look syntactically correct to the rest of the compiler.

Scope analysis checks the access rights of processes, monitors, classes, procedures, and with statements. It uses a stack to handle nested contexts. The top of the stack defines the identifiers declared within the current context. They are popped at the end of the context. Every identifier referred to by the program is looked up in the nested name table to see if it is accessible. Different uses of the same identifier in several contexts are replaced by unique integers. This pass also replaces constant identifiers by their values or addresses. Apart from this, scope analysis is only concerned about whether an identifier can be used within a given context, but does not worry about what kind of object it refers to.

Declaration analysis checks that declarations of constants, types, variables, and procedures are consistent and computes the length of types and the addresses of variables. It builds a table of identifier attributes and distributes them wherever the identifiers are referred to in statements. After this pass, declarations have disappeared from the intermediate code.

Statement analysis checks that operands and operators are compatible. This is done by means of a stack that simulates program execution by operating on data types rather than data values (Section 3.7). In this pass and the previous one, semantic errors are handled by replacing undefined types and incorrect operands by universal ones that are compatible with anything. This prevents an avalanche of error messages from a single semantic error.

Code selection selects code pieces to be generated and computes the length of procedure code and temporary variables. It leaves a table of program labels, stack requirements, and large constants in core store. (This is the only pass that transmits large tables in core store to its successor, in addition to the intermediate code stored on the disk.)

Code assembly outputs virtual code in which program labels are replaced by relative addresses. The generation of virtual code is straightforward; no optimization is attempted. It is interpreted by machine code on the PDP 11/45 computer (Section 9.2). This pass also prints error messages from the other passes (but does not generate code, if there are any errors).

Scope Analysis

It is the scope rules more than anything else that distinguish Concurrent Pascal from other programming languages (such as Fortran, Algol, Cobol, PL/1, and Sequential Pascal).

A Concurrent Pascal program consists of a hierarchy of abstract data types (classes, monitors, and processes). An abstract data type can only be accessed through procedures associated with it. A procedure can refer to its own temporary variables and to the permanent variables of the data type it operates on.

Data types and procedures cannot be recursive. This means that procedure entries associated with a single data type cannot call one another.

To enforce these rules, scope analysis associates an *access attribute* with every identifier [Hartmann, 1975].

Names with *external access* may only be referred to outside the scope in which they are declared. Example: monitor procedures.

Names with *internal access* may only be referred to inside the scope in which they are declared. Examples: monitor variables and procedure parameters.

Names with *incomplete access* may not be referred to until their declaration has been completed. Example: type declarations.

Testing

The compiler was tested using a technique invented by Naur [1963]. The passes were tested in their natural order starting with pass 1. For each pass we used a Concurrent Pascal text to make the pass execute all statements at least once.

During testing the compiler lists the source text and the intermediate code produced by each pass. A comparison of the input and output of a pass immediately reveals if something is wrong. The corresponding input operator usually tells in which procedure the problem is. After correction of the error the test is repeated.

This *test output* mechanism of about 20 lines is a permanent part of the compiler and can always be turned on to document compiler errors revealed by a particular program text.

The generated code checks that *subscripts* are within range, that *pointers* are initialized, and that references to *variant* records are compatible with their tag values. These checks were invaluable during testing of the compiler.

In a sample of 64 compiler failures during testing, 50 per cent were range errors, 20 per cent were pointer errors, and 28 per cent variant errors.

All made the compiler stop with a message of the form

pass 3 line 307 range error

(or something similar). Only one of the failures made the compiler go into an endless loop without any indication of what went wrong. Anyone who has tested compilers in assembly language will recognize the value of an abstract programming language that makes checking at compile and run time possible.

It took 4 months to write the compiler and 3 months to test it. This was done by Al Hartmann. The compiler has been used since January 1975 without problems.

A Sequential Pascal compiler was derived from the concurrent one in one additional man-month. It can compile its largest pass in 16 K words of core store. This compiler was moved from the PDP 11/45 computer to another minicomputer in another man-month.

Size and Performance

The following shows the storage requirements of the compiler when it compiles the Solo operating system — a Concurrent Pascal program of 1300 lines (Chapter 5).

	Virtual code (words)	Data (words)
common	1000	1300
pass 1	4000	5600
pass 2	5600	1200
pass 3	7800	6200
pass 4	5800	4800
pass 5	4000	300
pass 6	3000	650
pass 7	3600	650
compiler	34800	20700

The compiler runs in 16 K words of core store. This includes 2 K words of common input/output procedures and data buffers.

After an initial time of 7 sec the compilation speed is 240 char/sec (or about 10 lines/sec). The compiler is about 60 per cent disk limited.

THE NEXT STEP

The *process* and *monitor* concepts unify many things that were thought to be unrelated before (and were taught in different courses on programming)

> hierarchical programming (precise modularity)
> data abstraction (information hiding)
> scope rules (access rights)
> resource protection
> type checking
> concurrent processes
> process synchronization
> deadlock prevention

The minor inconvenience of the *class* notation (borrowed from Simula 67) is of little consequence compared to the general insight it has given us.

Where do we go from here? My feeling is that Concurrent Pascal can serve as a starting point for further development of *abstract concurrent programming* in several directions.

Model Operating Systems

The operating systems written so far in Concurrent Pascal are small. I would hope (and expect) that a larger system will turn out to be "more of the same." But it seems worthwhile to confirm this by using Concurrent Pascal to build a medium-size operating system, for example, a *terminal system* that gives each user the capability of Solo.

I would also expect that extensive control of access rights during compilation can be used to guarantee the integrity of a valuable *data base* kept on a large backing store.

Program Verification

Using the axiomatic method of Hoare [1969] it is possible to verify mathematically that small programs are correct. This verification can either be done manually [Hoare, 1971] or semiautomatically [Igarashi, London, and Luckham, 1975]. Formal verification is still limited to programs of about one page or less.

Since a Concurrent Pascal program can be composed of semiindependent components of one page each, there is reason to hope that the verification techniques for sequential programs can be extended to concurrent programs as well. Some of this work has already been started by Hoare [1972a, 1972b, 1974], Howard [1976], and Owicki [1976]. It would be a worthy achievement to verify parts of a working operating system, such as *Solo*.

The greatest value of a formal approach to correctness is probably the extreme rigor and structure that it must impose on the design process from the beginning to be successful. This cannot fail to improve our informal understanding of programs as well.

Language Design

Since hierarchical ordering of access rights is such a fruitful programming concept it should be studied from many other points of view.

One possibility is to use even tighter control of access rights and check that components only call a *subset* of the procedures within other components (for example, that a process only *sends* data through a buffer, but does not try to *receive* from it) [Wulf, 1974].

Another possibility is to check the *sequence* in which operations are carried out on abstract data structures (for example, that a resource always is *requested* before being used and is *released* afterwards) [Campbell and Habermann, 1974].

It may also be possible to *simplify* the access mechanisms of Concurrent Pascal (rather than extending them). If successful, this should reduce the size of both the compiler and the kernel [Wirth, 1976c].

Another idea would be to develop a simple, abstract language for *real-time applications* with critical timing constraints as suggested in Section 9.3.

But all these ideas must be tested in the design of real systems before they can be evaluated realistically.

Computer Design

The widespread use of Fortran, Algol 60, Pl/1, and Cobol illustrates the success of abstract *user programming*. Sequential and Concurrent Pascal show that suppression of machine detail also is the key to success in *system programming*. During the next decade, abstract concurrent programming may well simplify *computer design* as well.

New digital technology has already lead to the development of simple devices that are useful to everyone (calculators, watches, and fuel injectors). Eventually industry will be using complicated, specialized networks of microprocessors. We do not know how to build them systematically yet, but it is an intellectual challenge worthy of the best minds.

These dedicated computer systems may not be programmable in the sense that they can execute arbitrary programs. They may indeed owe their efficiency to fixed algorithms built into the hardware. But somebody must still write and verify these concurrent algorithms. In that sense, such computer systems will involve program development. And before these programs are nailed into hardware and mass-produced, they had better be correct.

It seems very attractive to write a concurrent program in an abstract language, test it on a minicomputer, and then derive the most straightforward multiprocessor architecture from the program itself.

REFERENCES

This is a complete list of the literature referenced in the text.

ALEXANDER, C., *Notes on the synthesis of form.* Harvard University Press, Cambridge, MA, 1964.

BELL, J. R., "Threaded code," *Comm. ACM 16,* 6, pp. 370–72, June 1973.

BRINCH HANSEN, P., and HOUSE, R., "The Cobol compiler for the Siemens 3003," *BIT 6,* 1, pp. 1–23, 1966.

BRINCH HANSEN, P., "The RC 4000 real-time control system at Pulawy," *BIT 7,* 4, pp. 279–88, 1967.

BRINCH HANSEN, P., "The nucleus of a multiprogramming system," *Comm. ACM 13,* 4, pp. 238–50, April 1970.

BRINCH HANSEN, P., "Structured multiprogramming," *Comm. ACM 15,* 7, pp. 574–78, July 1972.

BRINCH HANSEN, P., "Testing a multiprogramming system," *Software—Practice & Experience 3,* 2, pp. 145–50, April–June 1973a.

BRINCH HANSEN, P., *Operating system principles.* Prentice-Hall Inc., Englewood Cliffs, NJ, July 1973b.

BRINCH HANSEN, P., "The programming language Concurrent Pascal," *IEEE Transactions on Software Engineering 1*, 2, pp. 199-207, June 1975.

BRINCH HANSEN, P., "The Solo operating system," *Software—Practice & Experience 6*, 2, pp. 141-205, April-June 1976.

BRONOWSKI, J., *The ascent of man*. Little, Brown and Company, Boston, MA, 1973.

BROOKS, F. P., *The mythical man-month. Essays on software engineering*. Addison-Wesley, Reading, MA, 1975.

CAMPBELL, R. H., and HABERMANN, A. N., *The specification of process synchronization by path expressions*. Computing Laboratory, University of Newcastle upon Tyne, Newcastle upon Tyne, England, Jan. 1974.

DAHL, O. -J., DIJKSTRA, E. W., and HOARE, C. A. R., *Structured programming*. Academic Press, New York, NY, 1972.

DIJKSTRA, E. W., "Cooperating sequential processes," In *Programming languages*, F. Genuys (ed.), Academic Press, New York, NY, 1968.

DIJKSTRA, E. W., "Hierarchical ordering of sequential processes," *Acta Informatica 1*, 2, pp. 115-38, 1971.

ELSASSER, W. M., *The chief abstractions of biology*. American Elsevier, New York, NY, 1975.

HARDY, G. H., *A mathematician's apology*. Cambridge University Press, New York, NY, 1967.

HARTMANN, A. C., *A Concurrent Pascal compiler for minicomputers. Lecture Notes in Computer Science*, Springer-Verlag, New York, NY, 1977.

HOARE, C. A. R., "An axiomatic basis for computer programming," *Comm. ACM 12*, 10, pp. 576-80, 83, Oct. 1969.

HOARE, C. A. R., "Proof of a program: Find," *Comm. ACM 14*, 1, pp. 39-45, Jan. 1971.

HOARE, C. A. R., "Towards a theory of parallel programming," In *Operating systems techniques*, C. A. R. Hoare (ed.), Academic Press, New York, NY, 1972a.

HOARE, C. A. R., "Proof of correctness of data representations," *Acta Informatica 1*, pp. 271-81, 1972b.

HOARE, C. A. R., *Hints on programming language design*. Computer Science Department, Stanford University, Stanford, CA, Dec. 1973.

HOARE, C. A. R., "Monitors: an operating system structuring concept," *Comm. ACM 17*, 10, pp. 549-57, Oct. 1974.

HOWARD, J. H., "Proving monitors," *Comm. ACM 19*, 5, pp. 273-79, May 1976.

IGARASHI, S., LONDON, R. L., and LUCKHAM, D. C., "Automatic program verification I: Logical basis and its implementation," *Acta Informatica 4*, 2, pp. 145-82, 1975.

JENSEN, K., and WIRTH, N., "Pascal — user manual and report," *Lecture notes in computer science 18*, Springer-Verlag, New York, NY, 1974.

LAMPSON, B. W., "An operating system for a single-user machine," *Lecture notes in computer science 16*, Springer-Verlag, New York, NY, pp. 208-17, 1974.

LANGER, S. K., *An introduction to symbolic logic*. Dover Publications, New York, NY, 1967.

McNEILL, W. H., *The shape of European history*. Oxford University Press, New York, NY, 1974.

NAUR, P., "The design of the Gier Algol compiler," *BIT 3*, 2-3, pp. 124-43 & 145-66, 1963.

NORI, K. V., et al., *The Pascal P compiler: implementation notes*. Institut für Informatik, Eidgenössische Technische Hochschule, Zurich, Switzerland, Dec. 1974.

OWICKI, S., and GRIES, D., "Verifying properties of parallel programs: an axiomatic approach," *Comm. ACM 19*, 5, pp. 279-85, May 1976.

SIMON, H. A., *The sciences of the artificial*. M.I.T. Press, Cambridge, MA, 1969.

STOY, J. E., and STRACHEY, C., "OS6 — an experimental operating system for a small computer," *Computer Journal 15*, 2, p. 117, Feb. 1972.

STRUNK, W., and WHITE, E. B., *The elements of style*. Macmillan, New York, NY, 1959.

WIRTH, N., "The design of a Pascal compiler," *Software — Practice & Experience 1*, pp. 309-33, 1971.

WIRTH, N., *Systematic programming: an introduction*. Prentice-Hall Inc., Englewood Cliffs, NJ, 1973.

WIRTH, N., *Algorithms + data structures = programs*. Prentice-Hall Inc., Englewood Cliffs, NJ, 1976a.

WIRTH, N., *Programming languages: what to demand and how to assess them*. Institut für Informatik, Eidgenössische Technische Hochschule, Zurich, Switzerland, 1976b.

WIRTH, N., *Modula: a programming language for modular multiprogramming*. Software — Practice and Experience 7, 2, March-April 1977.

WULF. W. A., *Alphard: toward a language to support structured programming*. Computer Science Department, Carnegie-Mellon University, Pittsburgh, PA, Apr. 1974.

LIST OF PROGRAM COMPONENTS

This is a complete list of all *classes, monitors, process,* and *sequential programs* used in the model operating systems (*Job stream, Pipeline, Real-time,* and *Solo*).

Classes

Monitors

Processes

DANISH SUMMARY

Denne afhandling beskriver en systematisk metode for konstruktion af simple, paalidelige *multiprogrammer* — programmer der faar en datamaskine til at gøre flere ting samtidigt.

Bogen har baade teoretisk og praktisk sigte. Den forsøger at lægge grundlaget for *abstrakt* (maskinuafhængig) *multiprogrammering* ved hjælp af et nyt programmeringssprog *Concurrent Pascal* — det første af sin art.

Brugen af dette sprog illustreres af tre simple *operativsystemer* for en enkelt bruger, for smaa studenter programmer, og for industriel proceskontrol. Bogen indeholder en komplet udskrift af disse multiprogrammer der alle har været afprøvet paa en PDP 11/45 datamaskine.

Kapitel 1 opsummerer de generelle programmeringsprincipper bag abstrakt multiprogrammering. Simpelhed opnaas ved brugen af et maskinuafhængigt programmeringssprog, mens paalidelighed baseres paa omfattende oversaetterkontrol.

Kapitel 2 forklarer hvordan samtidige processer og monitorer kan anvendes til at konstruere et hierarkisk multiprogram.

Kapitel 3 giver et kort overblik over det sekventielle programmeringssprog Pascal der er udgangspunktet for dette arbejde.

Kapitel 4 indfører en sprognotation for hovedbegreberne i Concurrent Pascal (processer og monitorer).

Kapitel 5 beskriver et enkeltbruger system for en minidatamaskine skrevet i Concurrent Pascal. Det oversaetter og udfører brugerprogrammer skrevet i sekventiel Pascal. Programudførsel samt indlaesning og udskrift af data sker samtidigt. Pascal programmer kan kalde hinanden rekursivt, saaledes at Pascal ogsaa kan bruges som jobkontrolsprog.

Kapitel 6 praesenterer et system der oversaetter og udfører en strøm af smaa Pascal programmer indlaest fra en hulkortlaeser og udskrevet paa en linieskriver. Indlaesning, udførsel, og udskrift styres af samtidige processer der udveksler data gennem store diskbuffere.

Kapitel 7 beskriver et sandtidsprogram for proceskontrolanvendelser med et fast antal kontrolprocesser der udføres periodisk efter operatørens forskrift.

Solo systemet viser hvorledes et multiprogram paa mere end 1000 linier kan opbygges af en raekke processer og monitorer der hver isaer kun bestaar af en sides programtekst og som kan programmeres og afprøves enkeltvis.

Sandtidssystemet bruges til at vise hvorledes saadanne programkomponenter kan afprøves systematisk.

Jobstrøm systemet illustrerer hvordan et multiprogram kan konstrueres til at yde det bedst mulige paa den givne maskine.

Kapitel 8 definerer programmeringssproget Concurrent Pascal kort og praecist.

Kapitel 9 beskriver hovedlinierne i implementeringen af sproget: lagertildeling, kodeudførsel, systemkerne, og oversaetter.

Bogen slutter med at foreslaa en raekke muligheder for videre forskning af abstrakt multiprogrammering.

Concurrent Pascal er resultatet af 10 aars arbejde med multiprogrammering. Det begyndte i 1965 da jeg laeste Edsger Dijkstra's skelsaettende vaerk "Samarbejdende sekventielle processer" hvori han viser hvorledes samtidige processer kan synkroniseres ved at sende tidssignaler gennem *semafor* variable.

Peter Kraft og jeg brugte disse ideer i *RC 4000 proceskontrol* systemet i Pulawy, Polen [Brinch Hansen, 1967].

I praksis viste det sig at vaere vanskeligt at bruge semaforer rigtigt. Den mindste *programmeringsfejl* kunne gøre et multiprogram *tidsafhaengigt*, saaledes at det gav forskellige resultater hver gang det blev udført med de samme data. Det gjorde til tider programafprøvning vaerdiløs, idet man ikke kunne slutte fra programmets varierende opførsel hvad der var galt med det.

I *RC 4000 multiprogrammeringssystemet* forsøgte Jørn Jensen, Søren Lauesen og jeg at løse dette paalidelighedsproblem ved at lade samtidige processer sende *meddelelser* til hinanden (istedet for tidssignaler). Et maskinprogram, kaldet *monitoren*, sørgede for at disse operationer altid blev udført korrekt [Brinch Hansen, 1970].

Baade Dijkstra's T.H.E. system og Regnecentralen's RC 4000 system blev skrevet i maskinkode. Men mens Dijkstra antog at samtidige processer samarbejdede frivilligt, saa betragtede vi RC 4000 processer som værende saa upaalidelige at maskinen maatte overvaage dem konstant (ved hjælp af et beskyttelsessystem). Det første synspunkt er ofte urealistisk, og det andet er altid besværligt at arbejde med. Det forekom mig at der burde findes en bedre maade at gøre multiprogrammering baade simpel og paalidelig.

I 1971 fik Tony Hoare og jeg den ide at skrive multiprogrammer i et programmeringssprog der er saa velstruktureret at en oversætter til en vis grad kan garantere at programmeringsfejl ikke fører til tidsafhængige resultater. Vores hovedide var at erklære variable der bruges af flere processer som *fælles variable* og markere alle operationer paa disse variable som *kritiske sektioner.* Oversætteren og maskinen kan saa automatisk sørge for at disse kritiske sektioner udføres een ad gangen. Jeg foreslog tillige brugen af *proceskøer* til at gøre synkroniseringsoperationer mere effektive [Hoare, 1971 og Brinch Hansen, 1972].

Omtrent samtidigt foreslog Dijkstra [1971] at et multiprogram ville være nemmere at forstaa hvis en fælles variabel og alle operationer paa den var samlet paa eet sted i programmet. Denne kombination af en fælles datastruktur og alle de procedurer der har adgang til den kaldes en *monitor.*

I min lærebog om "Operativsystemprincipper" [1973] foreslog jeg en *sprognotation* for monitorbegrebet baseret paa *klassebegrebet* i Simula 67 [Dahl, 1972]. Jeg paapegede samtidigt at denne notation ville gøre det muligt for en oversætter at kontrollere at resten af et program kun udfører netop de operationer paa en fælles variabel der er defineret af dens monitor. Det er saaledes en mekanisme der beskytter en programkomponent mod at blive ødelagt af andre komponenter.

I en senere artikel illustrerede Tony Hoare [1974] dette monitorbegreb med simple eksempler.

For at prøve disse ideer i praksis udvidede jeg det sekventielle programmeringssprog Pascal [Jensen and Wirth, 1974] med samtidige processer og monitorer. Resultatet blev *Concurrent Pascal* [Brinch Hansen, 1975]. I januar 1975 fuldførte Alfred Hartmann den første Concurrent Pascal oversætter for PDP 11/45 maskinen. Samme aar udviklede jeg de tre eksperimentelle operativsystemer der er beskrevet her [Brinch Hansen, 1976].

Concurrent Pascal er et abstrakt sprog der skjuler de fleste af de detailer der gøre maskinprogrammering saa problematisk (registre og lagerord, bitmønstre og adresser, maskininstruktioner og hop, afbrydesignaler, samt tildeling af centralenheder og lager).

Proces- og monitorbegreberne forener mange ting der tidligere blev betragtet som værende uden forbindelse med hinanden (og blev indført i forskellige programmeringskurser):

> hierarkisk programmering (præcis modularitet)
> data abstraktion (isolering af detailer)
> resource beskyttelse

type kontrol
bevisførelse for programmer
multiprogrammering
synkronisering

Skønt klassebegrebet er ligesaa nyttigt til sekventiel programmering er det ikke noget tilfaelde at dets fulde potentiel først blev opdaget i forbindelse med den mest generelle og vanskelige form for programmering — multiprogrammering. Fejl i sekventielle programmer kan altid reproduceres og lokaliseres eksperimentelt. Men den mindste fejl i et multiprogram kan faa det til at køre saa tilfaeldigt at afprøvning bliver meningsløs. Man maa derfor indføre saa meget struktur i et programmeringssprog at en oversaetter kan finde synkroniseringsfejl (da ingen anden kan gøre det).

Før sekventielle programmører fandt ud af at hop og globale variable var problematiske havde multiprogrammører allerede erstattet parallelle forgreninger med samtidige processer og begraenset brugen af faelles variable til kritiske sektioner. Ting der ofte forekommer at være et spørgsmaal om smag og behag i sekventielle programmer kan betyde forskellen mellem success og fiasko i multiprogrammer I den forstand er multiprogrammering en rig kilde til en dybere forstaaelse af sekventiel programmering.

INDEX